SUDARSHAN SUKHANI was introduced to technical analysis in his late twenties when he read the book, *Technical Analysis of Stock Trends* by Edwards and Magee. He became a part-time investor, keeping charts manually, with pencil and graph paper. On a visit to the USA in 1988, he acquired the book *Technical Analysis of the Futures Markets* by John Murphy. This book introduced him to the world of computer based trading, with indicators, trading strategies, waves, cycles, scans, and more. In 1993, he changed careers and became a full time trader and developer of technical analysis software. Since 1999, when the first business TV broadcasts in India started with CNBC-TV18, he has appeared on thousands of market shows on CNBC-TV18 and Awaaz (Hindi language channel), providing in-depth and real-time analysis to investors and traders.

Sudarshan holds seminars for investors and traders all over India. He has presented more than fifty seminars on different aspects of technical analysis. In addition, he has participated in more than thirty investor camps throughout India, organized by CNBC-TV18 and ET-Now.

Sudarshan is President of the Association of Technical Analysts, India (www.ataindia.org), the country's professional body for technical analysts, which is affiliated to the International Federation of Technical Analysts (www.ifta.org). He is a Chartered Financial Technician (CFTe), a recognition given by IFTA.

Besides being a full time trader and regular TV guest, he writes a newsletter every day, reads as much as possible, remains involved in research and regularly interacts with individual traders and investors.

Sudarshan lives with his wife, Usha, in New Delhi. His business website is: www.s2analytics.com and he blogs regularly at www.sudarshanonline.com.

TRADING THE MARKETS

SUDARSHAN SUKHANI

www.visionbooksindia.com

Disclaimer

The author and the publisher disclaim all legal or other responsibilities for any losses which investors may suffer by investing or trading using the methods described in this book. Readers are advised to seek professional guidance before making any specific investments.

First Published 2012
Reprinted 2014, 2020

ISBN 10: 81-7094-845-2
ISBN 13: 978-81-7094- 845-2

A Vision Books Original

Published by
Vision Books Pvt. Ltd.
(Incorporating Orient Paperbacks and CARING imprints)
24 Feroze Gandhi Road, Lajpat Nagar 3
New Delhi 110024, India.
Phone: (+91-11) 2984 0821 / 22
e-mail: visionbooks@gmail.com

Printed at
Anand Sons
C 88, Ganesh Nagar, Pandav Nagar Complex
Delhi 110 092, India.

Contents

Chapter 1

Introduction

My Philosophy of Technical Trading

IN OR AROUND 1980, FRESH FROM COLLEGE, YEARNING FOR RICHES, I subscribed to a stock market letter which was written by a gentleman named Mr. Mansukhani. The letters talked about primary trend, secondaries, triple tops, basing formations and so on, while also identifying stocks to be bought and sold. Small handmade graphs were inserted in between the text. I do not remember actually taking any of the suggestions, but it was fun reading the letters which came by post, every fortnight, I think. In one of the letters, Mr. Mansukhani wrote about an American book called *The Technical Analysis of Stock Trends* which he said was being imported by an Indian publisher (Vision Books). I ordered the book, which duly arrived probably three to four months after the order. I still have that book. Printed on glossy paper, filled with charts, complete with references to the Dow Theory, *The Technical Analysis of Stock Trends* started my courtship with the stock market. In my life, I am grateful to God for my wonderful children, my understanding wife, and my parents. Apart from these gifts, the best thing that happened to me was technical analysis.

Technical Analysis is About the Markets

Let us try and identify what a market is. Markets are a mirror image of human nature.

Sounds good, doesn't it? But what does it mean? Do we have any images of human nature? I am not aware of nature having any shape or form. If nature does not have any visibility, how can there be a mirror image?

Let me try again.

For a trader, a market is an entity where buyers and sellers meet in perfect freedom to transact among themselves. This definition seems better, since we can relate to an environment, physical or electronic, where a number of people assemble to buy and sell.

The stock market is a specialized market where stocks are traded. The commodities market, on the other hand, trades only in commodities just as the vegetable market trades only in vegetables. All of these are markets where buyers and sellers trade in perfect freedom. I can buy vegetables from one vendor or from another vendor, and so on. The Bata shoe stores are also markets, but buyers and sellers do not move about in freedom. There is only one seller — the shoe store. Therefore, this is not a market in which we are interested. We are referring to markets with buyers and sellers in competition. I hope readers have understood that only liquid, freely traded markets lend themselves to technical analysis. This also means that many stocks and commodities with few buyers and sellers are not suitable candidates for technical analysis since they are not liquid.

Now, a market consists of buyers and sellers. These buyers and sellers can collectively be called traders. In fact, "traders" is a more relevant term since most market participants are buyers as well as sellers. Traders are humans. At least, till now. There is a lot of computer trading, but the computers need to be instructed, and the instructions are given by humans; so in spite of a recent trend towards computer based high frequency trading, it is safe to say that traders are humans.

What emotions do I feel as a trader when I make money in the market? Now, I know that the *Bhagavad Gita* tells us to do our duty and ignore the results, but we are mere mortals. So when my duty — which is trading in the markets — brings in profits, I feel pleased. Sometimes, I enter a trade only to see the market immediately go against me and stop me out. Oh, well, *Que Sera, Sera* — whatever will be, will be. My point is: our acts in the market come back to us and influence our emotions. Between the trader and the market, there is a one-way feedback loop — I do something in the market, the market does something. It may be something I like or do not like it. But whatever I do does not influence the market's emotions since the market is not a human. That's why, there is a one-way feedback loop — markets to me.

We have no control over the markets, even as the markets do and will continue to influence our emotions. Since market actions affect traders, the wise trader understands the need to keep her emotions in control. Just because the market opened gap down against your position, there is no need to shout at your spouse, scold your child or quarrel with your neighbour.

To sum up my understanding, the market:

1. Provides competition between multiple buyers and sellers,
2. Is run by humans, and
3. Affects our emotions.

The Basics of Technical Analysis

Over the years, I have refined my own principles of technical analysis. I cannot say if these are the best. For me, these are the ideas with which I am comfortable. The following is a brief discussion of these basic ideas.

Trends Make Money

Sneha buys a share at ₹ 40 and sells it at ₹ 50. She makes money on the investment. Why? She makes money because the share's price moved higher thus giving a profit. Could she make money if the price fell to ₹ 30? No, she would have lost money because the law of mathematics says that the only way to make money in the market is to follow the rule: Buy low and sell high.

The ideas that "trends make money" and "buy low, sell high" appear contradictory. In an uptrend, prices are going up. If they are going up, then how can you "buy low"?

So we ask, what is the low? If Sneha can sell her share for ₹ 50 then her purchase price of ₹ 40 is a low. After all, the purpose is to sell higher. If she anticipates that the price will rise, then the current price is a low since she may be able to sell higher.

Therefore, when we say "buy low" we are referring to a relative low.

Some time in 1989, Reliance's share price hit a low below ₹ 50. At the time of this writing it was trading at ₹ 1,000 (there were bonus issues also in the interim but we will leave that for now). Does the "buy at low" rule require us to wait for ₹ 50 in Reliance? I hope not, since this price may not be seen for a long time. **A low, therefore, is a price from where we anticipate higher prices.** If prices move up from our buying level, we have fulfilled the golden axiom "buy low, sell high", and, we have made a profit.

The move from ₹ 40 to ₹ 50 is an uptrend. **Buyers make money when prices go up. In other words, buyers make money when there is an uptrend.** The same principles apply to downtrends. Here, too, money is made with the principle "buy low, sell high" except that we first sell high and then, later, buy at a lower price. **Short sellers make money when there is a downtrend.**

Trends make money in the market.

When prices move from low to high, we have an uptrend.

When they move from high to low, we have a downtrend.

Either way, a trend is necessary in order to make money (Figures 1.1 and 1.2).

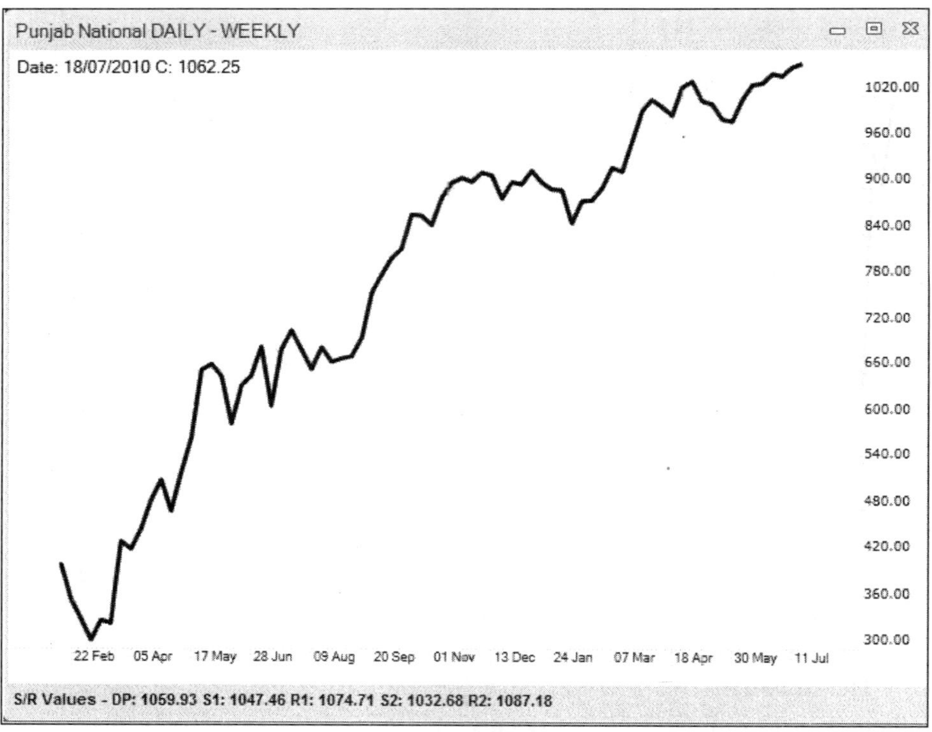

Figure 1.1: **Trends make money. The chart shows an uptrend in PNB as the price goes up from ₹ 350 to ₹ 1,050.**

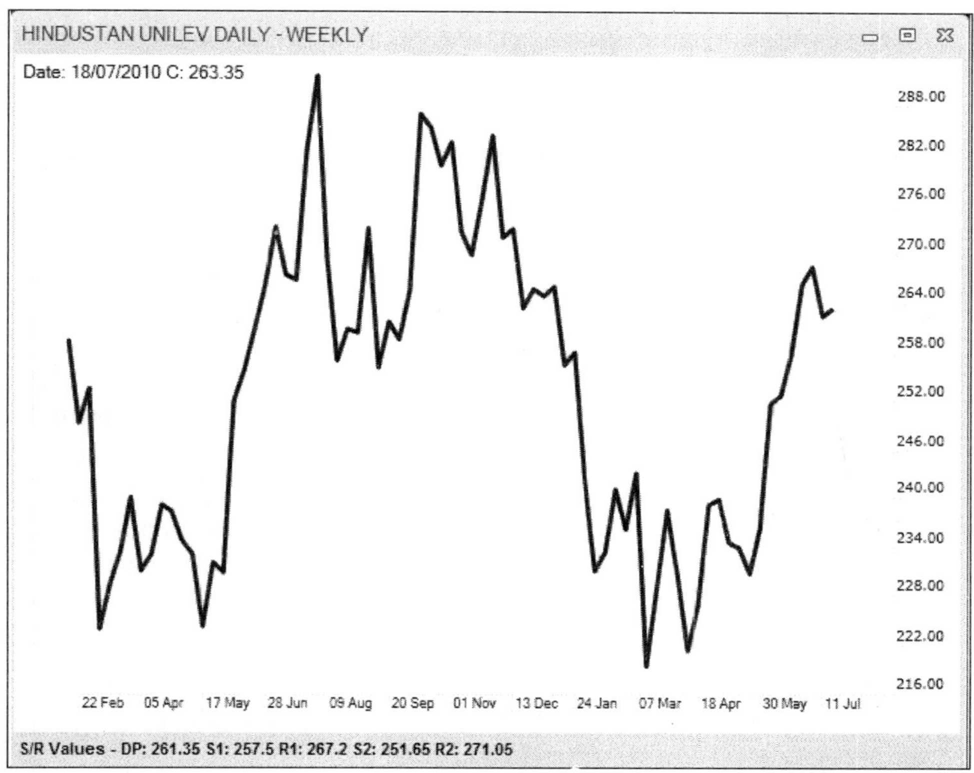

Figure 1.2: **No trend, no money. This chart of Hind Unilever shows the absence of any trend.**

The importance of trend must be understood. When share prices fall, there is a downtrend. Many investors will buy shares in a downtrend because they feel that prices have become too low. What they really mean is that, soon enough, prices will start rising. Therefore, they anticipate a change in trend from down to up. In other words, such investors are *anticipating* a trend reversal before the reversal actually happens. These investors are counter-trend investors. They are taking a position which is against the current trend.

Meanwhile, other investors will not buy. They wait patiently for prices to begin rising before they buy. This group is waiting for the trend to *actually reverse* before buying. This group comprises the trend following investors. This group of investors makes the most money.

The problem with anticipating a change in trend is that sooner or later the investor begins to "play God". Who knows the future? The counter-trend investor claims that he does. He is buying even before the trend has changed. He is saying that there *will* be a trend change and prices *will* go up. How can he be sure about that? What happens if prices do not go up?

The trend following investor, on the other hand, waits patiently for prices to actually begin moving up before he takes a buying position.

Assume That the Ongoing Trend Will Continue

We always assume that the ongoing trend will continue. After a sustained up move, many traders believe prices have risen so much that a retracement, or even a complete reversal, of trend is likely. Based on this belief, traders go and sell the market. Selling at what is currently the top of the market is an exhilarating experience. The trader feels like a king, announcing the end of a trend. We all love to catch the high or low of a move. It makes for good story telling. But, in reality, trends are persistent. Once a move starts, it can continue for longer than we imagine. When a market is in a trend, you should assume that the trend will continue. Trends make the big money (*see* Figures 1.3 and 1.4).

Typically, a strong trend will need a period of rest. In an uptrend, prices will stop going up and start moving within a trading range. When we find a trading range, which is essentially a pause in some trend or the other, there can be two different outcomes:

- Either the range will breakout in the direction of the trend (continuation);
- Or, alternately, the range will breakout in the direction opposite of the current trend (reversal).

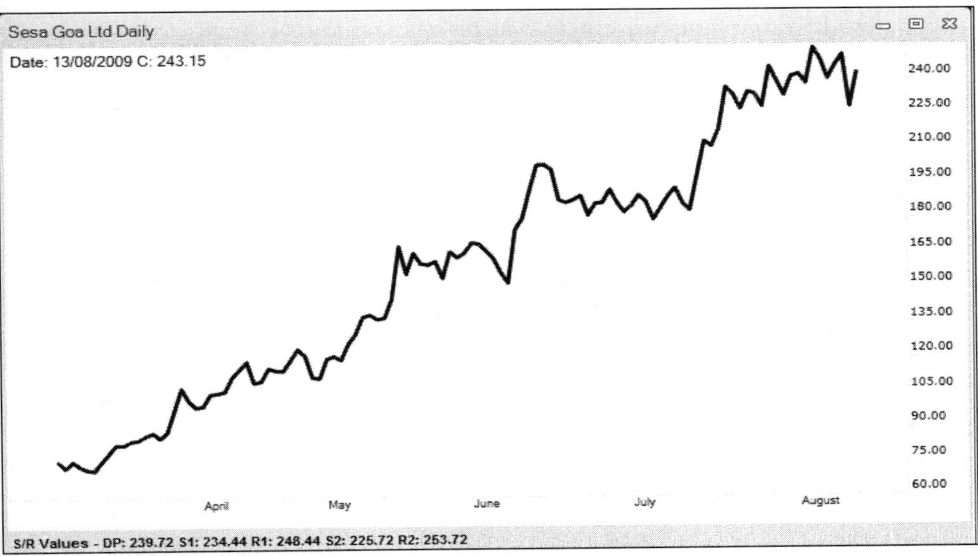

Figure 1.3: **The price of Sesa Goa moves up from ₹ 65 to ₹ 240, showing an upward trend. How much higher can it go?**

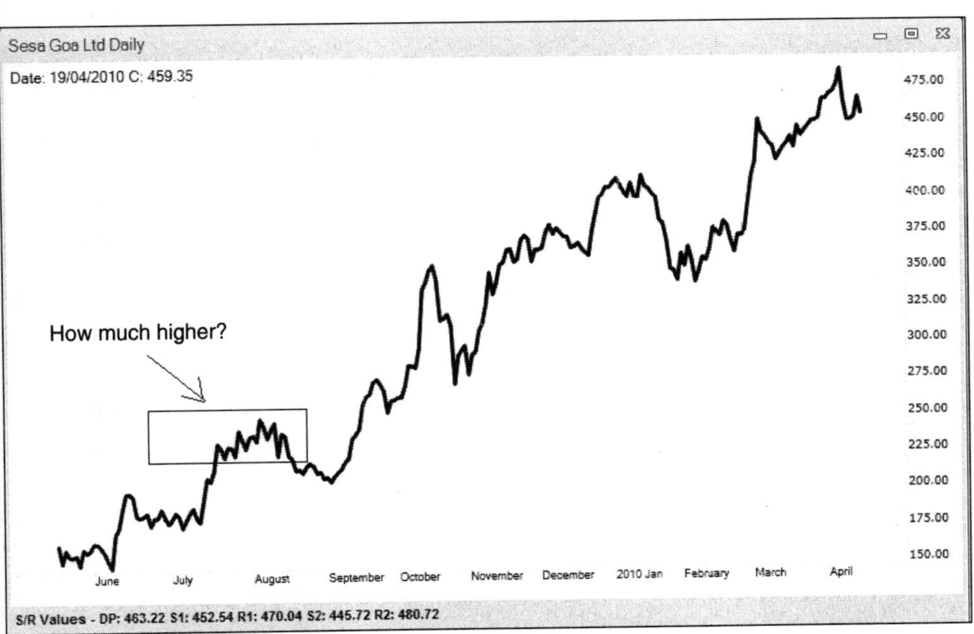

Figure 1.4: **Assume the trend will continue. The price of Sesa Goa tops out at ₹ 480. Remember at about or ₹ 225 (*see* boxed area in the chart), we had wondered how much higher it could go.**

Traders often make a mistake by believing that a reversal is imminent when they find a range. In Fact, Most trading ranges in strong trends will resolve themselves by breaking out in the direction of the original trend.

Just imagine a scenario in which prices are rising. Then prices move into a range. After a breakout from the range, prices rise again and a second trading range develops. Prices will often move in such steps; a trend, then a range, then a trend, and so on. Once an initial trend is visible, trading ranges should be taken as pauses in the ongoing move. They are periods of rest.

When a Trend Ends, Markets See a Climax or Distribution / Accumulation

An ongoing trend will usually end in a predictable fashion.

Usually, the market just runs out of buyers (in an uptrend) or sellers (in a downtrend). In other words, the market runs out of steam.

This process of trend exhaustion takes time during which prices remain locked in a range:

- The process is called accumulation when prices stop falling after a downtrend.
- It is called distribution when prices stop rising after an uptrend.

The other way in which a trend comes to an end is in a climax.

- In an uptrend, the market will witness a buying climax. Prices move up sharply and suddenly. There is a buying frenzy. Once everyone has bought, there are no further buyers left. The slightest disturbance can then cause prices to fall dramatically.
- In a downtrend, there is a sudden and sharp decline as sellers keep coming, while there is a general feeling that the world is about to end. The world does not come to an end. Instead, what usually ends is the selling. Once all potential sellers have sold, who is left to sell?

The process of accumulation and distribution is visible in different chart patterns, such as head and shoulders, triangles, wedges, trading ranges. These patterns are called reversals. When a trader identifies a reversal pattern, she gets a head start in identifying the new trend.

Selling and buying climaxes are more difficult to trade. They are easy enough to identify. In an ongoing downtrend, there is likely to be more than one selling climax. It is the final one that counts. Similarly, in an uptrend there will usually be more than one buying climax. When frenzy starts, it continues for a while. So, which one is the last? The fact that a buying or selling climax has occurred become clear only in hindsight after many days have passed.

We will see a phase of accumulation after a selling frenzy. This tells us that the selling we saw was a selling climax — an event in which all sellers sold out.

We will see a phase of distribution after a buying frenzy. This distribution will tell us that the buying frenzy we saw was actually a buying climax, an event in which everyone who wanted to buy, bought.

Buying and selling climax require reversal patterns for confirmation, so we really come back to distribution / accumulation as the basis for trading and investing decisions.

While many climax events will lead into accumulation / distribution patterns making them easy to identify, there is one special climactic frenzy that is different. This is the V-shaped reversal. And, the inverted V.

The V-shaped reversal begins with a downtrend, followed by a selling climax and there is then a sudden and sharp upswing; the process of accumulation is missing. Prices fall with a frenzy, then begin a sharp rally without any notice. The process of accumulation is a time consuming one which convinces traders that the selling may be over. Traders take tentative steps to buy. Those who were short will close their positions. But a V-shaped reversal does not give time. The market says — now I am down, now I am going through a vicious sell-off and, now, before you can say what happened — I am up, big time. V-shaped reversals are virtually impossible to catch. There are some who might catch them but that is mainly due to luck rather than chart reading.

The inverted V is the opposite of the V. Prices are going up, then a buying frenzy pushes prices even higher and, then, suddenly, without notice, the market falls with a big decline. The process of distribution did not take place as a rally was followed by a vicious decline. Again, like the V, this pattern is difficult to identify. Those who sold at the top just before the decline were probably lucky.

Markets Move from Range Expansion to Range Contraction — and Back

Markets continuously move from trading ranges to a trend — and then back from a trend to a trading range.

A trend is the phase of the market where money is made.

Trading ranges, on the other hand, are choppy, sideways movements which offer little scope for profitable trading. But these ranges serve a significant purpose — they alert us to a coming trend. We have a volatility cycle, where the range is followed by a trend, and then the trend is followed by a range. The trading range provides the signal that the next market phase will be a trend, which will come sooner or later.

A side issue with trading ranges and trending periods is the completely different nature of trading tools required to trade in each phase.

- **In a range, the strategy is to buy support and sell resistance.**
- **In a trend, the strategy is to take only one side trades (buy or sell) and try to let your profits run.**

Traders, therefore, need to identify the nature of the volatility environment and use technical tools suited for that environment (Figure 1.5).

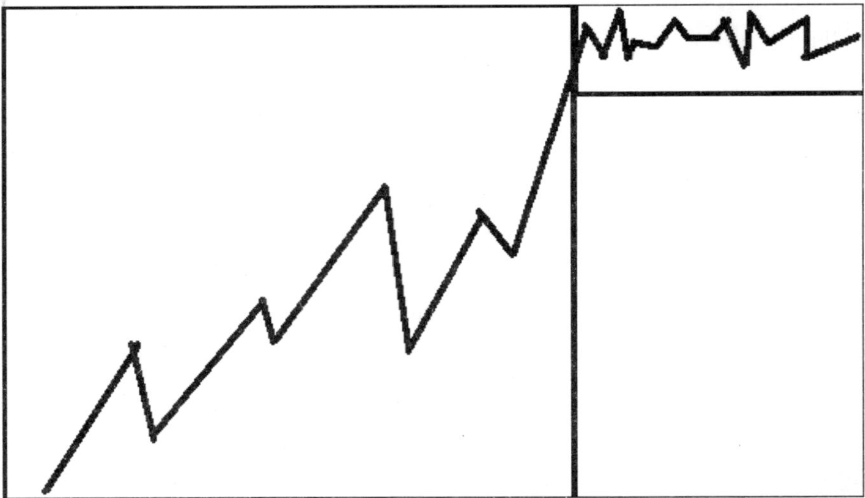

Figure 1.5: **Cycles of expansion and contraction. The volatility is increasing in the left panel and reducing in the right panel.**

Summary of the Basic Principles of Technical Trading

- Trends make money.
- Assume that the ongoing trend will continue.
- When a trend ends, markets see a climax or distribution / accumulation.
- Markets move from range expansion to range contraction and back

Inspiration from the Dow Theory

I have read hundreds of books on technical analysis, tried out thousands of ideas using Tradestation (from Omega Research), then come to the conclusion that my analysis is most compatible with the age old Dow Theory. Information on Dow Theory is available at thousands of web sites, apart from many books. Just Google "Dow Theory" and you can read for days.

The basic premise of the theory is trend:

- Higher highs and higher lows make an uptrend.
- Lower highs and lower lows make a downtrend.

In an uptrend, we buy.

In a downtrend, we sell.

When stock prices trade at their highest ever price, that is bullish.

New highs are bullish, new lows are bearish.

The latter idea is often a surprise to newcomers in the market, who cannot comprehend the idea of buying new highs. The idea goes against common sense, our instinct is to sell a stock that has rallied a lot — "How high can it go, after all?" — and buy a stock that has fallen to new lows — "How much lower can it go?". This thinking is wrong! I like to buy strength, sell weakness. This satisfies my basic principle.

"Buy low, sell high" is fine but remember that a low is a relative low. So we can also say, "buy high and sell higher", because the strong becomes stronger while the weak becomes weaker.

Actionable Analysis

It is very easy to analyze. But a lot of technical analysis does not result in actionable ideas. Such analysis is worse than useless. Here is an imaginary example:

"The ADX has gone above 25 while the RSI has just entered the overbought zone. There is resistance at 75 while there is support at 65. The MACD has given a buy signal but remains below zero."

What does it mean? After all, every trader or investor wants an answer to only one question: Should I buy or sell? Analysis that does not answer this question is of no benefit to users of technical analysis — people who trade or invest.

In my early days with technical analysis, I would ask the following question to anyone who used technical analysis: "What do you think of xyz stock?" I must confess that asking this question made me feel like an expert — one expert (me) talking high finance with another (the person whom I am asking). Typically, I would get a high sounding reply, like "The stochastic is at 40." "Ah," I would reply, well satisfied with a conversation between experts.

Now, looking back, I know there was at least one idiot in such conversations — me. The question "What do you think of xyz stock?" is silly. Investment and trading in stocks depends on the time profile of a trader or investor. The trend of a share will be different for a day trader, short term trader, position trader, or investor. In December 1999, I first started appearing on CNBC-TV18 television channel, by the time I had understood that the question "What do you think of xyz stock?" could not be answered without knowing the time profile of the enquirer. In numerous TV programs, I would ask what the time profile was before I could answer this question. Over the years, anchors and producers have understood the need to know this profile before the question can be answered.

My point is: every single effort at technical analysis MUST lead to an answer to the question: should you buy or should you sell. Many a time, analysis suggests that there are no clear patterns and it is best to stay away from the stock. So, maybe we can add one more option: Wait. The answer will depend on the trader / investor. A trader who cannot bear to take losses will require signals that have tight stop losses. Another trader who does not trade in the short term will have an answer that looks at the intermediate term trend. Therefore, the answers will be different.

Stop Losses

In my trading world, the use of stop losses is different for traders and investors.

Traders must use a stop loss.

Always.

A trader without a stop loss is like a soldier in a battle without a gun. Without stops, trouble is going to come soon enough. Traders make many trades over a year, hundreds or even thousands. Each trade is expected to make a small loss or a slightly larger profit. If losses are not kept small, this equation gets disturbed. If the trader allows one trade to pile up a large loss, that loss can eat away the profits from a number of successful trades resulting in a serious trading setback. One large loss can disturb the trading balance for a year.

How stops are placed is a very personal matter. There is no universal method of placing stops. It depends on the psychological make-up of the trader. It also depends on the circumstances surrounding a particular trade. Some traders want to give space to their positions. Such people have wide stops since they do not mind taking paper losses. Many traders hate taking losses, so their stops are tight. They will often suffer ten or more losses in a row before they get a profitable trade which, hopefully, wipes out their losses and ends up in a net gain.

Stop losses will also depend on the specific trade. Is your trade already in money with open profits? Then the risk of loss of capital becomes minimal since the capital is no longer at risk. The risk has shifted to current profits where traders can take larger risks. You may want to give such trades more space by keeping wide stops.

Stop losses also depend on the trading method that is used for a trade. If chart patterns are used to enter a trade, pivot points are most likely to be used as stops. The pivot level has to be accepted as a stop no matter how wide or narrow it is.

My point is: a stop loss is essential for traders, but the exact placement of stops is a matter of personal preference.

Trade with Stops, Invest on Themes

My investment philosophy does not include any stops at all. I go for a theme, then exit when the theme appears to be faltering. If I am using a stop loss, then I am trading. Most of my activity is trading, so that's fine — so long as I do not pretend that I am investing. But investments are made on themes.

For example, as I write this, I have a theme that shares of public sector banks (PSU) are available at low valuations, with their charts suggesting a sustained bull run. So I am investing in a PSU bank. So long as this theme is intact, I remain an investor. The theme can change if I decide that PSU banks may no longer outperform either due to higher valuations or deteriorating long term chart patterns, or both. Because a theme takes time to develop, prices can move up or down, or have sharp declines in the interim. As an investor, I have to accept such volatility as part of the investing cycle. If I am worried about deep corrections, then I should not be investing in the stock. I should then set up a trade where stop losses are an essential component. This also suggests that I do not go for "now or never" investments. My portfolio will typically consist of five to eight stocks which I hope will outperform the bank interest rate. It is possible that all the stocks in the portfolio can go into a free fall in prices. Usually this happens when long term chart patterns have started deteriorating, so I have enough time to reduce my exposure. But this decline can also sometimes take place suddenly.

Futures and Options are Not Investing

The stock markets all over the world were booming in 2006. In India, the Nifty had rallied from a low of 920 in April 2003 to a high of 3,774 in May 2006. I was fully invested. After all, the markets had no way to go but up. I purchased shares (which was the correct action) as well as loaded myself with stock futures and all kinds of stock options. Then a sudden decline saw the Nifty fall to 2,595 — a 35% decline in a month. The long term chart patterns did not deteriorate — there was not enough time — but the markets suddenly fell in an inverted V decline. My portfolio was badly damaged. I had large mark-to-market losses on the futures positions and zero values in options. Well, these stories usually end with liquidation. At what must have been the bottom of the decline, I closed all my futures positions, and sold the options for whatever I could get. I retained my equity holdings since these positions did not disturb me. We had seen a sharp dip but it was still a correction in an ongoing bull market. The markets revived, the Nifty saw a high of 6,315 in January 2008, my equities outperformed and, luckily were sold in the period from October 2007 to December 2007 when charts started looking toppy. I ended up with gains despite losses in my futures and options positions.

The moral of this story is: futures and options are not investing. Investing is done with your own money. Trading is done with leverage. I had initiated a trading position using futures and options pretending that I was investing. Consequently, I had no stop losses, i.e. no protection for these derivatives.

Taking Profits

Profit is the reason for all trading and investing. While the challenge of trading well is itself a good reason to trade, the end result of our efforts should result in profits. How much profit is sufficient? This rather silly question needs to be asked since traders often have fanciful ideas of what they can earn from the business of trading and investing.

I keep the bank fixed deposit rate as a benchmark. In my trading, I should earn more than the bank rate. I do not compare my returns to the market. If the market is down 15% and I am down 10%, then my performance is not better. I am doing much worse than the fixed deposit rate. If the market falls, I should be making money by going short in order to get a return on my capital, irrespective of what the market is doing..

If the market is up 40% and I am up 15%, I am quite pleased since I have out-performed the fixed deposit rate which could be 8% (for example). In fact, my approach is to get a net gain every year.

I treat trading like any other business, where we invest money and expect returns. By benchmarking the returns to the fixed deposit rate, I have reduced the volatility of my investment returns. This gives me peace of mind. My investments are "at the sleeping level" (I can sleep well!).

Just to clarify: I did not set about reducing the volatility of my returns. I slowly developed an investing method with which I was comfortable. Eventually, I realized that I was reducing volatility.

Trading is a high risk business so there must be a risk premium attached to this activity. What should be the risk premium? My answer remains the same. My trading returns should exceed the fixed deposit bank interest. The excess return should be enough to justify the risk inherent in trading. I do not have a formula for this. I do, however, feel that a trader should strive to get 20% to 30% return on capital per year.

A more important question related to profits is the strategy for taking profits. How do you exit a profitable trade?

I explained that a stop loss is a very personal experience. Fortunately, the profitable exit has generic rules which most traders can follow.

The first is the fundamental rule of all investing and trading: cut your losses short, let your profits run. If you take away just one idea from this book, it is that you can lose a lot by taking small profits.

It is the big moves that provide life and sustenance to traders and investors. By quick profits, you will drastically reduce the opportunity to catch the big move. How can you make ₹ 200 in a trade if you have taken a ₹ 10 profit? The best way to exit a profitable trade is to let the market throw you out of the trade. Therefore, use trailing stops. This allows you to participate in the trend. It also ensures that you keep on locking a part of your profits.

A trailing stop is installed once a trade has made a profit. Suppose you buy Infosys at ₹ 2,450 and your initial stop is ₹ 2,390. (Never keep stops at round figures). Infosys then moves up to ₹ 2,500. You move your stop to 2,460. The price moves up to ₹ 2,530. Your stop is moved up to 2,500. Then a sudden burst sees the price hit ₹ 2,590. You tighten your stop to ₹ 2,570. Infosys falls and you sell your shares at ₹ 2,570.

It is true that you did not catch the top, but no one catches the high and low of a move. By using trailing stops, you did not have to exit at an arbitrary price, say at ₹ 2,500. You ensured that your risk was covered, while you could participate in whatever trend was going on.

Summary

- Trend makes money.
- Traders must keep stop losses.
- "Cut your losses, let your profits run" is probably the only way to earn serious money in the market.
- The futures and options segment is meant to be used only by professional traders with adequate capital and experience.
- Technical analysis must be actionable — it should be able to answer the question — Buy, sell or do nothing? The answer will be different for each person, but there must be an answer.

Chapter 2

Real-Time Market Analysis

Writing a Daily Newsletter

I HAVE BEEN IN THE BUSINESS OF DEVELOPING AND SELLING TECHNICAL analysis software. I did a lot of analysis and study. Many years ago some clients suggested that I should also provide some guidance on the actual movements of the market. This led to the writing of a newsletter, provided to subscribers clients every evening. Since the letter was meant for the next day, it bore the next day's date. Thus, the letter analysing Thursday market action was written on Thursday evening, but with Friday's date stamp.

Writing a daily newsletter on the market is not easy because the forecasts are short term. When an analyst makes a long term forecast, chances are that the forecast as well as the analyst will be forgotten much before the forecast is expected to bear fruit. This is called "long term". Suppose an analyst comes on business TV and says "Suzlon is an excellent long term buying opportunity. We have a house target of ₹ 750 for the share in two years time". Now, if Suzlon is trading at ₹ 400, the target appears quite attractive (*see* Figure 2.1).

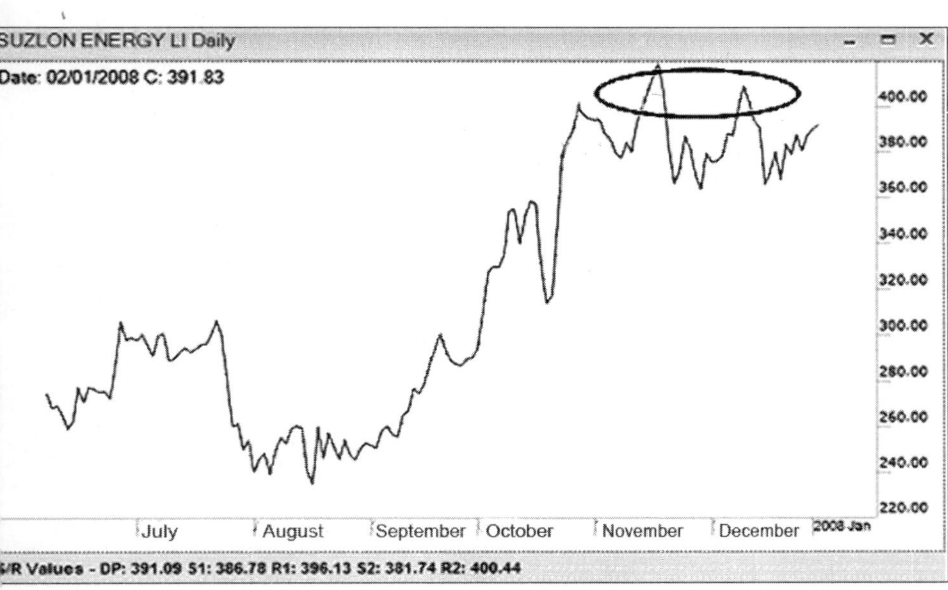

Figure 2.1: **In November 2007, the price of Suzlon touched ₹ 400 and analysts were falling over themselves with buy calls with a target of ₹ 750 in 2 years. [Note: This is a hypothetical example].**

Figure 2.2: **Actually the price of Suzlon fell from ₹ 400 in November 2007 to ₹ 58 in November 2009.**

Two years later no one remembers the analysts who recommended Suzlon. But the investor who purchased the stock simply on analyst-speak was looking at a chart that looks something like Figure 2.2.

For readers who do not like looking at charts, this is what the message is: stock prices of Suzlon fell from ₹ 400 in November 2007 to ₹ 58 in November 2009. What happened to the analyst who recommended this? We do not know and, frankly, it does not matter. My point is something else: When giving long term recommendations, analysts do not have to bear the pressure of accountability since, in the long term, everyone forgets. This makes the task of fundamental analysts much easier. They can pretty much say whatever they want without worrying about the consequences.

But when I write a daily column suggesting trades that will work out or not work out in the next few days or weeks, everyone remembers. The time span is too short to forget. Therefore, technical analysis "experts" who give short term recommendations have to carry a heavy responsibility of making sure that:

1. Their trades carry the least amount of risk (if the trade goes wrong), and
2. Have broad shoulders to accept responsibility for their actions.

Structure of the Daily Newsletter

My newsletter analyses the Indian stock market every day, using the NSE50 Index as the barometer of market action. The Nifty, as this index is popularly called, together with the BSE 30 Index ("the Sensex") are the two popular indices in the Indian markets. The Nifty is more broad-based comprising 50 stocks as compared to 30 for the Sensex. But, more importantly, futures are widely traded on the Nifty. For various reasons, futures on the Sensex never really took off. The Nifty futures account for about 99% of all futures traded; Sensex futures the remaining 1%. For this reason, it makes sense to analyse the markets based on Nifty.

I write this letter every day. My letters start with a newspaper style headline, which pretty much summarises my analysis of the market. If the market is inside a trading range with the current day ending with narrow movements, the headline may say — "Nifty in range, ready for big move, direction unknown". The lead explains the current market, with probable action. The action is to anticipate a big move in either direction. Readers of the letter are mainly professional traders who keep a watch on a breakout or breakdown. Not all days offer such self explanatory headings.

On 4 October 2007, with the Nifty making new highs day after day, I started with "Enter the Bubble". The analysis was fairly correct as Nifty topped out in January 2008. Yet, the lead itself did not explain what the trader should be acting upon. The letter explained this:

> "Such an up move is possible if it were coming at the beginning of a bull cycle. But at current levels, we can only assume that we are witnessing a period of euphoria.
>
> "Do all these warnings mean that we should sell?
>
> "Well, as an investor you should take profits. As a trader, your view should be to go with the trend, which is up. Be careful, as explained above. If and when you see signs of a down move, traders should take the trade."

In October 2008, when the financial world was falling apart as a result of the sub-prime crisis in USA affecting all and sundry, Indian markets too were falling by the day. For 7 October 2008, after a particularly vicious day of declines, the headline was "We are probably in the worst part of the bear market." In this message, the good news for investors was the possibility of a low coming in place soon enough. The low of the bear market was made 15 days later.

In other words, I try to prepare a heading which sums up the market's probable course of action.

Since the letter tracks the Nifty, I try to give a daily chart for the Nifty, marking out significant technical events on the chart. For the purposes of the letter, the primary technical events are support and resistance levels. I try to avoid the use of indicators in the broader analysis of the market. Price is the best indicator. If we can analyse price action, most of the work is done. Indicators have their own use, mainly in determining trading strategies. The letter discusses the big picture, for which the movement of prices, price patterns with support and resistance are enough.

A detailed analysis of the Nifty is carried out every day. This is relevant to investors, position traders as well as to short term traders. For investors and position traders, I identify periods of up- and downtrends. This enables entry and exits to be fine-tuned. For short term traders, the support — resistance levels with short term price patterns provide a road map of swing trades ranging from a few hours to a few days.

The letter also contains discussion of world events (sounds grand doesn't it!), identification of stocks that may move the next day, periodic analysis of sectors, and much more. In this book, the sections relating to Nifty analysis are reproduced since that is what identifies the market picture.

Primary Concepts Used in the Newsletter

Support

Support represents a price level where buyers should come in to buy (Figure 2.3). This price level is identified using one or several technical analysis methods*. Since markets do not offer any kind of guarantee, there is no assurance that buyers will, in fact, come in to buy at price levels identified as support.

---

* *See Technical Analysis and Stock Market Profits* by Richard W. Schabacker published by Vision Books for a detailed discussion of support and resistance methods.

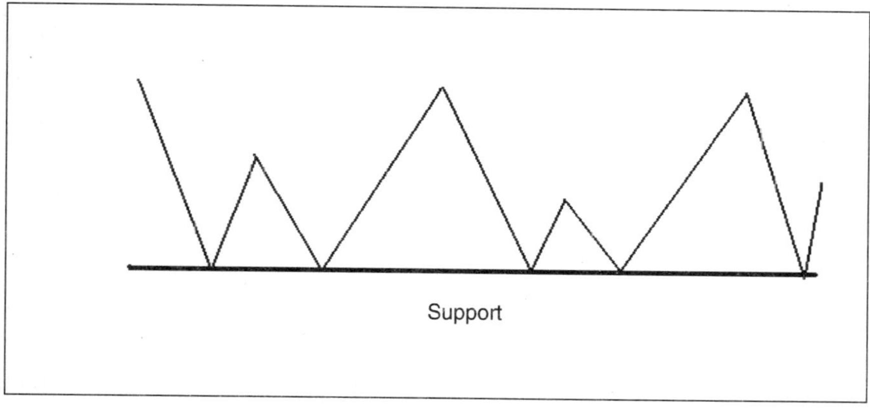

Figure 2.3: **An example of support level.**

Support levels are most useful when used in a strong uptrend, which can be considered as a bull market of some kind, whether a strong or a weak bull market, but at least the uptrend should be visible. When traders are convinced that prices are rising, then a minor decline in prices to support brings out the buyers who feel they can now get the shares at lower prices. Therefore, **support levels usually hold in an uptrend, offering a low risk buying opportunity.**

When markets are falling, support levels are of no use at all. The trend is down and the sellers are stronger than the buyers, which enables the sellers to break through any support levels that may appear on the chart.

Resistance

Resistance represents a price level where sellers are willing to sell (Figure 2.4). This price level is identified using one or several technical analysis methods.* When traders are convinced that prices are falling, then even a minor rally in prices which takes them to the resistance area activates the sellers who feel they would now be able to sell shares at higher prices. Therefore, **in a downtrend, resistance levels offer a low risk selling opportunity.**

---

* *Technical Analysis and Stock Market Profits* by Richard W. Schabacker is an excellent reference for chart patterns, including support and resistance concepts. In India, this book is published by Vision Books.

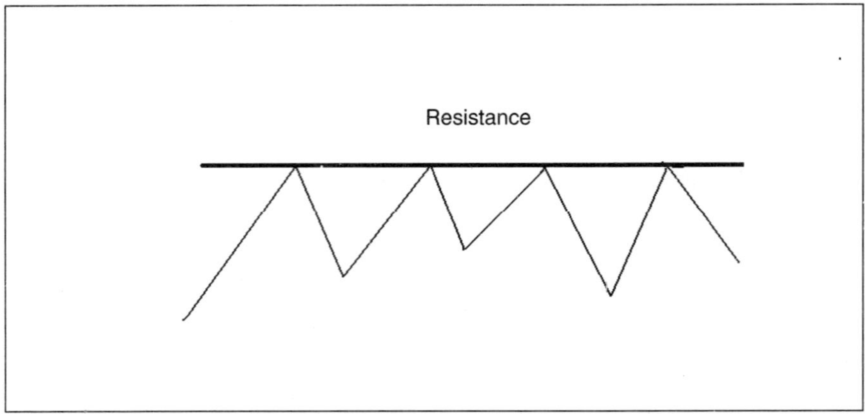

Figure 2.4: **An example of resistance level.**

Resistance is slightly different from support, since resistance levels are usually obeyed for some periods, even in bull markets.

Trading Range

Markets go through periods of expansion and contraction. When markets are in contraction, the price range, which is the difference between the high and the low of the price, comes down. In other words, during contractions the markets move less every day. Periods of contraction can last for just a few days or extend over many weeks.

The trading range is a special type of contraction (Figure 2.5). It has a distinctive characteristic — the price moves almost in a line during such a period of contraction. Prices, thus, take the shape of a narrow rectangle.

A trading range represents uncertainty. Both bulls and bears are equally matched, which is why prices neither go up nor down; they move sideways, instead.

Usually, the price will breakout of the trading range in the direction of the ongoing trend. If the range was made following an uptrend, then the breakout should normally be on the upside. The reverse applies in downtrends. But if only things were quite so predictable!

Sometimes, the breakout will be on the opposite side, which converts the trading range into a reversal pattern.

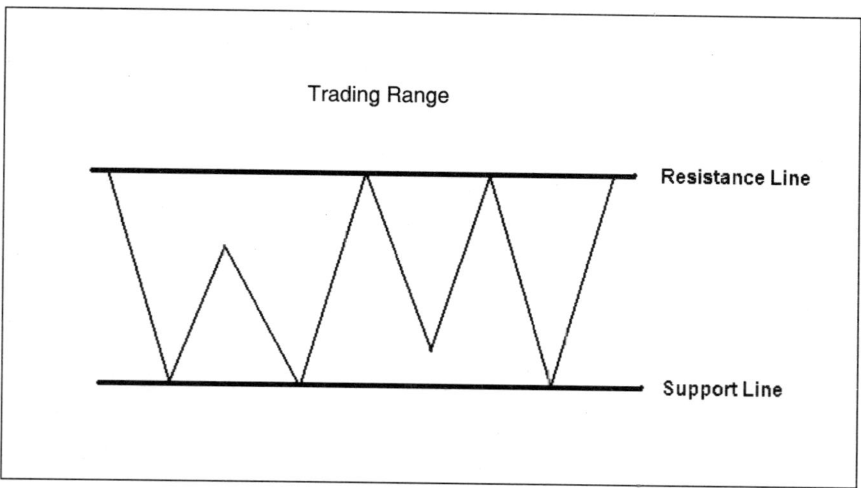

Figure 2.5: **An example of a trading range.**

Once a range is detected, the best approach for traders is not to trade inside the range. They should wait patiently for a breakout from the range.

The Doji

Price charts can be viewed in many different forms — line, open-high-low-close (OHLC) and candles. Candle charts are often called candlesticks. This chart form originated from Japan.

The Doji is a pattern found in candlesticks. On any given day, when the open and the close prices are almost equal, the pattern is described as a Doji. The Doji represents indecision because even after a full day of activity the price closes where it had opened. This happens when the bulls and the bears are equally matched.

Now, by itself, a Doji is not a big deal. There will be many days when the bulls and bears are equally matched; perhaps because a "big bull" went off on a day's holiday!

The Doji is significant when it comes about after a sustained up or down move.

Imagine a market which is going up day after day. The bulls are in full control. Suddenly, on a day when new highs are made, the close comes at or near the open. This means that bulls were not able to take prices any higher than the open. At such times, traders need to be alert. What happened? Was it just an off day or are the bulls getting tired?

The reverse logic applies when a Doji emerges after a downtrend. It could be an indication that bears are losing control (Figures 2.6 and 2.7).

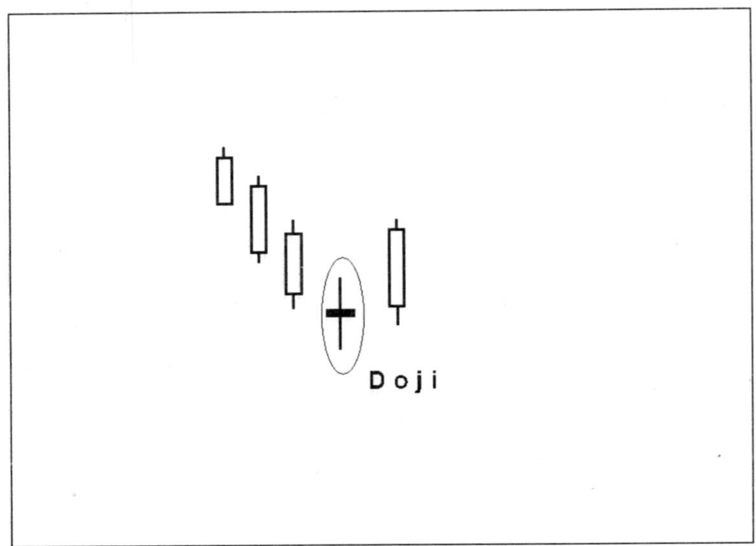

Figure 2.6: **The Doji in a downtrend — bears losing control.**

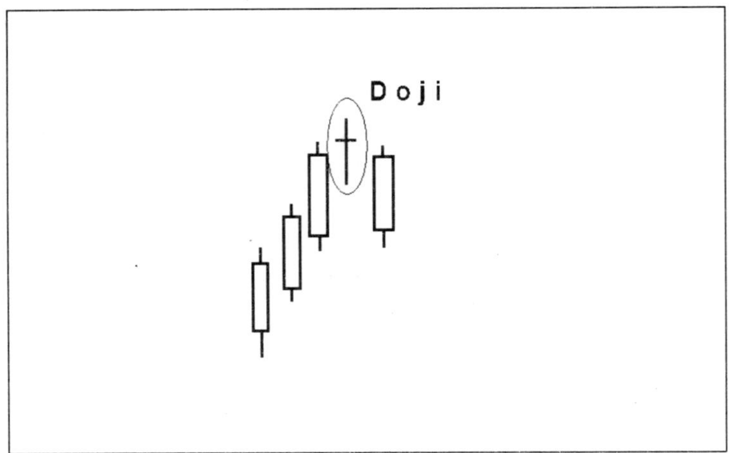

Figure 2.7: **The Doji in an uptrend — bulls losing control.**

NR7

NR7 stands for the "narrowest range in 7 days" (Figure 2.8). As already explained earlier, the range is the difference between the highest and the lowest prices of the day. A narrow range means that the price high and the price low were close together.

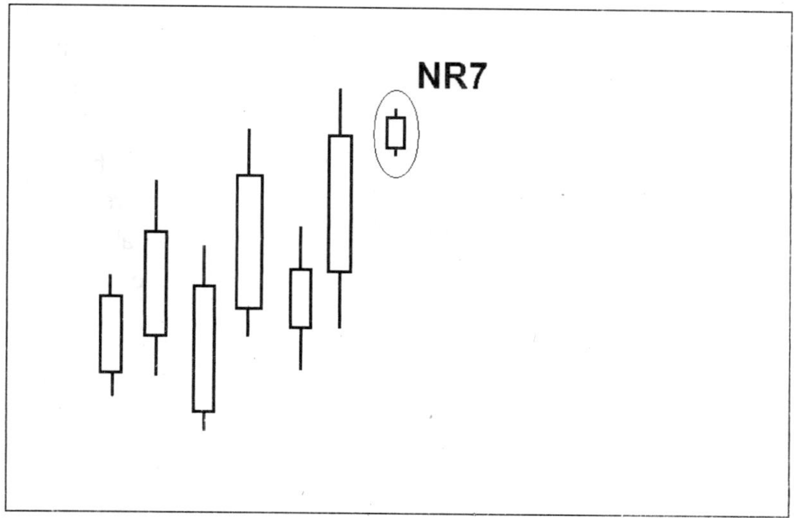

Figure 2.8: **Narrowest range in seven days.**

An NR 7 day reveals that the day's market moved much less as compared to the previous six days. NR7 days represent contraction, indecision and uncertainty.

Normally, when the markets are in a trend NR7 will be followed by a breakout in the direction of the ongoing trend. Suppose the market is moving up, and then we have an NR7 day. This is a day of consolidation. It offers a low risk entry into the uptrend. Traders should buy the next day when prices go above the high of the NR7 day.

The reverse applies for NR7 found in a downtrend.

Like with most good things, there are exceptions, however:

- NR7 days occurring inside a trading range have no technical significance. Avoid them.

- Sometimes after a long trending move, the NR7 day acts as the first sign of a reversal. In an uptrend, prices actually fall below the NR7 low suggesting that the bulls are becoming uncertain.

Inside Day

An inside day is another contraction patterns (Figure 2.9). Our search is to identify contraction, since contraction will eventually lead to an expansion in price. The inside day's price range is totally within the previous day's price range. Thus, the high of the inside day is lower than the previous day's high and the low of the inside day is higher than the previous day's low. The message is: today the bulls failed to take the price above the previous day's high, while bears also failed to take the price below the previous day's low. Essentially, a stalemate!

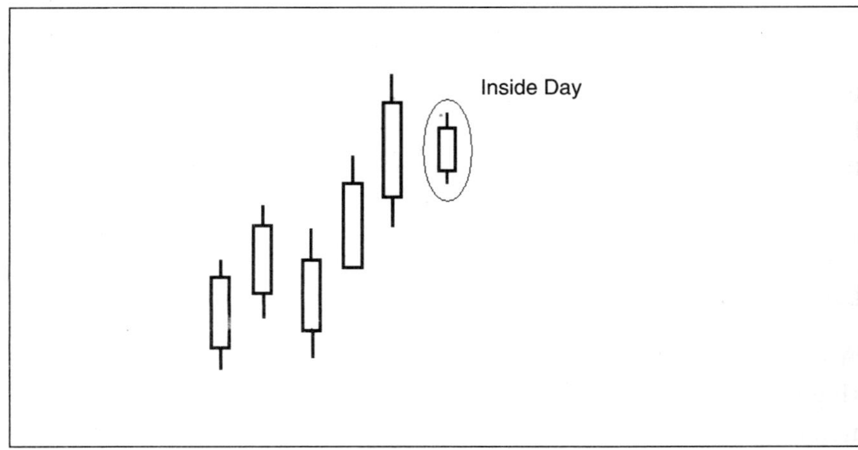

Figure 2.9: **Inside Day.**

The inside day follows the same rules applicable to NR7 days.

Higher Highs, Higher Lows

A higher high means that today's high is higher than the previous day's high (Figure 2.10). When the market displays a series of higher highs, an

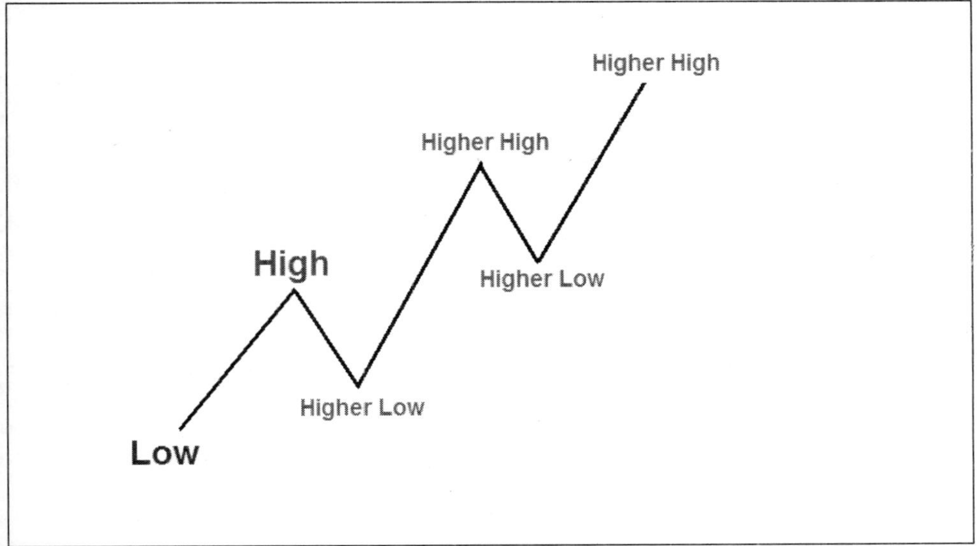

Figure 2.10: **Uptrend — higher highs and higher lows.**

uptrend is probably in progress. Investors are prepared to pay higher prices for the stock, trend followers are coming in, buyers are keen to get in the trend before the stock "runs away" on the upside.

Higher highs are usually accompanied by higher lows.

Lower Highs, Lower Lows

A lower low means that today's low is lower than the previous day's low (Figure 2.11). When the market displays a series of lower lows, a downtrend is probably in progress. Investors are either selling or staying away from the market, causing traders to go short in anticipation of even lower prices. Lower lows are usually accompanied by lower highs.

A word of caution: only professional traders should go short. Investors and amateurs should simply liquidate and stay away when they are confronted by a falling market.

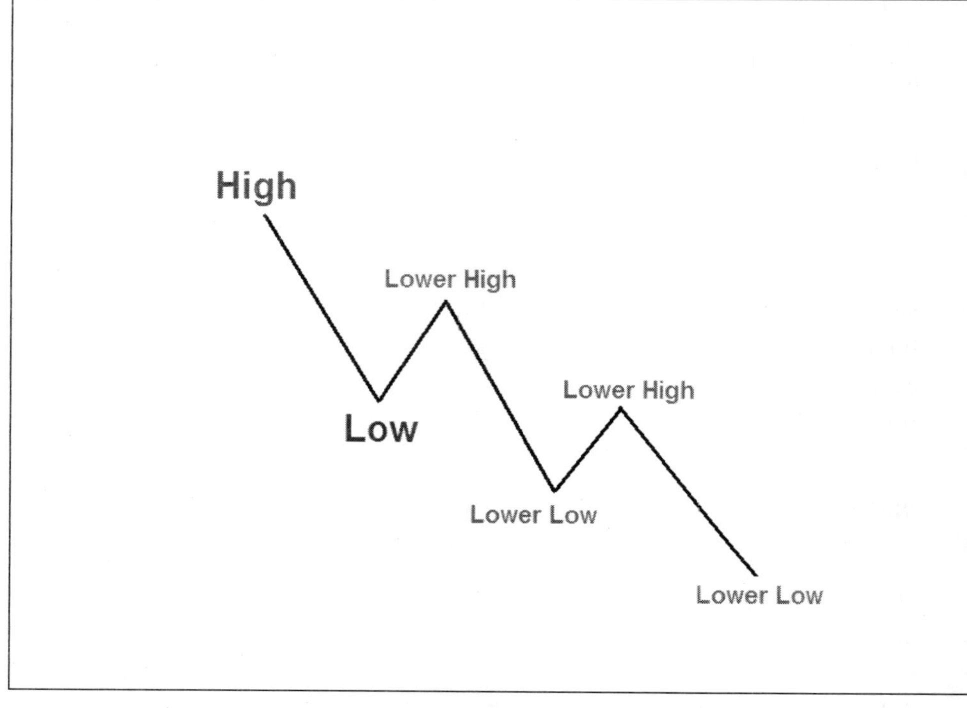

Figure 2.11: **Downtrend — lower highs and lower lows.**

Trend

A trend is a prolonged period of time when markets are moving in one direction. When markets are rising, we have an uptrend. When markets are falling, a downtrend is in progress.

There are many methods in technical analysis for identifying a trend.

The easiest of the methods is the five-second rule: Open a stock price chart. You have five seconds to say if prices are going up or down. If you do not have the answer in five seconds, then leave that stock alone, and move to another chart.

Classical chart analysis uses a series of higher highs and higher lows on a chart to identify an uptrend. A series of lower lows and lower highs denotes a downtrend.

Computer based analysis allows the use of complicated calculations to determine the trend. Moving averages, MACD, CCI, Trix are some technical indicators which identify the trend automatically for the trader.

A trend that lasts for many years is a primary trend. Bull and bear markets are examples of primary trends, many of which may last for a decade or more.

Within these primary trends, there are a number of smaller trend movements which are called intermediate, or secondary, trends. Thus, inside a primary bull market it is possible to have many intermediate trends, both up and down. The down moves are corrections where the trader stays away, while the up moves are in the direction of the primary trend, therefore, should be bought into.

Noise

A favourite phrase among TV analysts and anchors is "the market is choppy". Choppy markets exhibit "noise". Market noise is an erratic up and down price move that does not cause any final change in prices. Suppose the Nifty starts the month at 5,400, then during the month, falls to 5,200, goes up to 5,600, falls again to 5,250, and finally ends the month at 5,420. This is noise, where the market moved in different directions, only to stay where it was. Noise is far more prevalent in shorter time frames, where many days exhibit a lot of choppiness with the market closing where it opened, while moving all around during the day. Noise worries traders since there is no way to predict market movements.

The opposite of noise is trend, when the market moves steadily in one direction — up or down. There are corrections in between, but the direction is clear.

Background to the Newsletters in this Book

In 2003, the greatest bull market in Indian stock market history started. Like all good bulls, the market started in silence, almost in stealth. At 920, in April 2003, the Nifty was as low as it could get. Smart money started coming in, the market began to move up and, as they say, the rest is history. I have been writing these letters since 1998. The letters included in this book start in September 2007, when the bull market was still raging, almost four-and-a-half years after it had started. Wise men and women, coming on business TV, went on repeating five words: "This time it is different". The Nifty was then trading at 4,500, which was five times higher than its level in April 2003. So, we had had a five-fold gain in just four-and-a-half years. It could not be better. The trend was up, therefore, my own analysis was also upbeat. But the dark clouds, not yet seen on the horizon, were forming in the mind.

The letters start from September 2007 when the market was beginning to recover from a small correction. A new generation of investors, young and savvy, obviously unlike me, were asking, "What is a bear market, anyway?" All was well with the world. Market participants were heady with success. Later, much later, the public found that business TV channels were signing private "treaties" with companies planning IPOs.

My point is: when a business TV channel starts entering into "treaties" imagining itself to be like a sovereign nation, the bull market is probably living on borrowed time.

Anyway, my narrative starts in September 2007 when the market could do no wrong. It moves on to the time of great despair — the period from 2008 to early 2009 — when the market fell from 6,350 to 2,250, and then the start of a new bull market in early 2009.

Purpose of Publishing the Newsletters

I have already discussed the underlying philosophy behind my analysis. The purpose behind publishing these letters is two-fold:

- To share how analysis was done in real time, and
- To explain and illustrate how the classical theory of technical analysis is used for market analysis and trading.

Each letter contained a section called "Nifty Watch". It is this section which has been included in the following pages. To keep the narrative concise, I have excluded the Nifty Watch for many days to avoid repetitive commentary.

I would like to add that nothing of substance has been changed in the letters even when, in hindsight, my analysis of the market was incorrect. Only the language has been lightly edited keeping in mind the requirements of a book.

Chapter 3

Market live!

3 September 2007 – 28 April 2009

3 September 2007

Rally Continues, Strong Momentum Suggests New Highs Possible

Every Dip is a Buying Opportunity

Figure 3.1: **Nifty weekly chart. A brief correction may be over. Note the big move this week.**

Intermediate Uptrend

The Nifty is now in an intermediate uptrend. Investors should distribute their investment in different sectors. Here are some suggestions:

- Buy stocks which are breaking out to their 52 week highs.
- Buy stocks which may be coming out after deep corrections. These would normally belong to sectors undergoing a correction.
- Wait patiently for a small correction to come in. This is not impossible. All markets go through cycles which see peaks and troughs (lows). An investor who buys at the end of a correction makes the most amount of money.

But no short selling should be done. On breaking of support, we should step aside, avoid buying and wait for the correction to get over.

What could go wrong?

The trend may abruptly change due to:

1. Sudden instability in the domestic political scene.
2. Increased worries in the global markets on (the US) sub-prime or other issues.

Now, investors have no control over such external issues. Therefore, we should not worry about the things that we cannot change.

The charts tell us that the trend is up. We should follow market momentum.

14 September 2007

Nifty Closes Higher, Getting Ready for Breakout

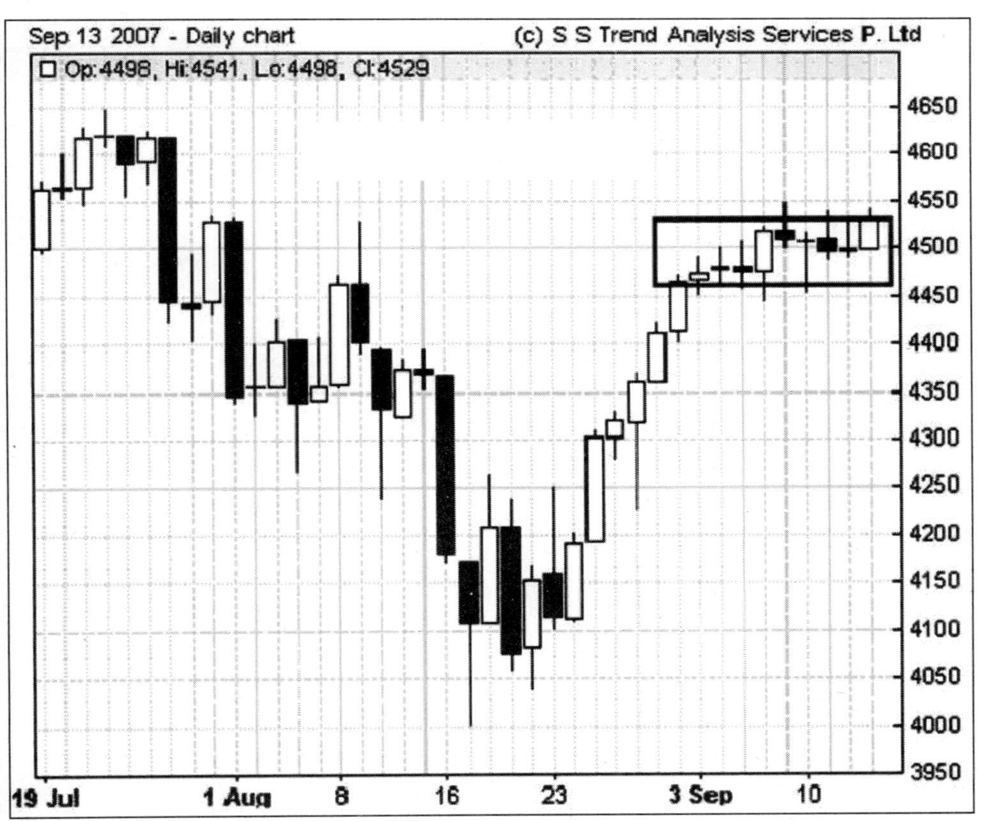

Figure 3.2: **Nifty on the verge of breakout from a trading range (boxed area in the chart).**

The CNX Nifty index closed higher today. Buyers came in from the start of trading. The market is in the top part of the trading range. Any close above current levels would reconfirm the current uptrend from the beginning of the month and forecast additional gains, while a move below new support in the 4,500 area would forecast a return to the recent lows in the 4,470 area. The primary uptrend is alive and well. The Sensex is within striking distance of its all time highs, while the Nifty needs just 100 points more to reach record levels again.

The short term trend remains up. Traders need to worry if the Nifty were to move below 4,470. Till then, buy on dips.

The trading range in the Nifty continues. It is on the verge of breaking up. On the downside, a close below 4,470 will be bearish.

20 September 2007

It is Official — The Bull Market is Alive

In a record breaking rally, Nifty moves to lifetime highs, cheers investors.

Optimism

The Indian rupee jumped to its highest level in more than nine years after the benchmark share index rose to a record, stoking optimism that overseas funds will buy more local (Indian) stocks.

The rupee rose 0.7 percent to 40.21 per dollar in Mumbai. That is the highest since May 1998.

It is party time! The Sensex has just moved above 16,000 — sweet sixteen! The Nifty is above 4,700, at levels we could not have imagined four years earlier. Stock markets the world over are in good shape. A rate cut by the Fed in USA has created quite a stir — almost as if the troubles around the world have been solved in one stroke. Cheers for the good times!

Life Time Highs are Bullish

Thus, even if there is some small sign of a dip, treat it as a dip, not a bear market. India is likely to face some turbulence in its political scene. While markets may react to such news, such reaction may just be short term in

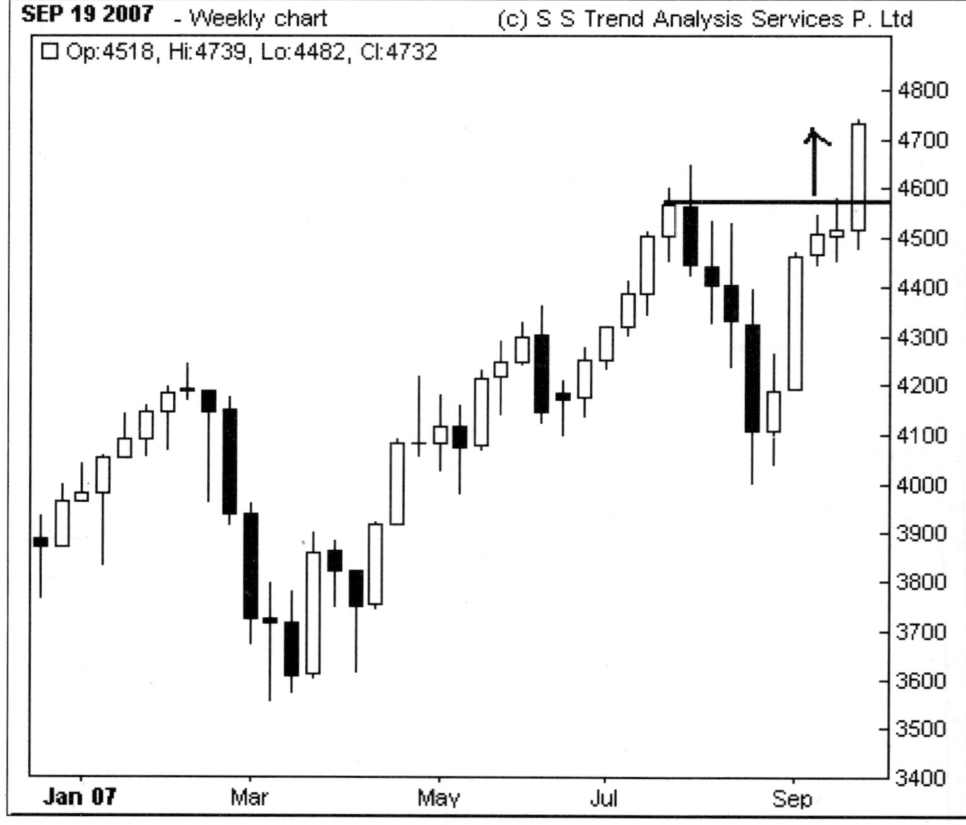

Figure 3.3: **Lifetime high of Nifty — buy on dips.**

nature. In summary, buy on dips. We need a lot of technical evidence to suggest that the intermediate uptrend is over. As of now, there is no evidence of weakness.

While target setting is not usually suggested, a simple glance on charts tells us this:

> The Nifty moved up 500 points from 4,050 to 4,550 before it started a trading range. An equal move is possible, after the trading range breakout, giving an eventual target of 5,050. Please remember that targets are just that — flights of fantasy. The market is reality.

25 September 2007

Markets in Euphoria

Traders should take profit and keep away from the market. Investors should take at least some profit.

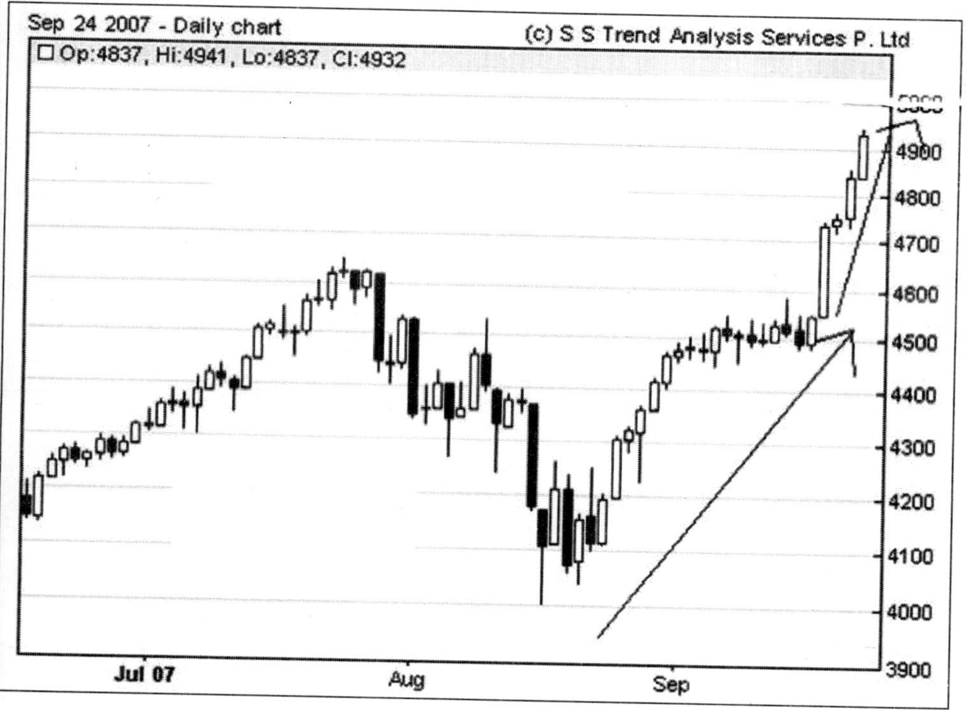

Figure 3.4: **Take care! Parabolic rally in Nifty shows signs of euphoria. Take profits on long positions.**

The Nifty has seen a 23% gain in less than a month — a remarkable achievement. This is a good time to book profits.

The Nifty is within striking distance of 5,000, while the Sensex needs just a few points to make it to 17,000. Assuming these magic numbers are touched, what happens next? At least in the short term, the current market euphoria cannot last much longer. Traders should take profits, keep away from the market for some days.

28 September 2007

A Landmark Day — Nifty Crosses 5,000

Slowly, Basic Support May Shift from 4,000 to 5,000

New highs are psychologically assuring, but markets will still correct.

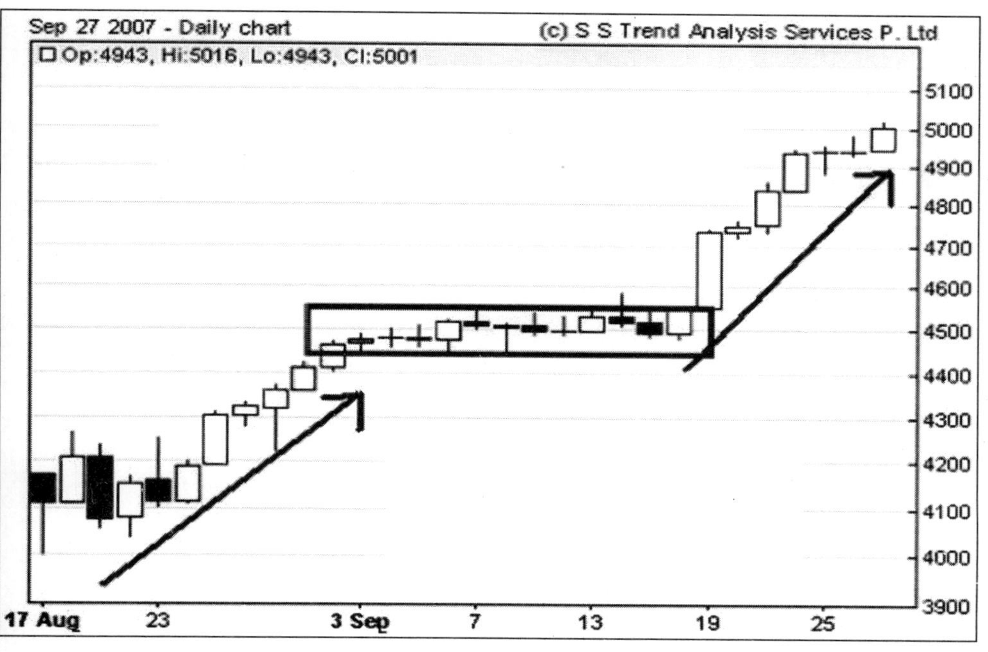

Figure 3.5: **The two Doji patterns are cancelled as Nifty closes higher.**

The Nifty crossed 5,000 rather easily. Two days of indecision as reflected by Doji patterns on the Nifty were cancelled today when the index closed decisively higher.

However, the market still remains under the threat of a short term decline / consolidation. I repeat this every day to warn traders not to get suddenly caught with big plus positions, or, even worse, to buy now only to find the market slipping away.

For long term investors, the going is good. What may come about is a consolidation — an event which should not frighten them. Thus, there seems to be no reason to lighten up. What investors should do is to switch from stocks that have given large returns to other stocks (not in the same sector!).

4 October 2007

Enter the Bubble

A 240-point intra day move in the Nifty is a sign of increased volatility. There is an intermediate top close by. Traders must be careful while trading.

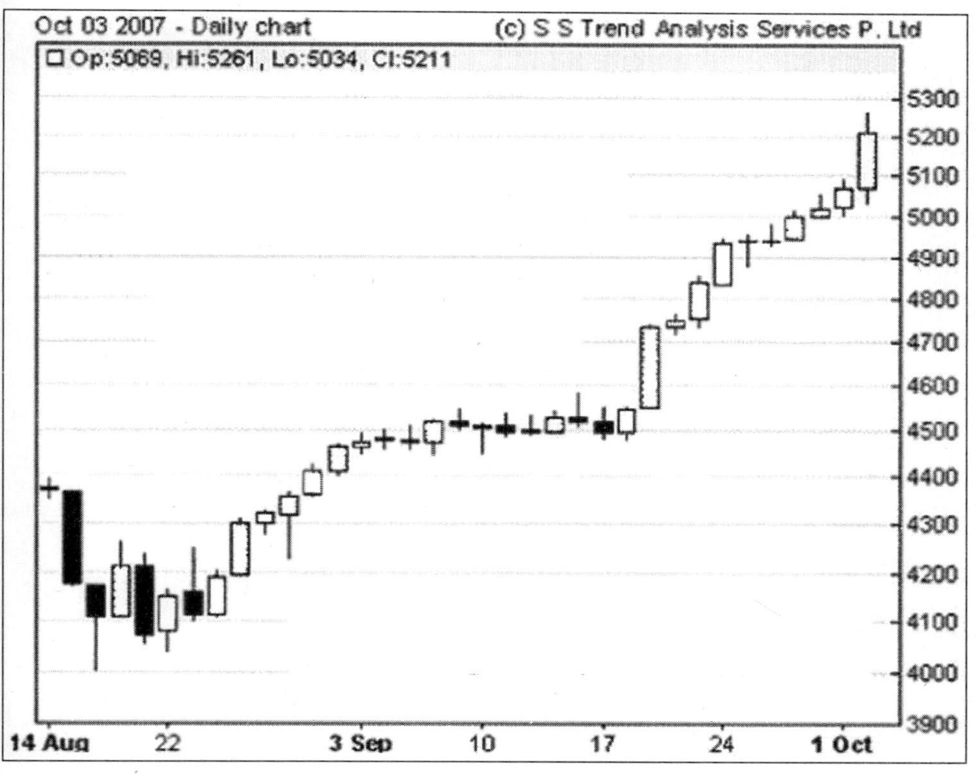

Figure 3.6: **Nifty gains 17%; 11 consecutive days of higher close. Look outside your window, there is a bear lurking nearby. Careful, please.**

The Nifty Today

From the open, Nifty futures moved up 130 points. Then they fell 250 points. Then again moved up 210 points. So the total movement was 590 points, about 12% of the Nifty's value. This is a lot of volatility.

The Nifty end of day chart displays a stunning rally, with 11 consecutive days of gains, and a 17% up move in the same period.

Such an up move is possible if it were coming at the beginning of a bull cycle. But, at current levels, we can only assume that we are witnessing a period of euphoria.

10 October 2007

Nifty, Sensex Surge 4% to Record Close

Markets have their own mind. When a trend starts, go with it or stay away. Never fight a trend, whether up or down.

Figure 3.7: **Nifty moves non-stop from 4,000 to 5,350 in 8 weeks. Such an event is unlikely. Thus we should expect a cooling off process, suddenly.**

The Indian stock markets set a historic record on Tuesday amid signs that the political uncertainty in the country may finally lead to some resolution, along with expectations that foreign funds will continue to come in India in large volumes.

The driver to this rally, Reliance, gained almost 8%. Big movers included telecom giants Bharti Airtel and Reliance Communications — both Index heavyweights. Most Nifty stocks notched gains over yesterday's close, thus helping the Nifty cross 5,300, and the Sensex cross 18,000.

What's Going On?

Well, there are buyers who feel that the markets will go up. The buyers presently have more money than the sellers. This tells us that funds remain buyers, while some professional and retail traders are sellers. Thus, the buying remains in strong hands, while selling is in weak hands.

This is also reflected by the intermediate trend which remains up. The short term trend, or the trader's trend, turned down yesterday, but quickly reversed direction today to become bullish again. That's the way of the markets — sometimes they are predictable, some times not.

What's Next?

The Nifty has gained 1,350 points in 36 trading days. This comes to 37.5 points per day. At this rate, over the next year, the index should pick up 9,000 points (given 240 trading days). Will the Nifty be at 14,350 after one year? Now, that is an unlikely scenario. Therefore, markets have moved up too fast. The small dip seen on Monday is not the end of the cooling off process.

A more comprehensive dip / correction / consolidation is inevitable.

Why do I keep writing about this?

Once markets reach a danger zone, professional traders should:

1. Bring down volumes, and
2. Be alert to sudden trend changes by always keeping stop losses.

Should we not always keep stop losses anyway? Why talk about it now?

At different stages in the market, stop losses have different use. When you sense that the market may be bottoming out or topping out, then your stops should be tight, since a reversal may occur any time. When you sense that you are in a strong trend, your stop losses are loose, since you want to avoid getting stopped out in any small whipsaw.

What is the Trading Strategy?

- Use dips to buy. Dips will keep on coming, day after day.
- Use stops to ensure that you are not caught when the dip becomes a full correction.

That P/E Ratio Again

After many months, there is a discussion on the P/E Ratio in this column. On 9 October, as per NSE web site, the P/E for the 50 Nifty stocks was 24.5.

Now, this is not on the lower side. Of course, valuations can keep on increasing. In Japan, the Nikkei peaked on 29 December 1989 at 38,915. P/E ratios for many stocks climbed to 80 and higher. The generally accepted explanation why this could be sustained was that Japan had become a new economy and could not be evaluated by outdated measures. ("It's different!"). The devastating bear market that followed felled the index by 63.5% to 14,194 by August 1992.

If the NSE P/E ratio were to double from 24.5 to 49 in a year, the Nifty would then trade at 10,700. A gain of 5,350 points will require an average daily gain of 22.30 points. Even by this measure, the current gains in the Nifty (37.5 points per day) are not sustainable.

12 October 2007

Nifty Above 5,500

Record Breaking Rally Sees 38% Gain in 39 Trading Days

This is 1% per day. In a trading year of 240 days, will this be 240%? Unlikely. Therefore, go with the up-trend, but be alert to any sign of reversal.

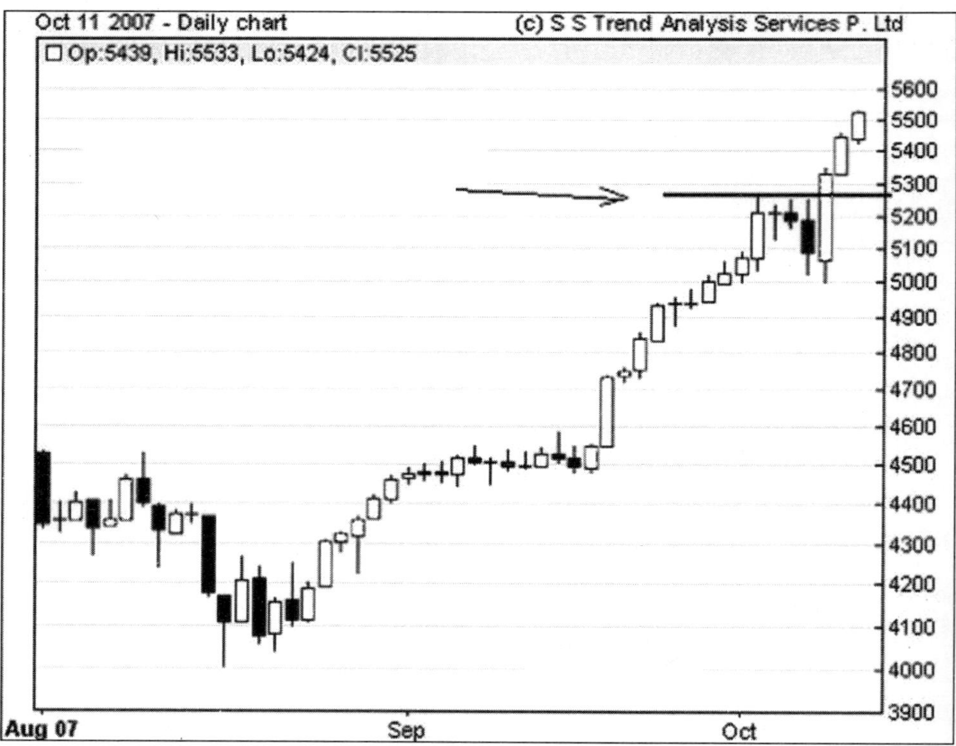

Figure 3.8: **Nifty daily — 5,270 is support. It is also a target for any correction.**

Keynes said: "Markets can remain irrational longer than traders can remain solvent." This means do not try to fight the market just because the market is at an extreme. Markets can remain at extreme point for long periods, but our money can get exhausted quickly. Irrational markets are a fact of life. These are cycles of optimism and pessimism. They reach extremes, but we can never say what the final point is. Thus, short term traders should go with the uptrend. Buy on dips.

Investors should either become traders or, better still, wait for a correction. In a bull market, every year there are 2 or 3 buying corrections.

Good News for Nifty Traders

With an increase in volatility plus an increase in absolute values, a 70- to 100-point intra day swing in the Nifty is quite possible. This opens up a number of possibilities for short term / intra day trading.

16 October 2007

A Bull on the Highway

1,000 Sensex Points in 4 Days, What's Next?

Strong bubbles can go on for more time than we imagine. The end result will always be a big bursting of the bubble, but when?

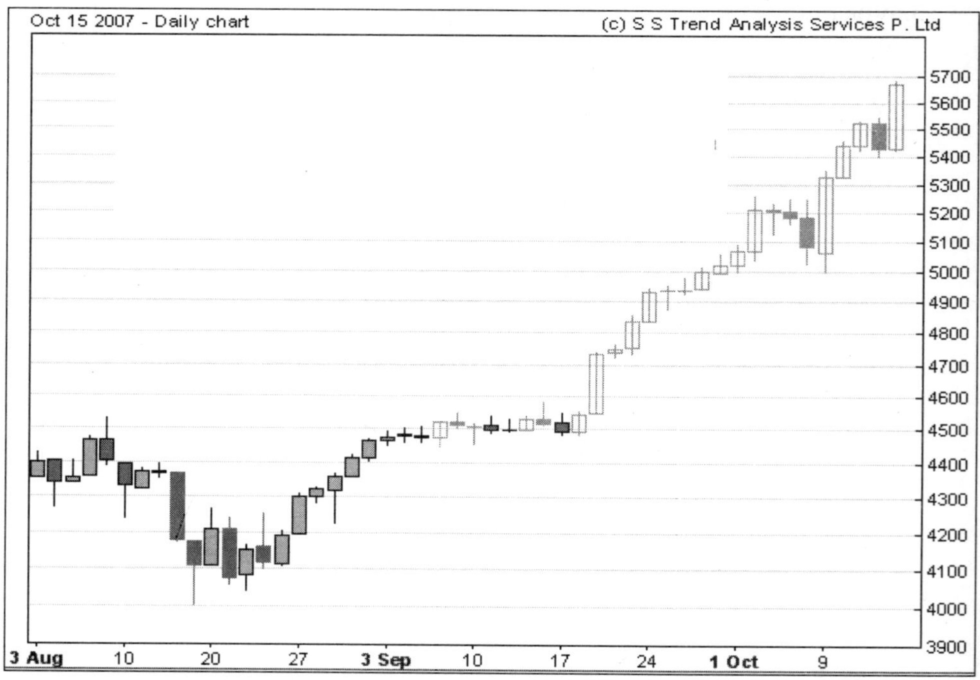

Figure 3.9: **Gains continue. Nifty gains 42% in less than 2 months. Follow the market, protect your positions — when a bubble bursts it can be harmful to your financial health.**

By pushing the index up, the FIIs feel they can make easy money in India. I think they are in for a surprise. The bull market in India will continue for sure, but probably not on the terms set by a few foreign funds. Well, we will watch this drama with a lot of interest.

For Monday, this column had written "A move above 5,549 on Monday will tell us there is a lot more upside left. " This seems to have worked out well.

The Nifty today had a 270-point range although there was no volatility — it was completely one sided.

After such a large range day there are three possibilities:

1. Follow through: Another big up move comes in riding on the momentum generated by this one.
2. Short term reversal. After trading above today's high, the market slides lower.
3. Volatility: The market remains direction less, causing a lot of intra day volatility.

Short term traders should be aware of these possibilities.

19 October 2007

Traders, How About Some Buying Now?

Big drama in the market creates havoc and panic. But IT stocks continue to hold on. The Nifty is almost 10% down from its intra day highs. Maybe, Friday could be a buy day.

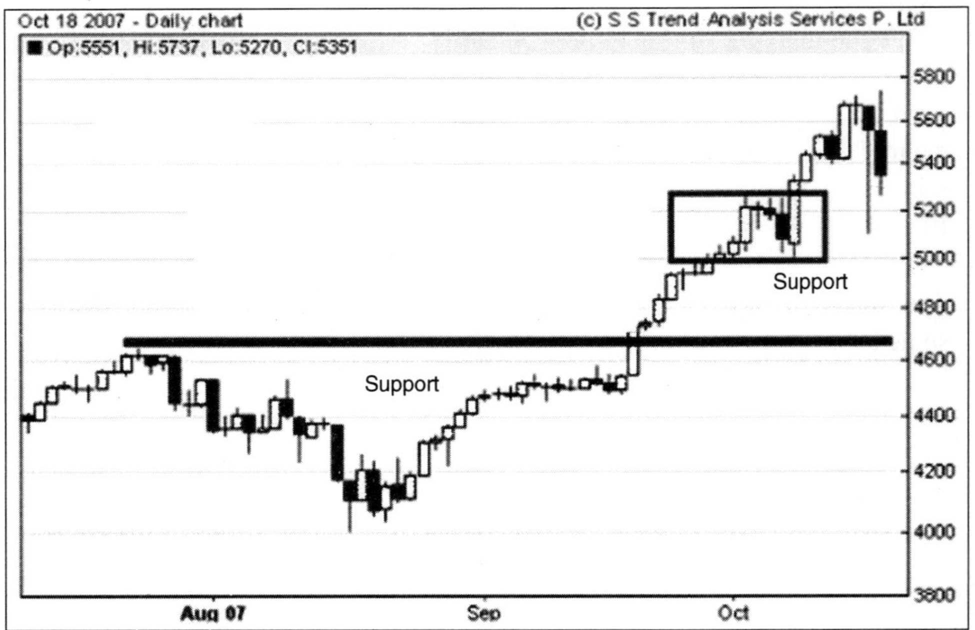

Figure 3.10: **Nifty has a zone of strong support 5,250-5,000 (boxed area in the chart). 4,650 remains support if we see an intermediate down move.**

Bulls Lose Control, But Increased Volatility Tells Us that Bears May Not Be in Control, Either

42 stocks advanced today, as compared to 28 advances yesterday. IT stocks were gainers, even after the big crash. This sector should now come in the lists of traders, as some changes seem to be happening here. But the overall trend seems to have changed, with the LR line* having 76 up-trending stocks and 134 downtrending stocks.

What Next?

The Nifty may see a lot of consolidation between 5,000 and 5,400 as this volatility ends. From this consolidation, will the index resume its up move, or will it move down even more — that's a question which cannot be answered now.

We are in a long term bull market. Now, after two volatile days, some of the excesses of the bull move have been removed. The Nifty is now in a short term downtrend. There may be more downside, but to some extent the market now carries lower risk. Traders and investors should follow the principle of buying on dips. There will also be short selling opportunities. But only professional traders should take such opportunities.

Last month, a straight line advance created a mini bubble in the market. This was a cause for worry as was pointed out many times. Now, there is some cooling off. To that extent, the market is safer.

* LR stands for linear regression, which is used in a manner similar to moving averages. When the LR line is moving up, the trend is up, and when it is moving down the trend is down. Its direction shows the trend.

30 October 2007

Sooner the Better, Up Move Continues

Nifty Races Towards 6,000, Sensex Touches 20k

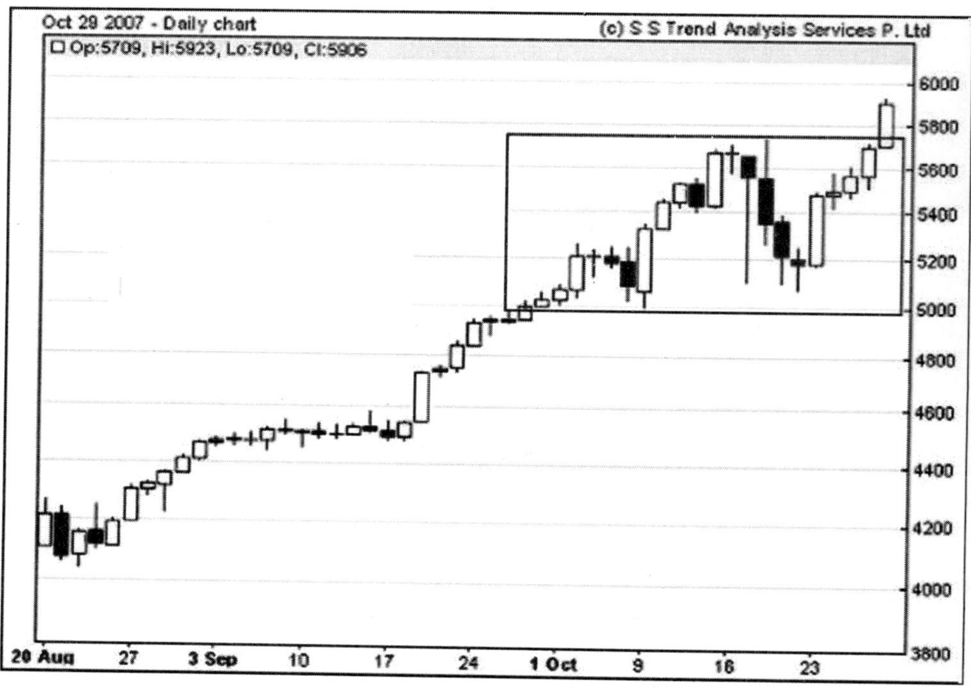

Figure 3.11: **Nifty breaks out from a large trading range (boxed area in the chart). Next target for Nifty is 6,400.**

Will there be a correction? Yes, of course, there will be one. The date and time is unknown, as also the levels at which this correction will start. With these two unknowns, traders should focus on the current trend, which remains up.

The Nifty moved up today, an event that of late seems to happen every day; therefore, it's no longer news. The Index has moved out of a fairly large trading range, giving a pattern target of 6,400 approximately. For the Nifty, these targets have usually been exceeded.

The last five days have seen the Nifty move from 5,100 to 5,920, a gain of 820 points, i.e. about 16%. While momentum can take us anywhere, it does appear that the Index may well take some rest soon. Within this bull market, dips should be used to buy.

No Crash, Please!

Many subscribers call us to say, "The markets are going to crash soon." Now, readers know that this was my own view, when the Nifty was rallying to 5,700. The market did crash, not once but twice, by 600 points each time. These two declines have removed most weak positions from the market, both long and short. There is no reason for a crash now. I assume there will be corrections and declines but a bear market move is unlikely.

6 November 2007

Resistance at Higher Levels Pushes Nifty Below 5,900

More Downside Possible

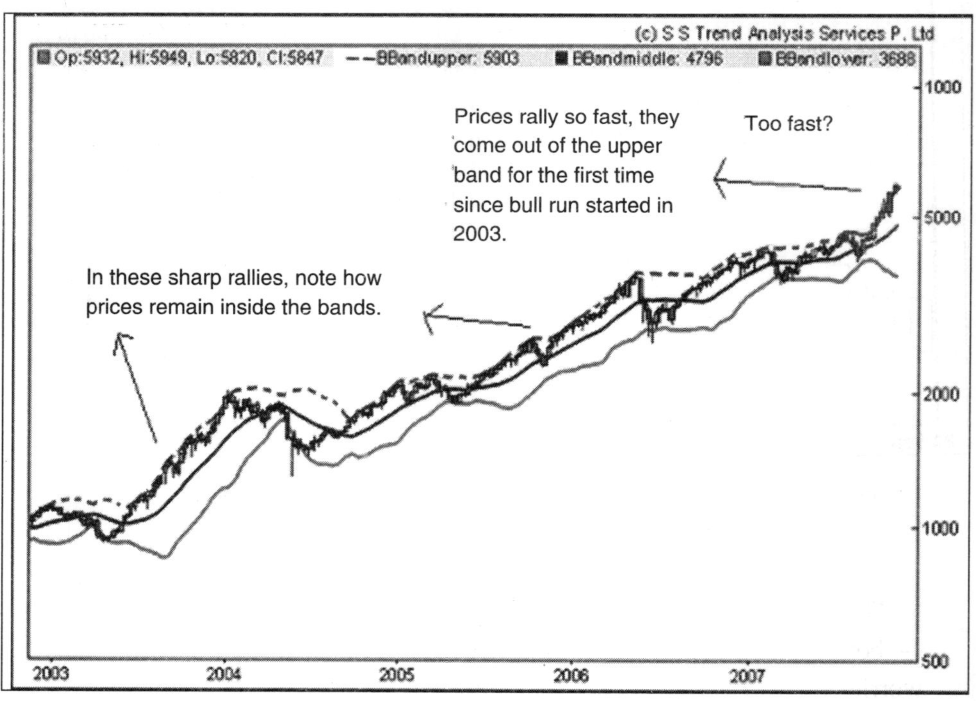

Figure 3.12: **Nifty weekly chart with Bollinger Bands.**

The current bull market started in 2003. Since then we have seen many sharp rallies. The weekly chart given here shows how each rally was broadly contained by the upper line of the Bollinger Bands. But, this time, the rally has been so rapid, prices have gone above the bands. This may be an indication of unsustainable momentum.

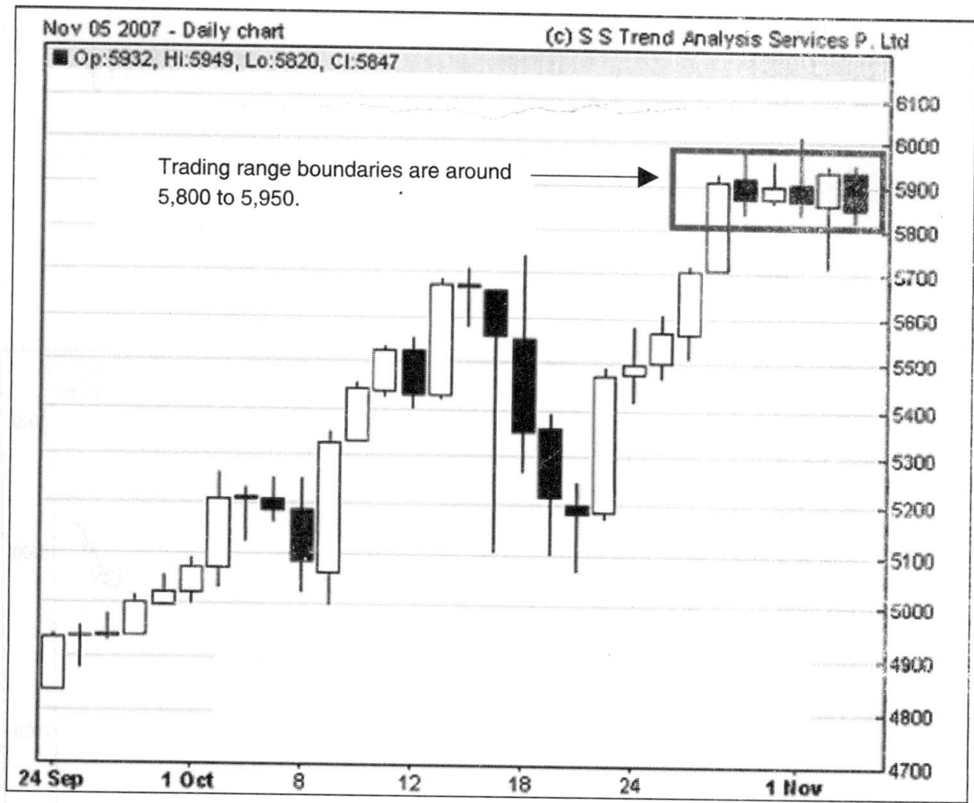

Figure 3.13: **Nifty spends five days in a trading range. Index may be ready for big move — up or down.**

The Nifty continued its roller coaster ride with large intra day swings — both up and down. For some reason, the Index disregarded American worries on Friday. Today (Monday), the market opened lower, then never really recovered from its gap down. A mid-afternoon sell off saw the Nifty go below 5,900, then reach 5,810, finally close at 5,847 with large losses over Friday's close.

So, what's happening? The Nifty chart tells us that the Index is in a trading range for the past five days. This trading range will eventually lead to a trending move — up or down is unknown. Taking the width of this range to be around 150 points (upper boundary = 5,950, lower = 5,800), if and when any of these boundaries break, we can look for a move to 5,650 on the downside or 6,100 on the upside.

The market is going through a period of increased volatility. This means that your stop losses must be wider than normal. If necessary, reduce volume. Avoid taking overnight positions that are losing money.

8 November 2007

Decisive Close Below 5,800 Starts a Down Trend in the Nifty

The short term trend is down, with the Nifty closing below 5,800, then breaking down from an intra day triangle. All in all, these are signs of weakness. Now, there is a sense of hesitation in calling a down move since the market has this tendency of suddenly changing direction, making a mockery of all prevailing bearish chart patterns. When will this down

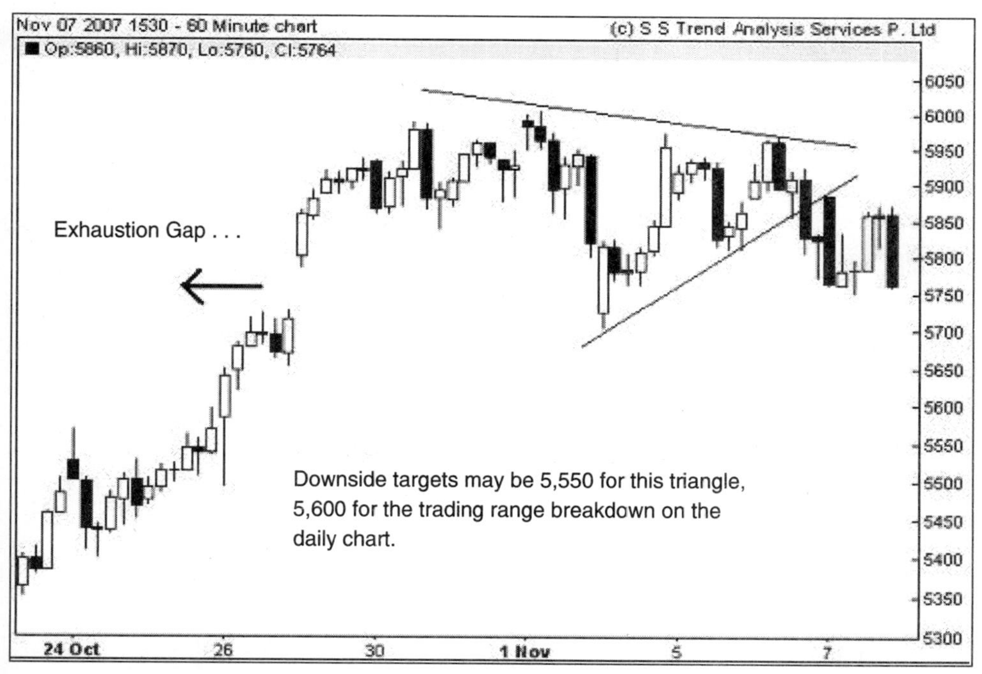

Figure 3.14: **Nifty 60-minute chart. In closing below 5,800 the Nifty broke down from a triangle (upper right hand portion of the chart).**

move be cancelled? If the Nifty were to go above 5,950, then the down move is no longer valid. Closer to current price, there is a pivot high at 5,880 approximately. A close above this number will be a warning signal for bears. In the intermediate term, the Nifty has fairly strong support around 5,500. A dip to this level will represent a buying opportunity.

The Golden Age of Volatility Inspired Opportunity

The increase in volatility is a big benefit to traders. Volatility can provide opportunities for an active trader that would not exist if the asset were to appreciate along a steady trend line. Price swings are an aspect of markets that both traders and active investors could truly learn to love.

What Happened to Our Earlier Talk of Unsustainable Rallies?

We have seen many non-stop rallies in this market; day after day the market going up without any respite. Such rallies are not sustainable. For this reason, when a feeling developed that "this time it is different", this column warned against assuming a perpetual uptrend. I think later events have proved us to be correct. We have seen severe declines after the sharp rallies. Now the market is moving in both directions. It is volatile, no doubt, but we are having both up and down swings. This is the sign of a healthy market. Therefore, we no longer talk of unsustainable rallies.

Gazing into the Crystal Ball

We remain optimistic on equities. While target setting is not an easy task (not required also), a Nifty at 10,000 is within the realms of possibility over the next 2 years. Markets will undoubtedly remain volatile thanks to:

(a) World wide credit worries, and,
(b) A faster than required momentum in our own market, which needs to cool down.

Emerging markets should remain the flavour of the season, with India leading the pack. We will have the inevitable and necessary corrections during this up move. It is possible that some of these corrections may be severe. That's the law of nature — it balances irrational exuberance with severe declines. Please remember, lower prices imply higher prospective returns.

13 November 2007

Bullish Reversal Day Protects Nifty from Downside

Support Comes in Around 5,500

After a gap down, the Nifty did manage to recover lost ground closing with only minor losses. The day was fairly bullish with a long lower shadow in the candlesticks suggesting a possible low. The Nifty was touching its 20-period moving average. The centre black line is this average in the chart. This average has provided support on three earlier occasions. This may well happen again.

Indications that support has broken: If the Nifty were to close below the average again, this will be an indication that the moving average support is not holding. In case the support breaks, we may be looking at a dip to the lower Bollinger Band around 5,200+. Traders should try to go long with a mental stop loss based on the breakdown of support as detailed above. If the MA support breaks, then there should be no long positions. Going short is a preference for each individual trader.

Trade with a View

Traders must have a view on the market where they wish to trade. This view can be bullish, bearish, or no view at all. If you are bullish then you

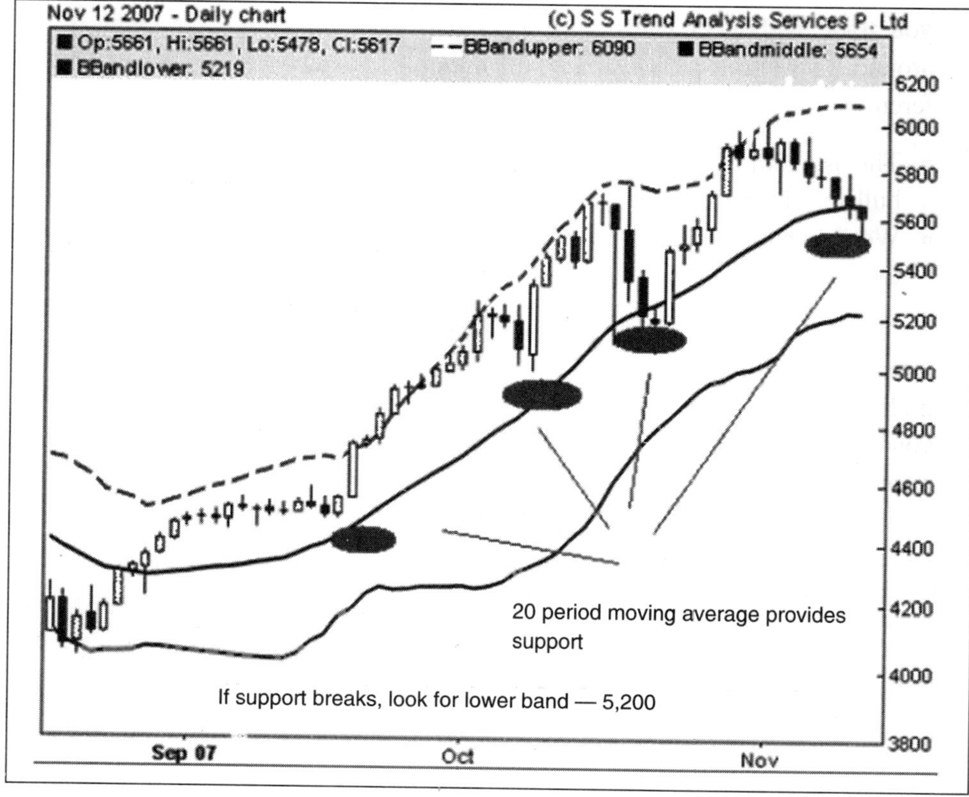

Figure 3.15: **Nifty with Bollinger Bands.**

look for dips to take low risk entries. If you are bearish then you look for rallies to take low risk shorts. Your view can be based on charts — higher highs and higher lows are bullish, lower highs and lower lows are bearish. You can also form your view based on an indicator — the Alligator, MACD, direction of a linear regression line, etc. Be prepared that often your view will be wrong. This is not your fault. The markets are not predictable to the extent of 100%. If your view is wrong, then your money management procedures will ensure that you take only small losses. But if you trade without a view, then there will be havoc and confusion all around. I write this today since at this point it is possible to have two different views on the market:

- This is a bull market. Any dip is a buying opportunity. Here the view is bullish. The trader looks for opportunities to go long.
- We may be in for a sharp correction, maybe all the way to 4,500. Here, the view is bearish with the trader looking for shorting opportunities.

At some point in the future, one of these views will be accepted as wrong. But, currently, each scenario has some possibility. Now, you can trade with either view and make money if the market remains volatile. But you cannot trade by wishing to capture all moves, up and down. So, please have a view, then try to trade in that direction.

21 November 2007

Nifty Corrects, Seeks Lower Levels

Significant Support Comes in Around 5,600

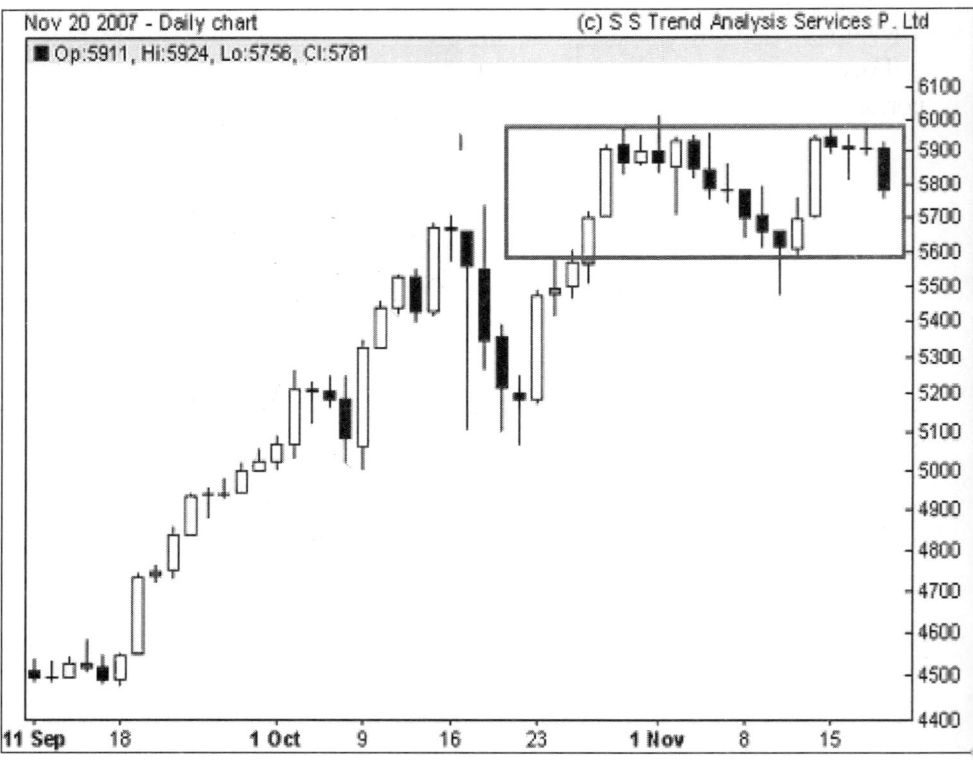

Figure 3.16: **Nifty is in a trading range between 5,600 to 6,000. Inside this range, traders should identify low risk spots to trade — dips to buy, rallies to sell. Use oscillators like tm Stoch to identify such points.**

Three days of narrow range movements set the pace for a breakout / breakdown. Today this big move came about, with the Nifty falling 140 points from its intra day high to an intra day low. The decline itself changes nothing much. The intermediate trend remains up. A close below 5,600 is required to change this to sideways.

The Nifty is now inside a fairly narrow range, bounded by 5,600 and 6,000. Inside this range, there will be up and down movements likely to be limited by the outer boundaries of 6,000 and 5,600. Traders should seek to buy on weakness, then exit on rallies. A move above 6,000 is certain to see another 400 to 500 points, whenever it happens.

Range bound trading is not fun. But the market goes through cycles. The current cycle is for a consolidation.

Focus should be on mid cap stocks, where dips can provide buying opportunities. Always use stops.

4 December 2007

Trend is Up in All Time Frames

Figure 3.17: **Nifty's pattern of lower highs and lower lows changed to one of higher highs and higher lows, confirming that the trend is up in all time frames.**

A breakout above 6,000, if and whenever it happens should see 6,500.

The Index continues to move up. Following classical Dow Theory (as modified by my own understanding), a pattern of higher highs, higher lows tells us that the intermediate trend is up. Therefore, the primary trend is up, the intermediate trend is up and the minor trend is also up. All said, buy on dips. The trend is in trouble if the Nifty were to close below 5,600 — a swing low. As time goes by, these levels will change.

12 December 2007

Nifty Makes All Time Highs

Breakout to Upside from the Range of 5,500-6,000 as Nifty Closes at 6,092

Figure 3.18: **Upside breakout of Nifty after trading in a range. Nifty's new target is likely to be 6,500.**

A large trading range was finally (and decisively) broken on the upside as the Nifty gracefully moved above 6,000 and closed well above this level at 6,092. The uptrend resumes after a period of consolidation. A target for the current breakout is 6,500 approximately.

The key question is: will this be a genuine breakout or will the Nifty return back inside 6,000? On the charts, the breakout has come after a period of consolidation. This zone of consolidation (5,900 to 6,000) will act as support for any decline. Therefore, by the charts, this breakout should be sustained, eventually leading to 6,500.

But the Indian markets are coupled with the international markets. Therefore, what happens to the US markets after any Fed announcement is likely to affect the Indian market. Thus, the trend determined in USA will be what eventually happens here. If USA decides to fall, then we are likely to follow suit. Chart patterns will change. Traders should, therefore, have an open mind. The trend is decisively up. In case of an international reversal, be prepared to reduce long positions and become neutral. Do not fight the market.

31 December 2007

Doji Appears in Uptrend

Nifty is Facing Resistance

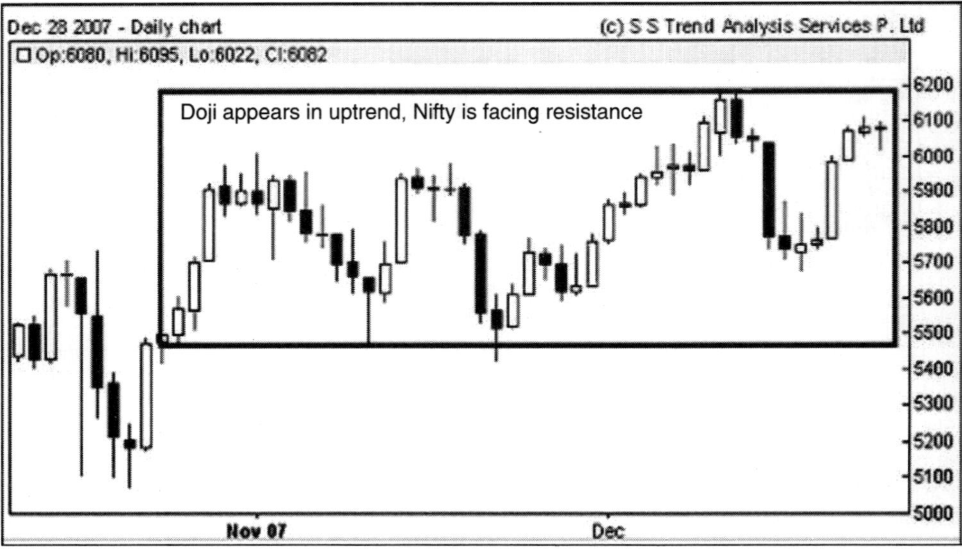

Figure 3.19: **Nifty touches higher end of trading range. Expect some consolidation in the next few days. A move above 6,100 should eventually see 6,500.**

The short term trend for the Nifty is up. The short term trend changes to down if the Nifty closes below 5,900. This level may change with time.

The intermediate trend for the Nifty is up. The trend changes to down if the Nifty closes below 5,700. The long term trend for the Nifty remains up. We are in a long term bull market. But readers must understand that this market has moved up without any significant correction. Therefore, the chances of a deep correction remain high.

4 January 2008

Narrow Movements in the Nifty

Consolidation / Choppy Intra Day Moves Suggest Uncertainty at Higher Levels

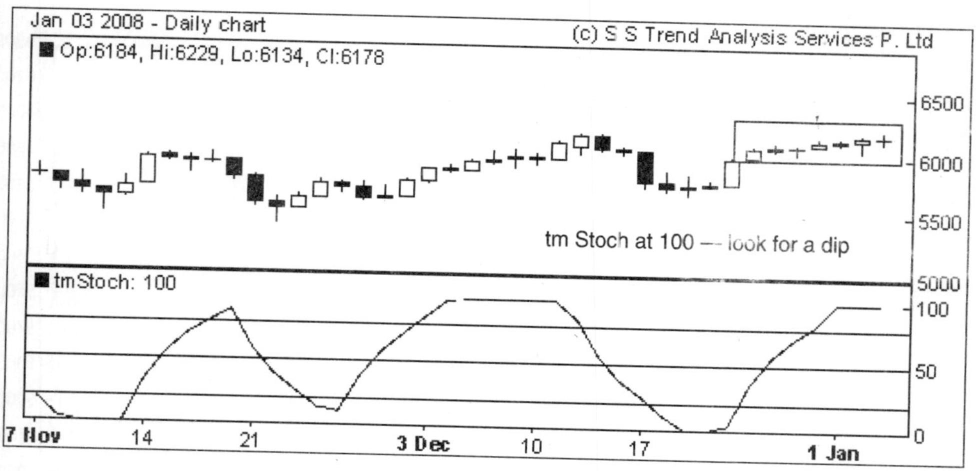

Figure 3.20: **Narrow range bars suggest uncertainty at higher levels.**

The Nifty proved to be the strongest among emerging markets. While most markets saw declines, the Indian market was almost unchanged. This relative movement does have a message: The trend is up, buy on dips. A rally from 5,700 has seen a 500-point gain. The market is providing us with confusing signals. We have narrow range days, high wave candles, then Doji — all of these suggest uncertainty. While individual stocks may still go their own way, it makes sense to wait for some kind of a cooling off before creating new swing trading positions.

Nifty Trend

The short term trend is up. A close below 6,060 will change this trend to down. The intermediate trend remains up. The Nifty will enter a downtrend if it closes below 5,700.

16 January 2008

Nifty in a Correction, Breaks Down from Trading Range

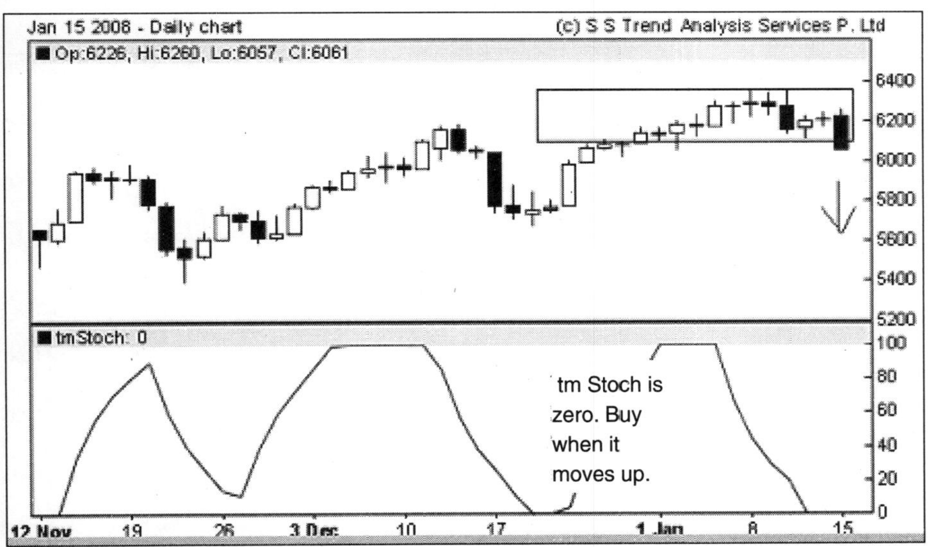

Figure 3.21: **Nifty breaks down from a trading range; pattern target is 5,850.**

A narrow range fell apart today, with the Nifty seeking lower levels. Momentum is no longer favouring the bulls. Traders should stay away, while investors are still waiting for a dip. They should hold their patience.

Nifty Trend, Support and Resistance

The short term trend has changed to down from up. This happened today when the Nifty closed below 6,100 giving a trading range breakdown.

The intermediate trend is up. This trend changes to down, if and when the Nifty closes below 5,700.

21 January 2008

Markets See a Big Correction

India affected by sharp decline in world markets. Nifty comes close to strong support around 5,500.

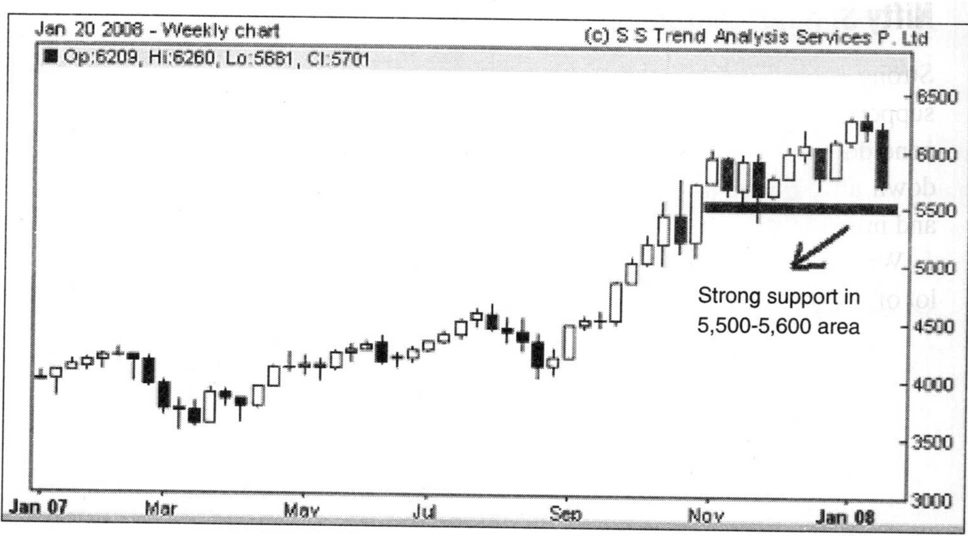

Figure 3.22: **Weekly chart of Nifty; the 5,500-5,600 zone should provide support. Wait for the market to become steady.**

Corrections and dips are buying opportunities. This remains a long term bull market. But the intermediate trend is down, so investors should be patient and wait for markets to become steady.

Nifty Trend

The short term trend is down. This trend changed to down when the Nifty fell below its trading range support at 6,100. This is the trend that should be followed by traders.

The intermediate trend changed to down on Friday. This happened when the Nifty fell below 5,800. This is the trend that investors should be tracking. In a downtrend, avoid making new commitments. Investors should wait patiently for this decline to be over.

Nifty Support and Resistance

Strong support for the Nifty comes in the 5,500 area. Think of this as a support zone rather than a number. This support should hold. But if this zone does not hold, then we are looking at a bear market that may take us down all the way to 4,500. This is a very unlikely scenario. But, traders and investors should be aware of the possibilities.

Where is the resistance? The first level is 5,800, then 5,960. There is a lot of resistance at different levels.

22 January 2008

Black Monday — Markets Take Big Hit, Go into a Free Fall

The intermediate downtrend strengthens, but this massive decline tells us we must be near an intermediate low.

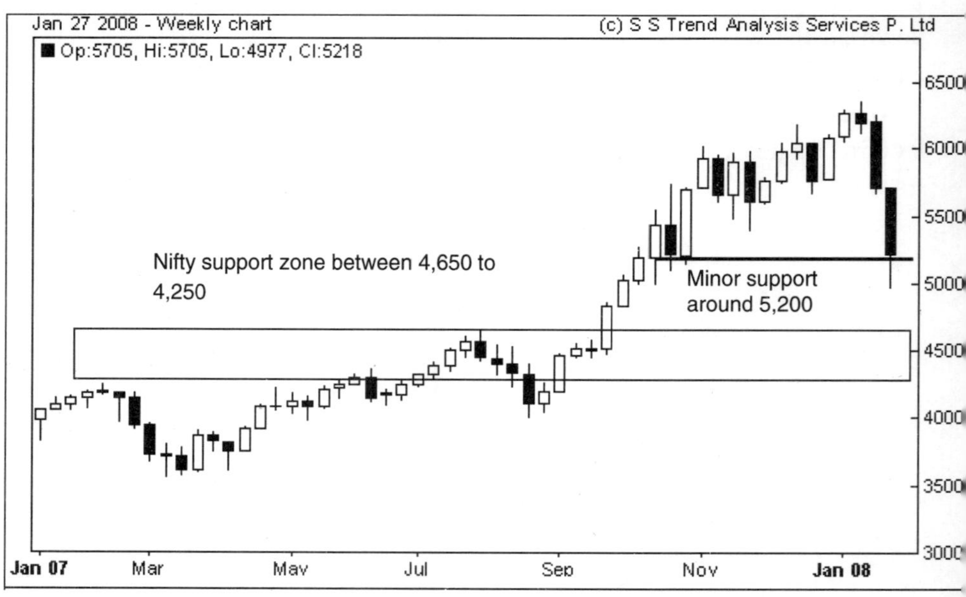

Figure 3.23: **A breakdown from minor support will probably see the Nifty drift down to the 4,650-4,250 support zone.**

Nifty Trend

The short term trend is down. This trend changed to down when the Nifty fell below its trading range support at 6,100. This is the trend that should be followed by traders. This trend remains down. If today's lows around 4,950 continue to hold, then we should be getting ready for a bounce back. Since these will be buying signals after a sharp down move, there is always the possibility that the trend may revert back to a down move. Therefore, the use of proper stops is essential. Stops should be placed below the lows made in this down leg (hopefully these have been made today).

When should you exit? If the trade is stopped out, then the exit is automatically done. In case the trade moves up, exits should be done when:

1. Trend Energy gives an exit signal by making a blue bar or a normal bar after a brown bar, or
2. tm Stoch crosses below 90, or,
3. Short term trend changes to down.

   (Trend Energy and tm Stoch are momentum indicators in the software which I use, and which most readers of my newsletter also use. When a trader buys into an uptrend, he should exit when momentum turns weak. A turn in the RSI after it goes above 60, or in Stochastics after it moves above 80 would give the same message — namely, the momentum is becoming weak.)

The intermediate trend changed to down on Friday. This happened when the Nifty fell below 5,800. This is the trend that investors should be tracking. In a downtrend, avoid making new commitments. Investors should wait patiently for this decline to be over. The intermediate trend entered into an exaggerated phase on Monday when the Nifty moved below 5,000 before rallying a bit. This does appear to be a sign that the worst is probably over, or nearly over. Investors should position themselves to take advantage of buying opportunities that are likely to emerge soon enough. At this point, they should ensure that they have cash to buy equity or derivatives. Remember, cash is king.

Nifty Support and Resistance

We had written:

> "But, if this (5,500) zone does not hold, then we are looking at a bear market, that may take us down all the way to 4,500. This is a very unlikely scenario. But, traders and investors should be aware of the possibilities."

The 5,500 support did not hold at all, triggering a free fall and pushing the Nifty all the way down to 4,950. Now, there remains a possibility that the eventual low may be formed near 4,500 where substantially strong support comes in. I do not say that 4,500 will be touched. It is quite possible that a low has already been made today. Frankly, we will let the market decide. The summary is: we now do not have any significant support for the Nifty. Strong support comes in only around 4,500. But it is possible that the Nifty may define a new support level.

Where is resistance? The first level is 5,450. There is a lot of resistance at different levels.

The Big Picture

Let us look at the reasons for the American stock market crash in 1929:

> "The crash followed a speculative boom that had taken hold in the late 1920s, which had led hundreds of thousands of Americans to invest heavily in the stock market, a significant number even borrowing money to buy more stock."*

This position has not yet come in India. Retail is far away from the stock market. Only a few million investors and traders are in the market. These are mainly affluent middle class people. Moreover, a bubble was developing in 1929, with share prices having no relationship with earnings. That is not so in India. My view then remains the same: This is a long term bull market. Corrections and dips are a part of the process. These should be considered as buying opportunities.

**Source:* http://en.wikipedia.org/wiki/Wall_Street_Crash_of_1929.

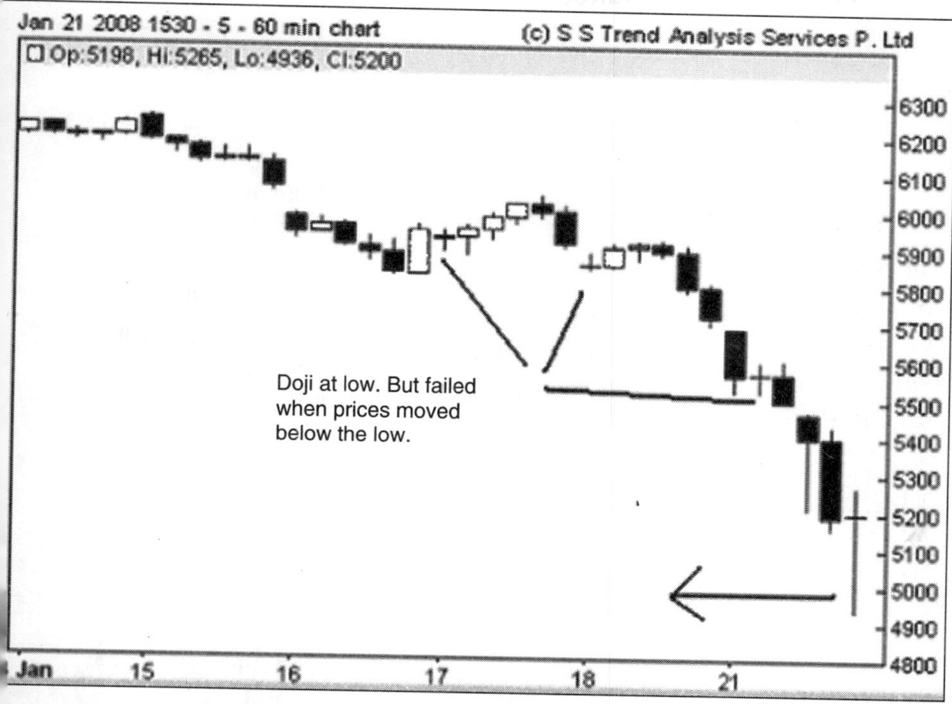

Figure 3.24: **The 60-minute chart of Nifty indicates that selling may be exhausted. A Doji combined with high wave candle with long lower shadows suggest a possible reversal. Earlier, a Doji was formed at the lows but failed as the prices moved even lower.**

The last bar was a high wave candle with long lower shadows. It was also Doji. This may well signal at least a short term reversal.

23 January 2008

Carnage in the Market

The market remains in an intermediate downtrend. A sharp dip saw the Nifty touch 4,500 before recovering a bit to close slightly better.

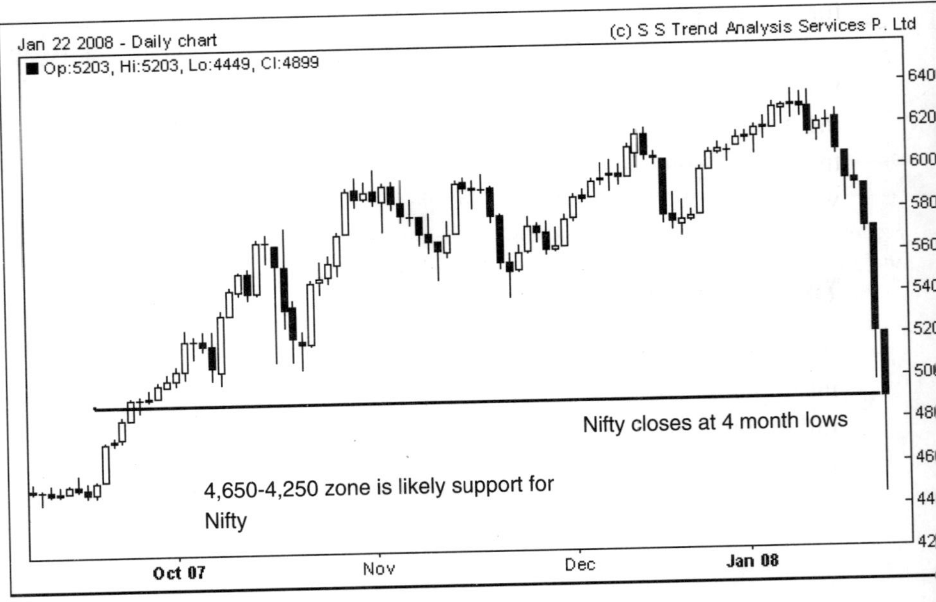

Figure 3.25: **Index likely to remain volatile as market tries to find support.**

Nifty Trend

The short term trend is down. This trend changed to down when the Nifty fell below its trading range support at 6,100. This is the trend that should be followed by traders. Yesterday's lows were broken quickly and easily. The Nifty fell all the way to 4,449 before a small bounce back saw a recovery. While it is early to say, all of this volatility is probably putting a low in place. As the markets revert back to some kind of stability, the short term trend may turn up.

The intermediate trend changed to down on Friday. This happened when the Nifty fell below 5,800. This is the trend that investors should be tracking. In a downtrend, avoid making new commitments. Investors should wait patiently for this decline to be over.

The intermediate trend is likely to remain down for some time. As of now, the trend will change to up when the Nifty closes above 6,360. Do not panic, these levels will change with time. But it will require some time for this to happen.

Position traders and investors should now be ready to go into the market and buy. The market has gone through a correction. While some buying can be done at current levels, it may be wise to wait for the short term trend to become positive. Please follow the rules suggested for buying with the short term trend, given above.

The Big Picture

A sharp decline, such as the current one, is unlikely to suddenly change into a rally. This means that we may see a sideways market with decent rallies, but eventually the Nifty may come back to test the 4,500 low made today. Investors should begin buying in small lots. Traders should go with the flow, which will provide both buying and selling opportunities.

30 January 2008

Nifty Fails to Hold Gains

A small trading range is visible between 5,200 and 5,400. A move out of this range will give trading opportunities.

Figure 3.26: **Nifty in a narrow range between 5,200 and 5,400 (boxed area in the chart). Traders should wait for a breakout, one way or the other.**

Nifty Trend

The short term trend is down. This is the trend that should be followed by traders.

The intermediate trend is down. This is the trend that investors should be tracking.

The Big Picture

As the Nifty continues to consolidate, we have the possibility of a process of base building. This process takes its own time. A large trading range between 4,500 to 5,500 is possible. I refer to 4,500 as the lower part of the range since this number was touched during the recent decline. There is a fair amount of support at 5,200, and then at 5,000. Therefore, it is always possible that 4,500 may not come under test. Let us see. Inside this consolidation, oscillators (i.e., mean reversion indicators) will offer the best tools to trade since these will identify short term extremes. Traders should use tm Stoch, RSI, CCI, CMO, Money flow index, or Stochastics to identify trading set-ups.

12 February 2008

Down Trend Continues

Reliance Power Listing Adds to Selling Pressure

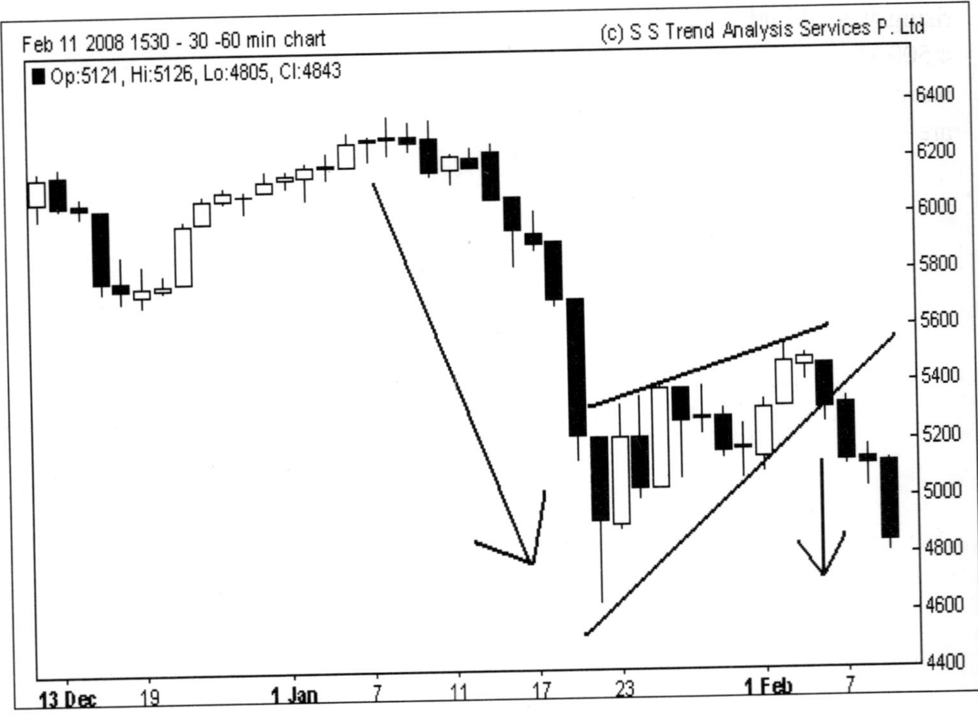

Figure 3.27: **Rising wedge breaks down suggesting lower levels in the Nifty.**

Nifty Trend

The short term trend is down. This is the trend that should be followed by traders. As of now, a close above 5,550 will change the trend to up. This is far away from current level, therefore we really have to wait for new pivot levels to be made. Traders will find it difficult to track these rapid changes in momentum. It is wise to have a view — up or down, then take the trades in that direction.

The intermediate trend is down. This is the trend that investors should be tracking. Daily charts are slowly becoming bearish. These patterns can easily change, and this is a long term bull market. But even in a bull market, there will be periods of sharp corrections. We are probably going through such a period and the end may not be near. An up sloping channel in the Nifty has been broken on the downside. This takes the form of a rising wedge and after its breakdown the suggestion is that a test of the 4,500 support level is quite possible. Please understand that such a scenario may or may not come about. Yet, we should discuss what the charts are saying.

21 February 2008

Sharp Decline in Nifty

Resistance at Higher Levels

As the index approaches 4,800, there will be opportunities to go long — watch your charts!

Nifty Trend

The Nifty moved into a short term downtrend, retreating from higher levels. The Index lost over 120 points today, the selling coming in from tired bulls (my perception!). The Nifty is locked inside a wide trading range. Inside this range, it is likely to oscillate up and down, offering opportunities to buy on dips and sell on rallies. As the index moves down towards 5,000, or maybe lower, there will emerge opportunities to buy in the market for a swing trader.

The intermediate trend is likely to remain down for some time. The ideal method of trend change is for the daily chart to begin a process of higher lows, higher highs. This will take its own time happening.

22 February 2008

Nifty Support Comes at Lower Levels, Remains Volatile

A Sharp and Sudden Dip Will be a Buying Opportunity

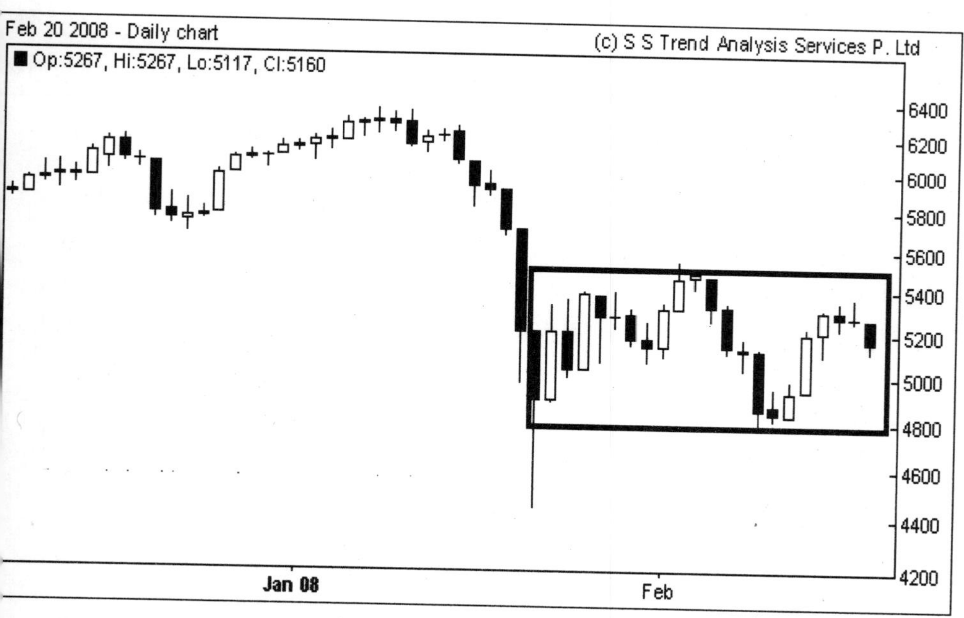

Figure 3.28: **Nifty is inside a wide trading range between 4,800 and 5,500 (boxed area in the chart). Support should come in above 5,000 and that would be a buying opportunity.**

The Nifty moved into a short term downtrend, retreating from higher levels.

The intermediate trend in the Nifty is down. This is the trend that investors should watch. There should be no hurry in buying. The Nifty is building a base, a process that can continue for many weeks, or even longer.

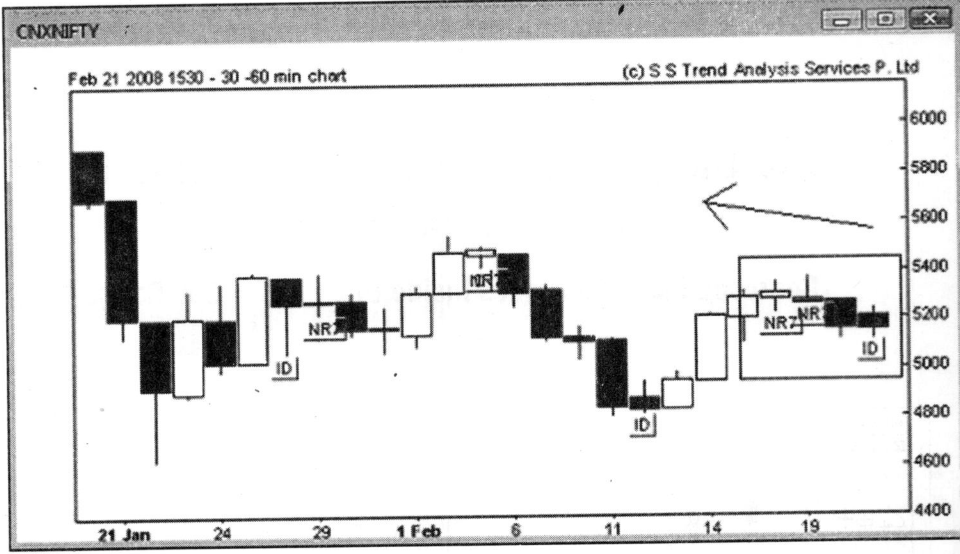

Figure 3.29: **Uncertain Nifty — 21 February was an inside day with two narrow range bars. Expect big move soon, do not fight it.**

A gap up in the Nifty did not work out, with the Index seeing a decline of 130+ points intra day before recovering most of its losses to close with minor gains. The short term trend remains down. This is the trend that traders should watch.

Just like it happened today, when the Nifty continues to wind its way down, there comes a point when bargain hunters enter, triggering a relief rally. Short term traders should watch their intra day charts, waiting for a sharp or sudden reversal to the upside. Trend Energy* may provide such a buy signal. When such signals come, it is worthwhile to take them and go long.

Over the past four days, two have been NR7 days (narrowest range day in seven days) while today was an inside day. NR7 and inside days reflect uncertainty in the market. It is possible that the bears may be getting uncertain! Or, the bulls! For the trader, expect a big move to come in the next few days. If a strong trend starts, do not try to confront it.

* Trend Energy is a momentum indicator similar to RSI and Stochastics.

3 March 2008

The Budget Comes and Goes, Markets Remain Uncertain

Confused Index Continues Inside the 5,100-5,300 Range

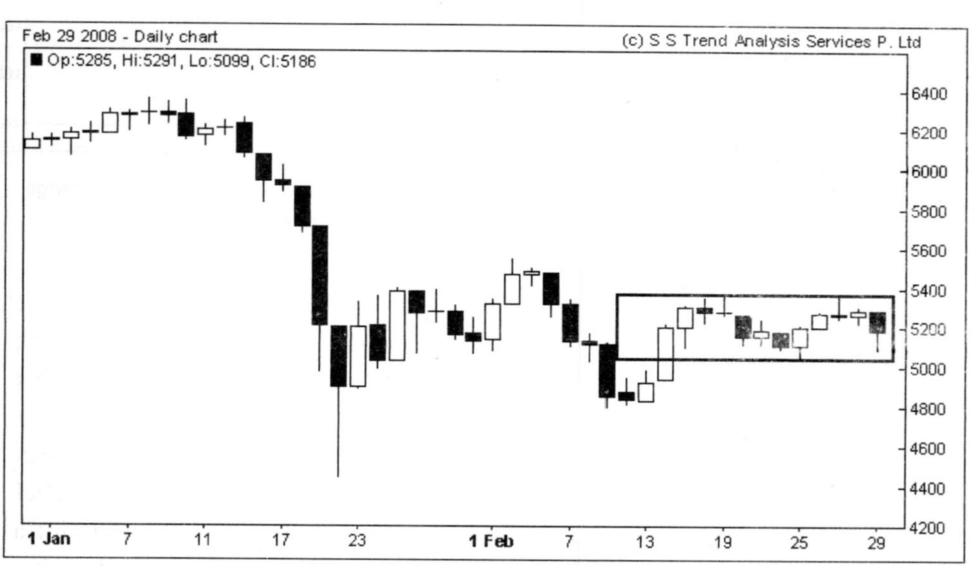

Figure 3.30: **Nifty daily. Index continues inside a trading range. Buy above 5,300, avoid if Nifty falls below 5,100.**

Nifty Trend

The short term trend turned sideways, thanks to a sharp decline in the market on budget disappointments. This is the trend that traders should track. While the Index has turned sideways, more important is the trading range within which it is moving. The Nifty continues to move in:

1. A narrow daily range, and
2. Inside a well defined trading range — between 5,100 and 5,300.

The trend changes to down if and when the index closes below 5,100. The index had exhibited almost similar chart patterns in early January. What came after the narrow move was a big down thrust. Now, again the index is making a similar pattern. Again, the direction of the breakout is unknown. But traders should go with the flow, wherever it moves to.

The intermediate trend remains down. This is the trend that investors should track. Narrow range moves will eventually lead to big up moves. We have been suggesting that investors should buy, with the understanding that this is more of a trading entry. Keep tight stops. If Nifty falls below 5,100, then suspend any further buying. Also remember that March is usually a difficult month to trade. A new trend emerges in April.

10 March 2008

Big Declines in Nifty as Explosive Move Comes on the Downside

Significant Support at 4,800 Breaks Down

Nifty Trend

The short term trend in the Nifty continues to be down. A vicious bout of selling has pushed the Nifty below a significant support level. There is no purpose in trying to catch falling knives. Let the short term trend change to sideways, then swing traders should consider buying. Day traders / intra day traders should have a different approach and watch for a relief rally to begin. If and when buy signals come in, it is worthwhile to enter since bear market rallies can be sharp and sudden.

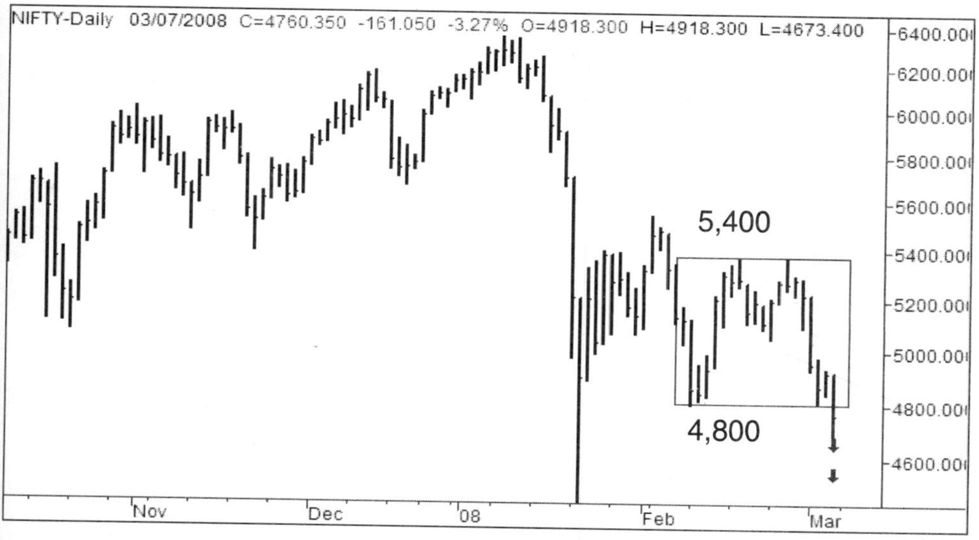

Figure 3.31: **Nifty breaks down from the 5,400-4,800 range giving a target of approximately 4,200.**

Now, for most traders, the 1,650 point sell-off, from 6,350 to 4,700, is giving the impression of a bear market. I continue to think of the decline as a deep correction — after all the market did rally from 920 to 6,350. After this stupendous rally, a correction is also likely to be as stupendous. But, for today, we will call this decline a bear market.

My point is — bear market rallies are sharp and sudden. Day traders should understand this phenomenon:

- First, they should not try to sell in a rally until sell signals come in. Higher levels by themselves are not a justification to go short. You need a clear sell signal.
- Second, a buy signal is worth taking. At worst, you will be stopped out. On the other hand, if you catch the relief rally you may get a decent ride up.

The intermediate trend continues to be down. This is the trend that investors should track. A breakdown of the 5,400-4,800 trading range gives a downside target of 4,200. A lot of support comes in around 4,200. I am not suggesting that the Nifty will fall to this level. But it may. Thus, as on date, there is no buy signal. This is not yet the time for bottom fishing.

14 March 2008

Nifty Closes at Lowest Levels Since Correction Started

A Bearish Head and Shoulders Pattern is Visible

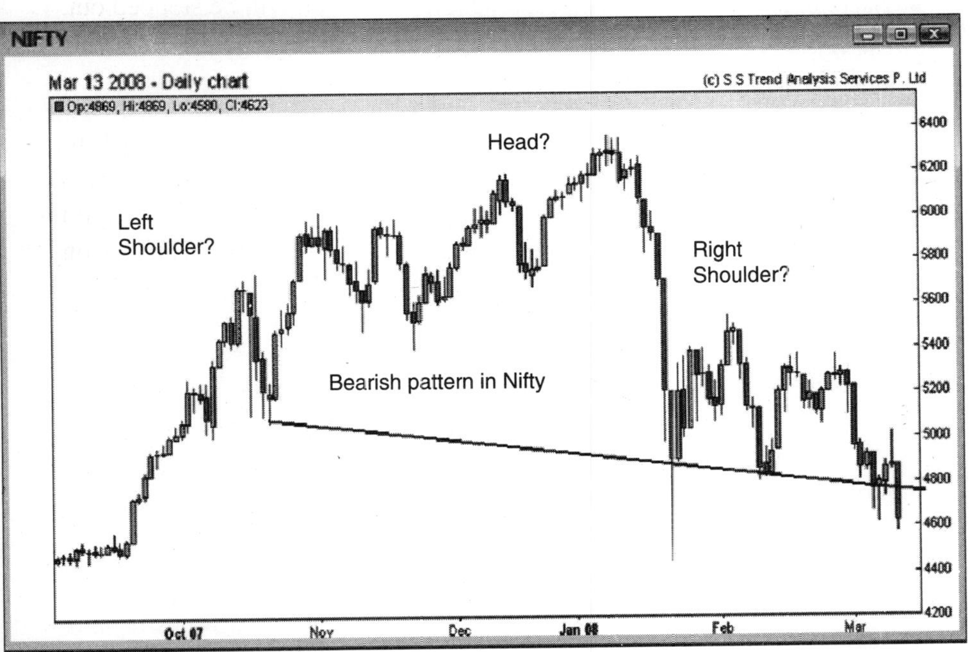

Figure 3.32: **A bearish head and shoulders pattern in Nifty; price targets are 3,600 and 3,200. Now, these patterns can also fail. A move above 5,500 will be a failure signal.**

- Investors should wait for specific buying patterns before entering the market.

- Traders should not try to go bottom fishing — they have to wait for consolidation.

The short term trend remains down. The Nifty has been regularly breaking down from support. The first breakdown was at 6,180. Then the Index broke 5,500, then 5,100, 4,800 and finally it is now on the verge of breaking below 4,600. What comes after 4,600? We have support at 4,200 which is also a pattern target for the 4,800-5,400 range breakdown.

With some imagination, it is possible to visualize a bearish head and shoulders in the Nifty which has been confirmed today when it closed below the neckline. If this pattern is followed, then there are two targets:

- First, the distance between the top (6,400) and the neckline (4,800) is about 1,600 points. From the neckline, we subtract 1,600 points and get 3,200.
- The second target is calculated as a percentage. 1,600 points is 25% of the top. Then we calculate 25% of the neckline which gives us 1,200 points. The target here is 3,600.

Now, this price level may or may not be touched. We cannot make price forecasts. Our task is to go with the trend. The trend is down, therefore we should not be buying until the trend changes.

The intermediate trend remains down. There is no support near current levels. Support comes in only lower — at 4,200. We have the slim possibility of a new support getting created around 4,600, but this is only a possible scenario. We cannot buy on this scenario. There is minor support around 4,550, but why should a minor support hold in a major breakdown? Then we have 4,200 where stronger support comes in. The 4,200 level is also the pattern target for the trading range breakdown. Thus, it may be wise to step aside, and wait for the market to tell us where it wants to stop.

28 March 2008

Narrow Range Moves Continue as Nifty Takes Some Rest

Dips in an Uptrend Should be Used to Go Long

Nifty Trend

The short term trend for the Nifty remains up. Two days of narrow range moves tell us that the market is taking a breather after a big blazing up move on Tuesday. This is all for the better.

The 60-minute chart of Nifty provides us with an interesting pattern — which is good for the bulls. The chart is given below.

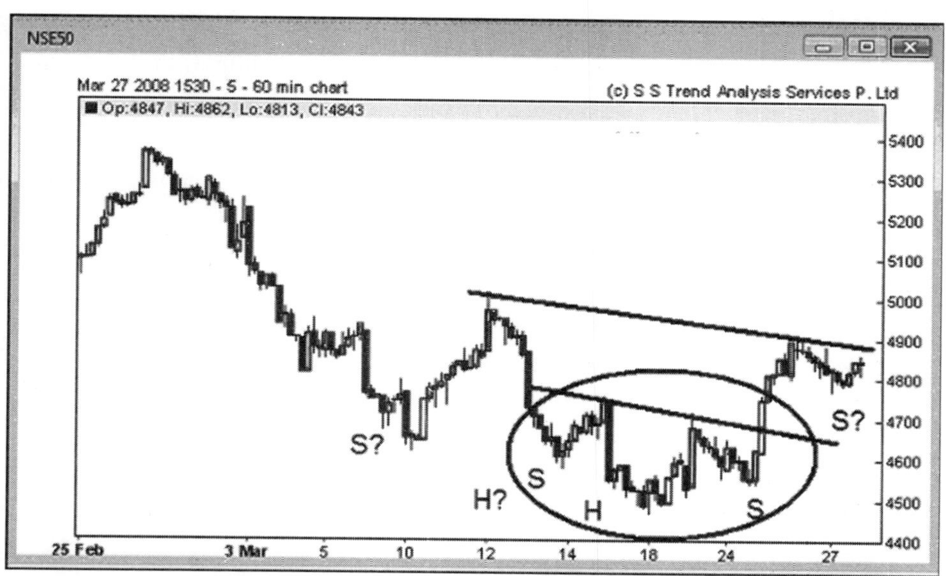

Figure 3.33: **60-minute chart of Nifty suggests a possible bullish head and shoulders pattern. The neckline gives a target of 5,300.**

A small bullish head and shoulder pattern was formed, initially. This is shown inside a circle. The pattern worked, as prices broke out of the neckline and touched 4,900, which was the target. Fine. Now the head and shoulders pattern can also be viewed as the head of a larger pattern, with two shoulders on either side. This pattern is not complete. If prices do break out of the neckline around 4,880, then the pattern target will be 5,300. As always, we have no idea if this will work out, but based on the patterns, traders should be looking to buy on dips.

A close below 4,750 will tell us that bulls are losing steam. While this is not a short signal, it will be an exit signal for traders.

The intermediate trend remains down. There is a minor pivot at 4,912. A close above this number will be a message that the bulls are gathering strength. It will also be an aggressive buy signal for investors.

7 April 2008

Stock Market Remains in Correction

A close above 4,900 in the Nifty is required to change the trend to up.

Belligerent bears have taken control of the stock market. Prices have been falling as though regulated by clockwork.

The bulls do not feel well. Everything is going wrong. The market is rife with stories of gloom and prospective disasters. Fear is overcoming hope.

Fears of Inflation

It is a fact that poor and middle class households have been badly affected by the rise in prices of essential commodities. With the inflation rate touching 7%, there are fears of more government intervention to control the price rise. There may be pressure on large companies to bring down prices of their products (as is happening in steel). While a decline in prices will be beneficial in the long run, there may be pain in the short term. The stock market is probably discounting all the bad news that could be coming in the next few weeks.

The Coming Weeks

As the Nifty moves inside a trading range, the market gives no opportunity to buyers or sellers for making money. There is a lot of volatility, resulting in adverse overnight gaps and intra day reversals. All in all, this is a good time to reduce trading volumes and take some rest.

At some point, the 400-point trading range in the Nifty will come under test. Either the Nifty will fall below 4,500, or it will go above 4,900. This will be a breakout or breakdown, depending on the way it goes. When the

Nifty moves out of this trading range, the chances are that the resulting move may be between 500 to 1,000 points — a strong trend.* If there is a breakdown below 4,500, no bottom fishing should be attempted. Investors should simply wait for a base to be visible. If the Nifty moves above 4,900, we can expect a strong rally that could surprise most people.

Nifty Trend

The intermediate trend continues to be down. The Nifty has been making a pattern of lower highs for the past three months. This pattern continues. An intermediate uptrend will begin if and when the Nifty closes above 4,900. This level will change with time.**

Figure 3.34: **Nifty continues its pattern of lower highs. A close above 4,900 is required to change the trend to up.**

---

* Nifty fell from 5,500 to 4,500, i.e. by 1,000 points. In a smaller trend, it fell from 5,000 to 4,500, i.e. by 500 points. The next movement should be equal to one or both of the previous moves.

** Support and resistance levels change as newer highs and lows emerge which become more important than the previous high / lows.

10 April 2008

Nifty Locked in Very Small Range for Past 4 Days

Ready for a Big Move

Inside the larger range between 4,900/4,950 and 4,500, the Nifty has made an even smaller range, one between 4,600 and 4,800. Such narrow moves cannot be sustained for long. We can look for a break of this range, soon enough.

Nifty Trend

The short term trend remains sideways. After two days of staying in an extremely narrow range, it is probably time for the Nifty to start a trending move. In the last 4 days, the Nifty has been in a range between 4,600 and 4,800. A move out of this range should give a trending move. Traders should buy above 4,800. This is the easy part. But for selling, 4,600 is quite far away. Perhaps a short position may be taken below 4,670.

Figure 3.35: **Nifty goes inside a small range between 4,600 to 4,800. You can trade a move out of this range.**

The intermediate trend continues to be down. The Nifty has been making a pattern of lower highs for the past three months. This pattern continues. An intermediate uptrend will begin if and when the Nifty closes above 4,900. This level will change with time.

16 April 2008

Nifty Breaks Out Above a Minor Trading Range

This is a buy signal for short term traders. Buying should be done only on dips.

Figure 3.36: **Head and shoulder pattern forming? 5,350 is target for a bullish head and shoulder pattern if the pattern is made and confirmed.**

Nifty Trend

We assume that this is a corrective rally in the downtrend. Counter-trend rallies during corrections are by no means a signal for new investments. Bear market rallies can be sharp to the upside and come back down even faster. If you look at the Nifty chart, notice how it has been repeatedly held back by its 50-day moving average which is acting as resistance. I might become more bullish if the Nifty can clear this line and stay above it with some convincing price / volume action.

Remember, markets can rally even with all the gloom and doom out there. It's their nature to fool the majority of the people.

Possible Scenario

The Nifty may be making a bullish head and shoulders pattern. A move above 4,950 will confirm this pattern and will give a target of 5,350 or thereabouts. While the Nifty may not reach these targets (if it crosses 4,950), an up move will represent a trading opportunity to go long. An eventual exhaustion of this up move may give a signal to go short. Thus, there are trades likely to be available now.

For long term investors, the trend remains down.

30 April 2008

Big Up Move in Nifty

Narrow Range Leads to Expansion

The Index is now reaching its first target around 5,300. Short term traders should tighten stops or take partial profits.

The short term trend is up. This is the trend that traders should be tracking. While the trend is intact, the Index has seen a rather large run of gains. There is also resistance at 5,300 which is close by. Traders may like to use intra day charts to tighten their stops on long positions.

Figure 3.37: **intermediate trends are up. Buy on dips, consolidation or narrow range; resistance at 5,300 (the horizontal line in the chart).**

The intermediate trend is also up. This trend will change if the Nifty closes below 4,950, an event that does not seem probable as of now.

Is This a Bear Market Rally?

We don't know if a strong rally after a sharp decline is a bear market rally, the extension of a secular bull market, or an entirely new bull market. But we ought to be careful in concluding that simply because stocks have been rising recently, an economic recovery is just around the corner and that sub-prime issues around the world have been solved.

The point I should really like to emphasize is that a rally after a serious break frequently leads to a false sense of security and confidence among the investment community in the belief "that the worst is over" because stocks are rebounding strongly. Moreover, because business conditions do not deteriorate very badly during the first phase of a bear market, economists and well-known market observers remain optimistic about the future.

We simply don't know how the world will look in a year's time.

The best method is to follow the charts. So far the charts remain bullish, and so it is wise to go with the bullish sentiment. Therefore, the question — "Is this a bear market rally" — does not have an answer. In fact it does not need to be asked at all. Just go with the flow of the market.

5 May 2008

Here Come the Buyers . . .

Market up on improved sentiment. The intermediate trend is up. Nifty faces strong resistance around 5,300. If this resistance is overcome, the next target for the Nifty is 5,500 or thereabouts.

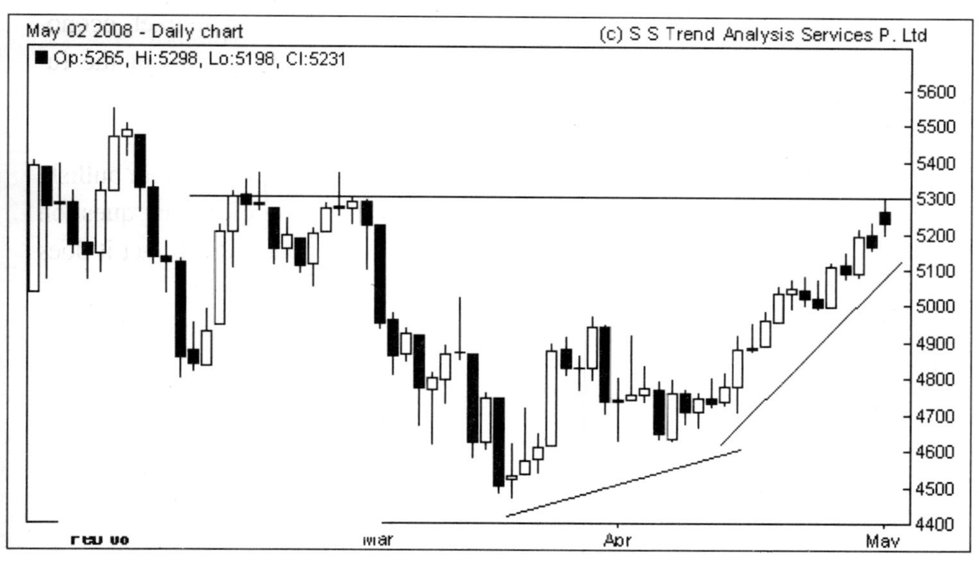

Figure 3.38: **Nifty faces strong resistance around 5,300. Traders should take positions after a dip.**

It appears that the Nifty may consolidate at current levels before making another up move above 5,300. This is the time to take profits, and wait for a dip in the Index before taking any new long positions. Investors can stay invested but fresh buying should be done only on dips.

The Three Stages of Primary Bull Markets

Hamilton* identified three stages to both primary bull markets and primary bear markets. These stages relate as much to the psychological state of the market as to the movement of prices. In both primary bull markets and primary bear markets, there will be secondary movements that run counter to the major trend:

Primary Bull Market Stage 1 — Accumulation
Primary Bull Market Stage 2 — Big Move
Primary Bull Market Stage 3 — Excess

In which stage is the Indian stock market now? We have already seen Stage 3 — excess — in December 2007-January 2008.

Thus, either we are in Stage 1 or in the process of completing Stage 3. If this is still Stage 3, then sooner or later the Nifty will see a breakdown of support. Therefore, until that happens we assume that the bull market has resumed. If support breaks, we should liquidate all our trading positions and wait for new signals. This has not happened so far.

---

* William Peter Hamilton, editor of the *Wall Street Journal* from 1903 to 1929 articulated the Dow Theory in numerous editorials in the paper.

9 May 2008

Nifty Correction Continues, May Now See a Rally

If this is a bull market, then the Index is close to strong support. Higher American markets could easily trigger a rally tomorrow.

The short term technical picture is still bullish. While the brief correction is good for the bulls, the RSI remains above 40, suggesting that this dip is just a bull market correction. Now, if the markets fall, all of this could change. But we have to go by the evidence that we have at present, which is — the current dip may be just that, a dip.

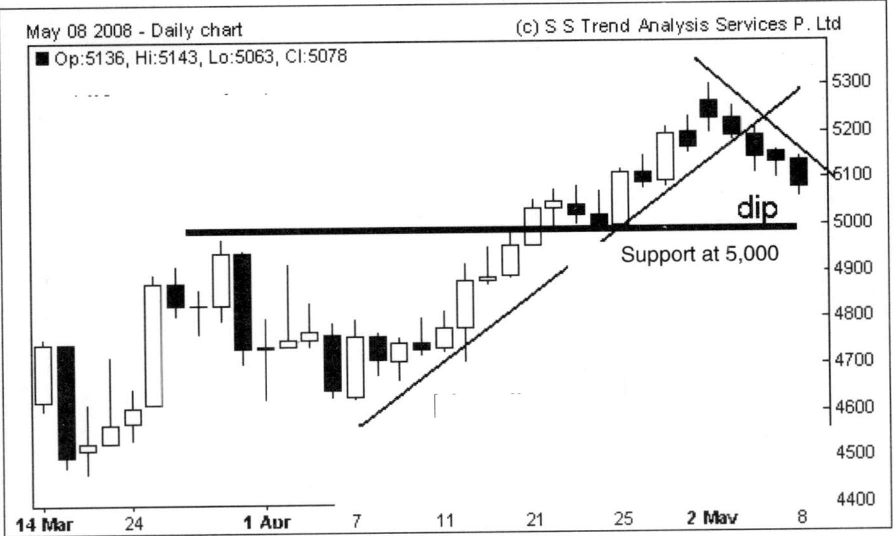

Figure 3.39: **Nifty records 4 consecutive lower closes after a 2-month long big rally. This could just be a dip after a big rally.**

How Should We Plan Our Trading?

For the Nifty, short term support held at 5,075 today. If this support breaks, then traders should close their long trading positions [this refers to deliveries or futures positions set-up for taking advantage of the up move, not being long term in nature]. While there is support at 5,000, and support again comes in at different levels below 5,000, it may not be wise to wait for a test of those lower levels. On the other hand, cheerful US markets tonight could trigger a rally tomorrow thus removing any need for protective measures.

Buying is suggested if US markets close higher. If there is a gap up on Friday, then traders should follow the fifteen minute rule.

15-minute rule: When markets open, wait for 15 minutes, then identify the high and low of this period. Buy only when prices go above the first 15 minute high. Sell only if prices go below the first 15 minute low.

12 May 2008

Nifty Breaks Down from Significant Support Levels

Avoid Buying

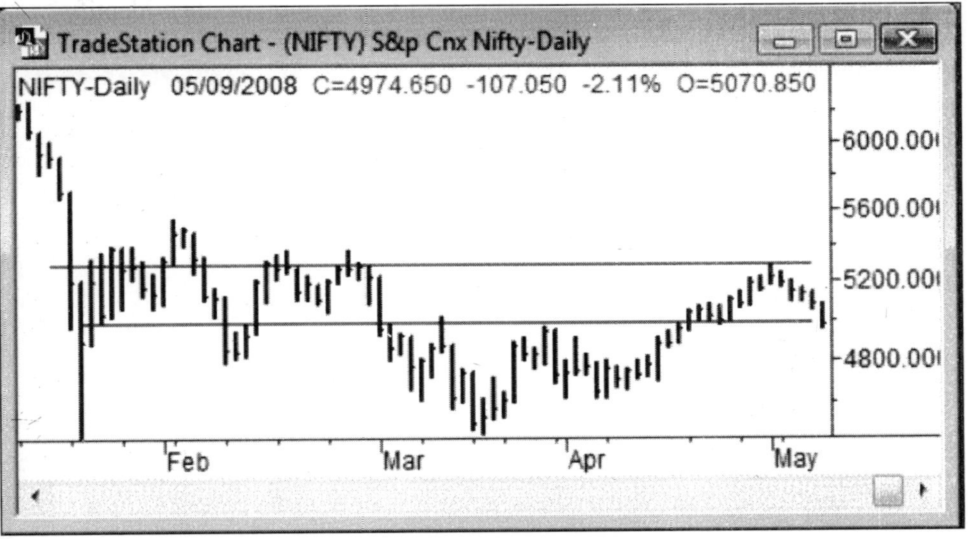

Figure 3.40: **Nifty faces strong resistance at 5,300. Support at 5,000 is broken — avoid buying.**

As the Nifty closes lower for the fifth day in succession, important support levels are broken. The key level at 5,000 has now been breached. With such breakdowns, it is wise to stay away from any further buying. The Index will eventually find its own level where support comes in. It is not possible to forecast these levels, now. However, after 5,000, there is support close by, near 4,900-4,950. If these levels break, then we can expect a test of the much lower levels at 4,600, or even 4,450.

14 May 2008

Nifty Falls Again

Faces Prospects of An Intermediate Down Move

A breakdown below 4,950 will signal that the uptrend is finished.

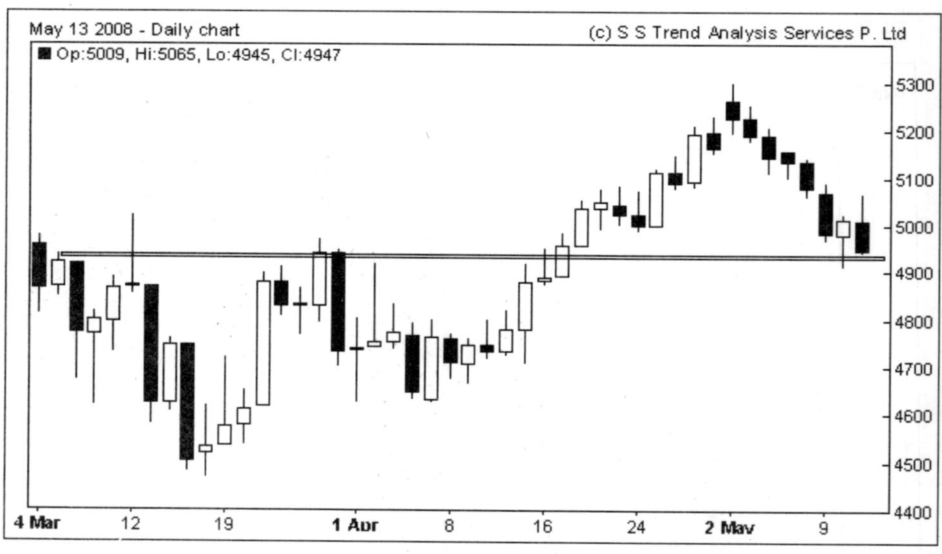

Figure 3.41: **Nifty at critical support — 4,950 support holds for now. A breakdown will signal an intermediate downtrend.**

With uncertain environments, buying should be avoided. The Nifty has fallen in six out of seven days — including today. This is not the sign of a bull market.

There is support coming in at 4,950. If this support breaks, we are looking at a free fall, with support, possibly, coming in at 4,750 and then at 4,600. This may not happen, but as of now this is what the scenario is.

15 May 2008

Choppy Nifty Marks Time in a Narrow Range

A breakdown below 4,950 will signal that the uptrend is finished. Also, a move above 5,100 will suggest a resumption of the up move.

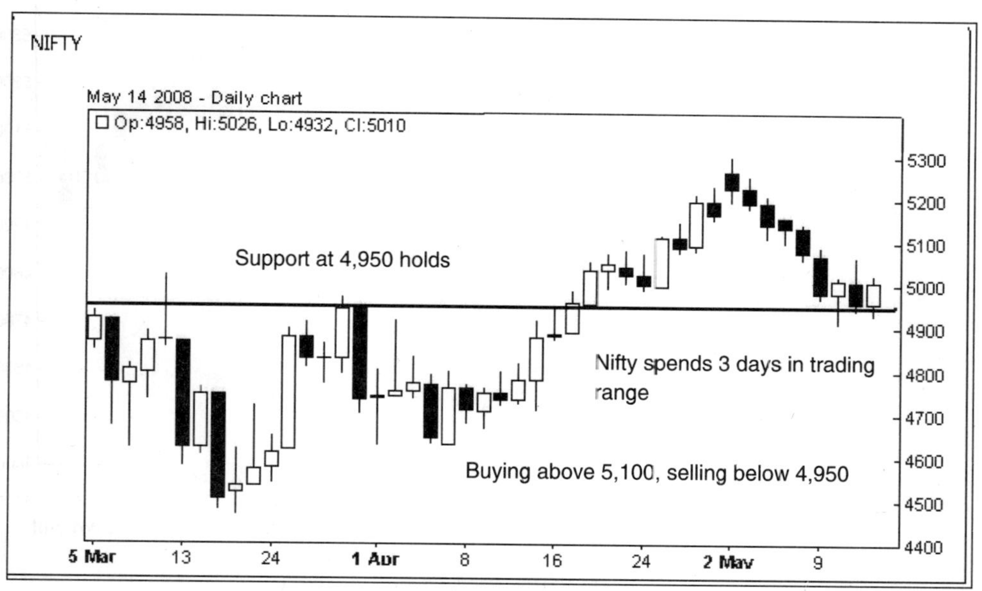

Figure 3.42: **Is the support holding? It seems so far now though choppy markets do not give clear signals.**

There is support coming in at 4,950. This support has held well today. If this support breaks, we are looking at a free fall, with possible support coming in at 4,750, and then at 4,600. This may not happen, but as of now this is what the scenario is. Earlier, the 5,100 zone was offering support.

Traders would know that support becomes resistance. A move above 5,100 will probably be a reaffirmation of strength, also a buying opportunity.

The Nifty is not giving any clear directional signals. The short term trend is down, while the intermediate trend will become down if it closes below 4,950. This has not happened till date. Therefore, a breakout / breakdown from the support and resistance levels (mentioned earlier) is presently a better way to trade the Nifty.

22 May 2008

Nifty Consolidation Continues

Intra Day Rally Suggests Bulls May Be Getting Stronger

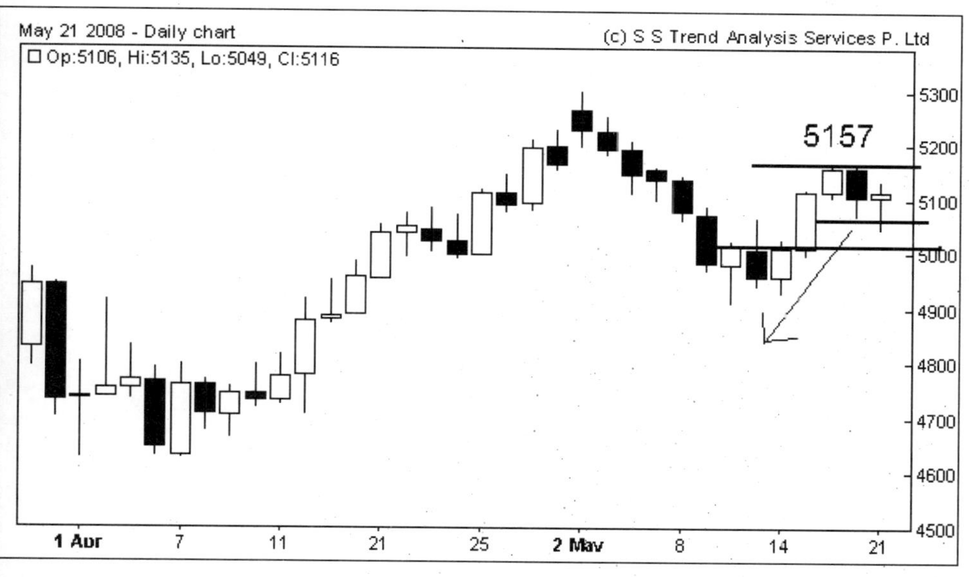

Figure 3.43: **5,157 is resistance. A close above it should mean 5,300. Support at 5,050, then 5,000. Wait for Nifty to move above 5,150 or below 5,000.**

A gap down open in the Nifty was also the low of the day. After the gap down, the Nifty began to recover finally erasing all its gap down losses to close in the green, higher than the previous day by 12 points. Much of today's rally was caused by oil stocks which seem to be moving up every day, thanks to the gains seen in crude prices. The sector could easily stop its momentum if crude begins a sudden decline. As traders, we cannot worry about what may or may not happen.

The intra day rally does suggest that bulls may be getting the upper hand. This is not confirmed, though, since the Index remains inside a narrow trading range, between 5,050 and 5,157. A short term trend will be visible when the Nifty closes either above 5,157 or below 5,050.

23 May 2008

Dow Blues Affect Nifty Sentiment

Falls 96 Points

Figure 3.44: **A big move will come when Nifty moves out of the trading range between 5,160-4,950 (boxed area in the chart).**

As the American markets continued to fall for the second day, the Nifty was finally affected by this gloom. Index futures opened about 60 points lower, then continued to drift down, finally closing at 5,025, near the 5,000 support level.

What does the chart say?

The Nifty remains in a trading range. A breakout above 5,160 is a buy, while below 4,950 is a sell. Inside this range, small moves are possible based on oscillator movements.

26 May 2008

Market Faces a Setback

Nifty Falls Again

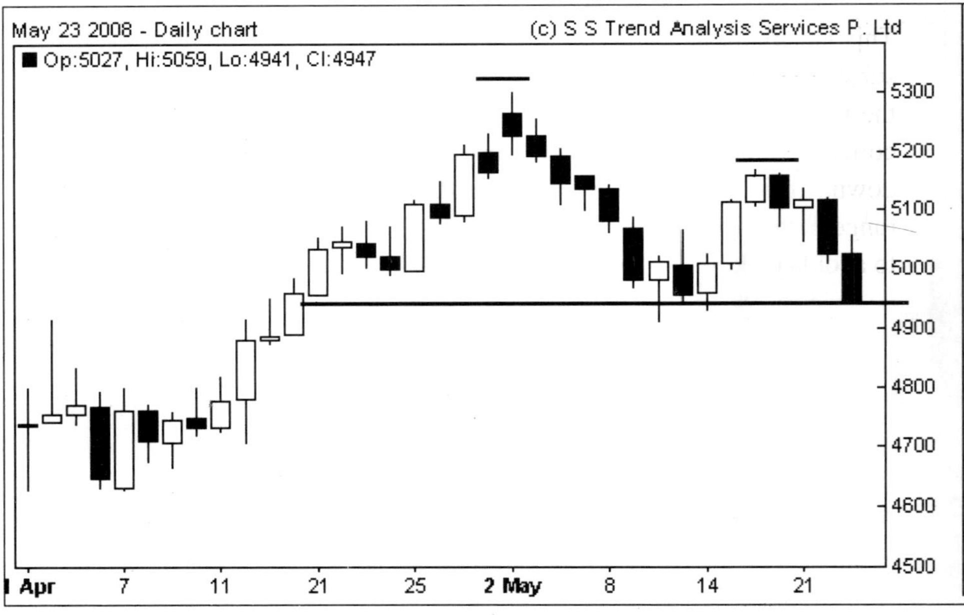

Figure 3.45: **Lower highs in Nifty. There is support at 4,950. Below this support, next level comes in at 4,750. Avoid buying and consider selling on rallies.**

The current week saw markets give up most of their gains. Inflation numbers were not acceptable to traders. After falling on account of weak international markets, on Friday the Nifty fell due to higher than expected inflation. In the process, the Index broke down from a critical level of 5,000.

The chart picture is no longer attractive for the bulls. The Nifty is now on the verge of breaking down below 4,950, thus triggering an intermediate term downtrend. Now, at some point this decline will end. But we do not know when that point will come. Thus, it is safer to go with the current trend — which is down.

On the downside, there is support coming in at lower levels. First, at 4,650, and then at 4,500. We cannot say that the Nifty will fall to these support levels. But we do know that the market has broken down from support. In such an eventuality, it is wise to stay away from any kind of buying.

Stock Prices Will Never Become Zero

This is certain, that prices of shares will never become zero. If there is a substantial fall, a lot of bargain hunters will step in. The point is: With all the bearishness, the downside is limited. What is possible is an extended correction in terms of time. The market can continue drifting sideways to down, for months. Traders and investors can get frustrated, watching this range bound movement. For this reason, as of now, our suggestion will be to avoid any kind of buying.

27 May 2008

Nifty Enters an Intermediate Downtrend

Figure 3.46: **Lower highs, lower lows confirmed. Nifty enters an intermediate downtrend again. The market will turn bullish only above 5,150.**

The Nifty fell again, breaking the 4,950 support, and also printing a pattern of lower highs, lower lows. This is the sign of a resumption of the intermediate downtrend. All of this is worrying since a downtrend can extend in time as well as in price. We may be looking at a long, protracted bear market.

Worrying

Question: Is there a guarantee that the Nifty will fall?

Answer: Surely not. After making a pattern of lower highs, the Nifty can turn back and begin an up move again. No one can predict the markets. We can only work on the most probable scenario. Currently, the trend is down, with lower levels likely.

Correction in Terms of Time

The bull market that started in April 2003 lasted till January 2008 — i.e., for 4 years and 8 months. A one-third correction in time can mean 19 months — giving us a time target of September 2009 for the end of this bear market or correction.

Correction in Terms of Price

The bull market saw a rise from 920 to 6,350, i.e. a gain of 5,430 points. A one-third correction can see a decline of 1,810 points with a target of 4,540 points. The good news is that this correction has already taken place.

The bad news then is that to complete the correction in terms of time, the market may simply drift in a 1,000-point range for another one year. If this happens, brokers will become an endangered species while people will ask: What is CNBC? Well, whatever will be, will be, will be . . .

28 May 2008

"There Was a Time When . . .

A fool and his money were soon parted, but now it happens to everybody" — Adlai Stevenson

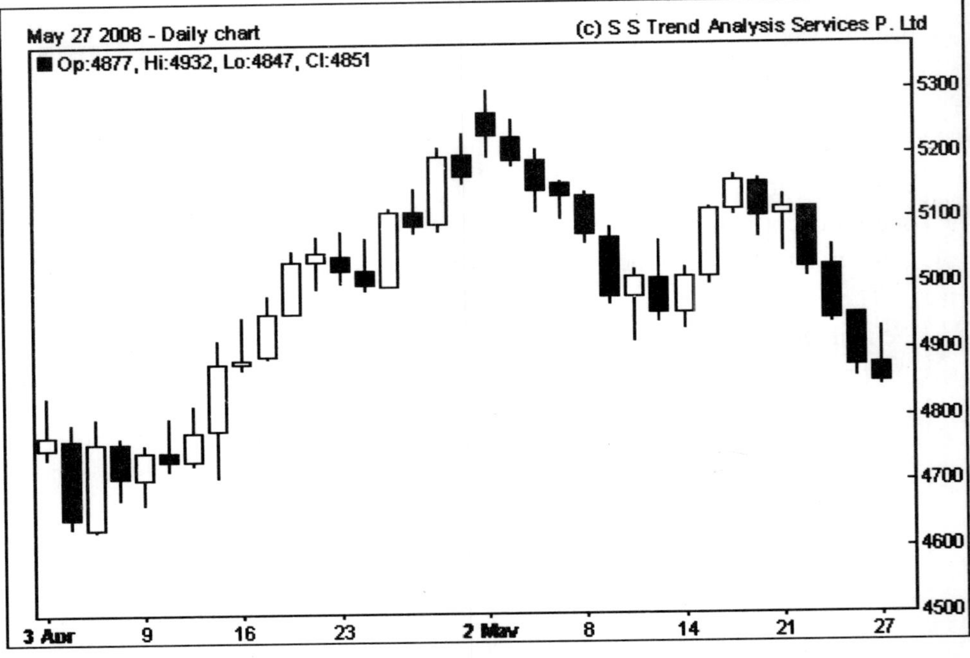

Figure 3.47: **Downtrend continues. Nifty is in a bear market. Support around 4,750. Previous lows at 4,450 may be challenged.**

No matter what momentum stock was purchased, it is now a big loser. At the risk of stating the blindingly obvious, perhaps the most critical observation is to restate the fundamental counsel: invest only what you can afford to lose. Bound up within this core advice is the requirement to identify an appropriate time horizon for investment. An unrealized loss from a quality equity investment, for example, may be nothing more than a reflection of market noise. But if the capital tied up in that investment is soon required to set off against short term liabilities, something has gone awry with the investment process.

In the same way, your capital in trading should be "free" money, i.e. money that you can afford to lose. If you are trading with this money, then trading success will surely come to you.

30 May 2008

Nifty Falls Again

F&O Expiration, Bear Pressure Pull Down Prices

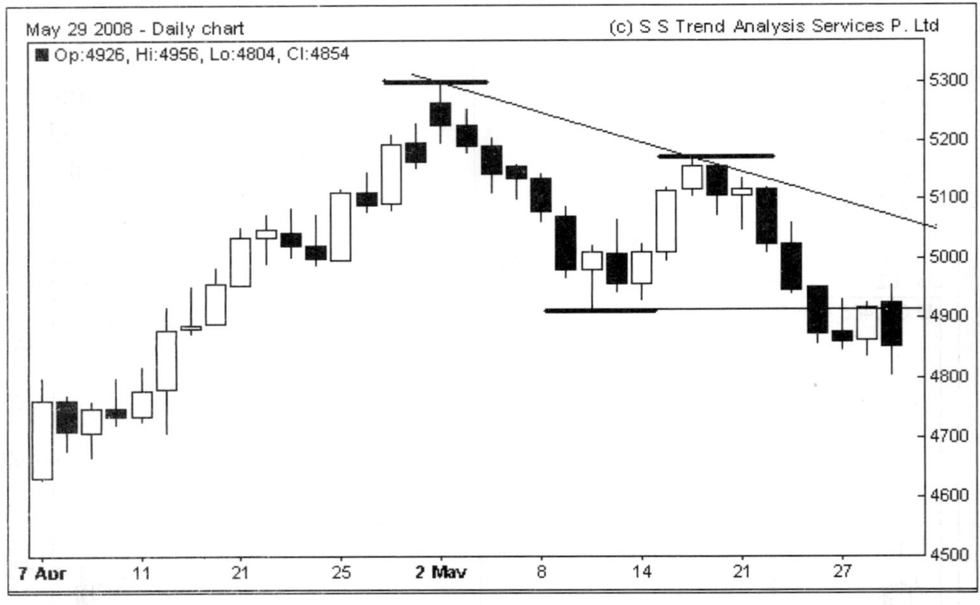

Figure 3.48: **Nifty displays a pattern of lower highs and lower lows. This is an intermediate downtrend. Avoid bottom fishing.**

Downward pressure on the Nifty continued with prices not sustaining early morning highs. By end of the day, the Index slipped to close lower at 4,854, down almost 64 points from yesterday. Some of the decline may be due to the F&O effect. But the fact is that the intermediate trend is down.

A close above 5,000 will change the short term trend to up, and a close above 5,150 will change the intermediate trend also to up. These levels will change over time.

3 June 2008

Nifty Decline Continues

Prospective Buyers Should Stay Away — Avoid Catching Falling Knives

Markets will usually follow the intermediate trend. This seems to be true even now. A big decline in the Nifty saw the Index fall below 4,800, and almost touch 4,700, with Nifty futures trading at 4,695, i.e. below the 4,700 mark.

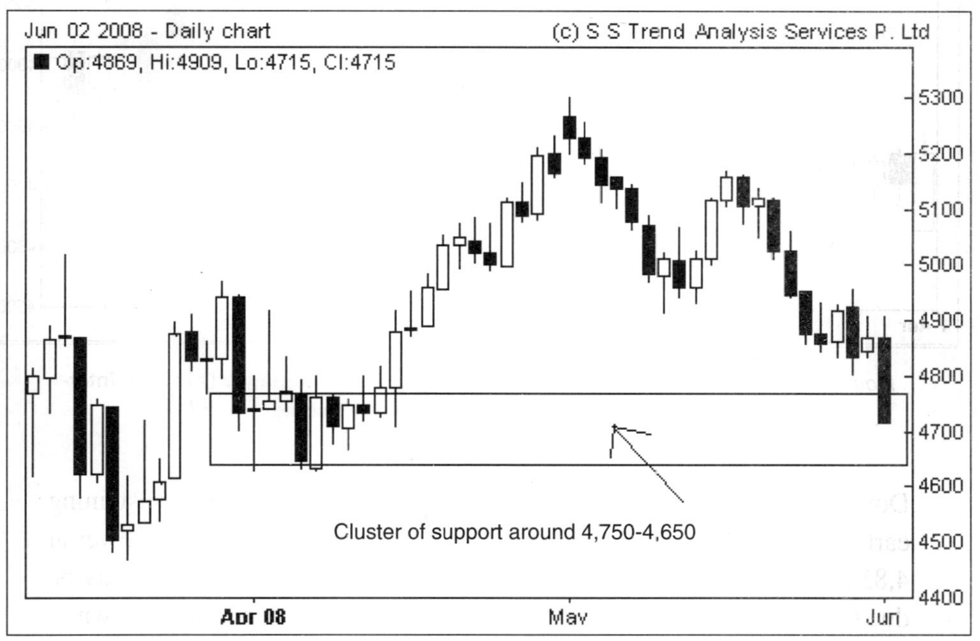

Figure 3.49: **Nifty reaches a significant support zone.**

This decline should not come as a surprise. After all, in a downtrend prices are supposed to move down.

The Nifty has now entered a significant zone of support in the range between 4,750 and 4,650. It is possible that this zone will prevent any further slide in the Index, at least in the short term. A breakdown below 4,650 should see the Nifty test its earlier lows at 4,450. Below 4,450, there is a free fall.

Buy Dips, Sell Rallies

One way to keep on the safe side is only to buy dips, and sell rallies. Avoid breakouts and breakdowns.

5 June 2008

Big Decline Again

Nifty Comes Close to March Lows

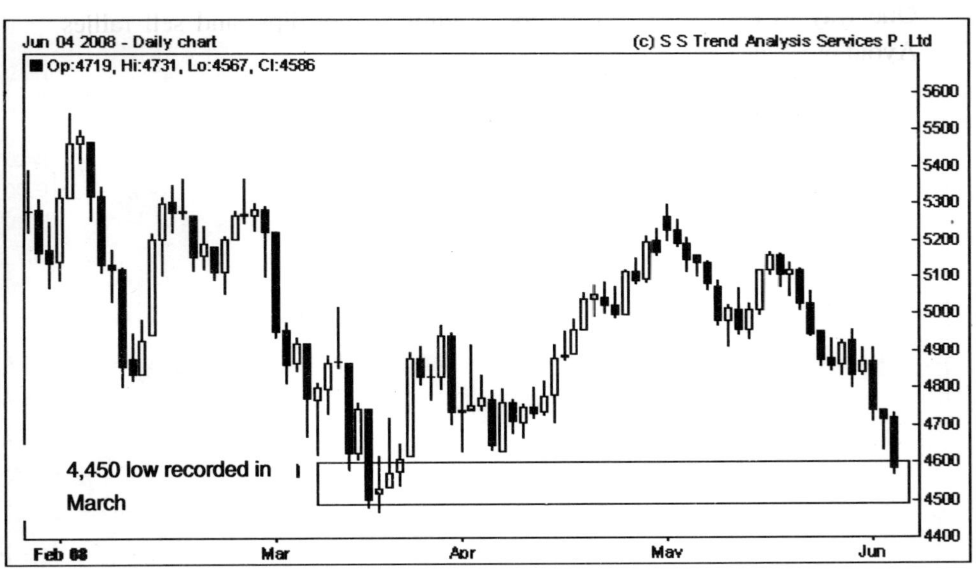

Figure 3.50: **Nifty falls again, comes to a test of March lows.**

A test of the March lows at 4,450 was expected. This has come to happen. If the support holds, then we should expect a base building process to begin. If 4,450 support breaks, then much lower levels seem possible.

11 June 2008

Big Decline, Then Sharp Recovery Leaves Traders in Confusion

Is This a Bear Market or Start of a New Rally?

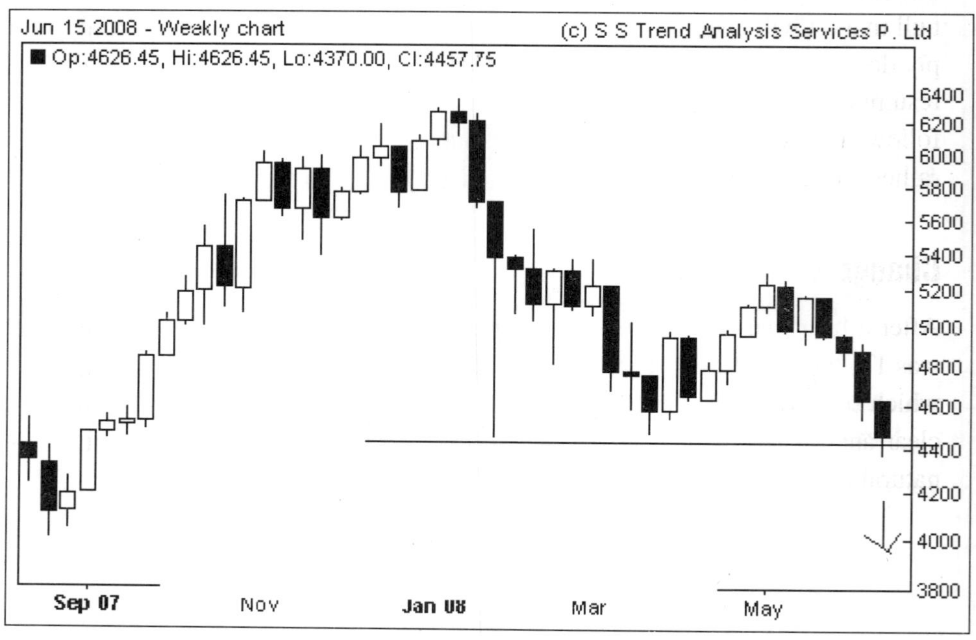

Figure 3.51: **Nifty breaks below its January / March lows. This is not bullish. Treat up moves as bear market rallies.**

A last hour intra day rally saw the Nifty move up by almost 100 points from its intra day lows, closing with just minor losses at 4,450.

Marc Faber wrote:

> "For a market, which has become very over-sold, it is only natural to rebound, but frequently these rebounds are merely bear market rallies, which are subsequently followed by vicious declines."

In 1930, after the famous 1929 market crash, stocks were trading at low levels. Irving Fisher, the best known economist in America, thought that stocks were "ridiculously low" (subsequently they fell another 80%). In between, there were sharp rallies but these rallies eventually fizzled out.

When we encounter a big up move, we must beware that bear market rallies are often sharp and sudden. They give the impression that the downtrend is over, but this is often a deception. On the other hand, a new bull market will eventually start with a rally of some proportions. We simply do not know if a rally after the sharp decline is a bear market rally or a resumption of the bull market. With this imperfect knowledge, it is wise to follow the existing trend. The current intermediate trend is down. Thus, rallies are assumed to be bear market rallies, until proved otherwise.

Change of Leadership

After a bear market, leadership among sectors usually changes. Earlier, it was IT, then banks and capital goods. Now, we are in a bear market, but which sectors are likely to lead once the decline is over? While there is no clear answer to this question, some possible leaders are: pharma, cement, natural resources (Cairn, Neyvelli).

12 June 2008

Choppy Market with Bear Pressure

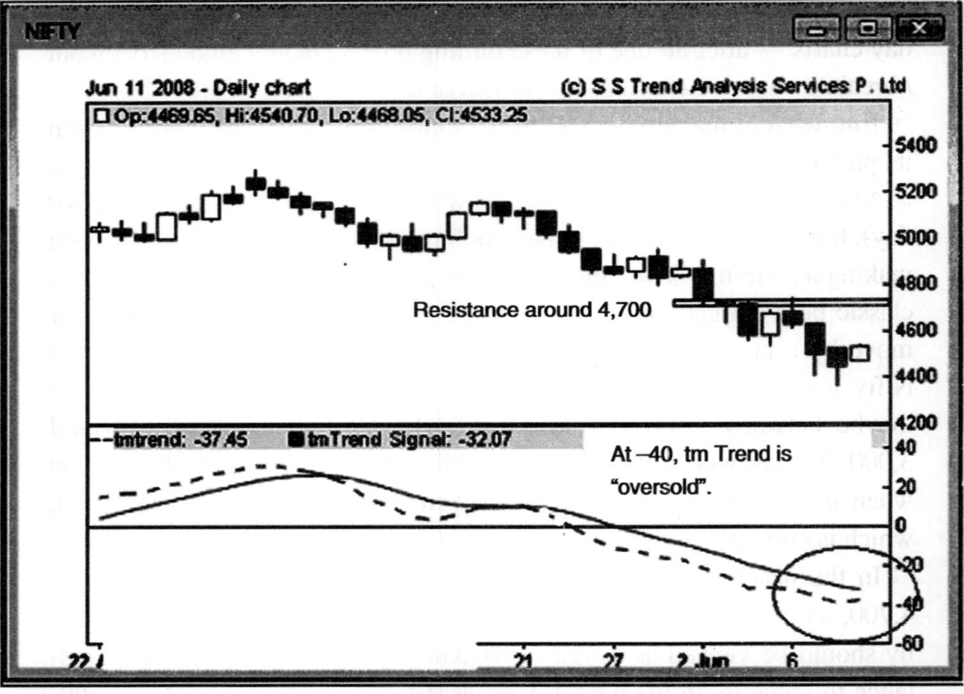

Figure 3.52: **Nifty relief rally may have more upside.**

Investopedia.com tells us, "The choppy market is a stock market condition whereby prices swing up and down considerably but with no resulting overall price movement in either direction."

Helpfully, it adds that "the term is derived from the phrase choppy seas, where a boat will move a lot but not over any large distance as waves prevent it from moving any meaningful distance. The DJIA, for example, may start a six-month period at 10,500 and over the six months move all over the 10,000 to 11,000 range but end the period at around 10,500."

Today's Nifty trading saw a choppy market with the Index first moving up 25 points, then down 25 points, and so on throughout the day. After the initial euphoria when the Nifty was up 100 points, the trend was down, although conditions remained choppy.

Once it is clear that the market is moving sideways, the wisest course of action is to stay away. The only way to trade in a trading range (which is what a choppy market really is) is to anticipate tops and bottoms. This is easier said than done, because it requires us to call a turning point on intra day charts — after all one of these turning points could well be a breakout / breakdown point, causing a great deal of discomfort.

But, what of the Nifty itself? Well, it closed at 4,534, up 85 points from its previous close. The Index closed near the highs for the day, which was at 4,541.05. There will be many days when the market moves up (like today), but such rallies do not make a bull market. So far, the Nifty has been making a pattern of lower highs and lower lows on its daily chart. This is a classic bear market pattern. Ideally, the Index will come out of this bear move by a process of base building. The key question is: between what Nifty levels will this base be developed? Between 4,200 and 4,800, or maybe between 3,500 and 4,000, or, who knows, between 2,600 and 3,000. The answer to this question is easy: wait for the market to tell us when it is likely to stop falling. Till then, follow the intermediate trend, which is currently down.

In the near future, the Nifty could slowly and steadily see a rally to 4,700, where substantial resistance exists. A failure to reach 4,700 or close by should be viewed as a sign of weakness. Traders should expect resistance to come in, in the next 2 days, as the Nifty has already seen a 200-point rally in just one day (from yesterday to today).

17 June 2008

Short Term Trend Changes to Up

13 June's NR7 Gives a Bullish Breakout

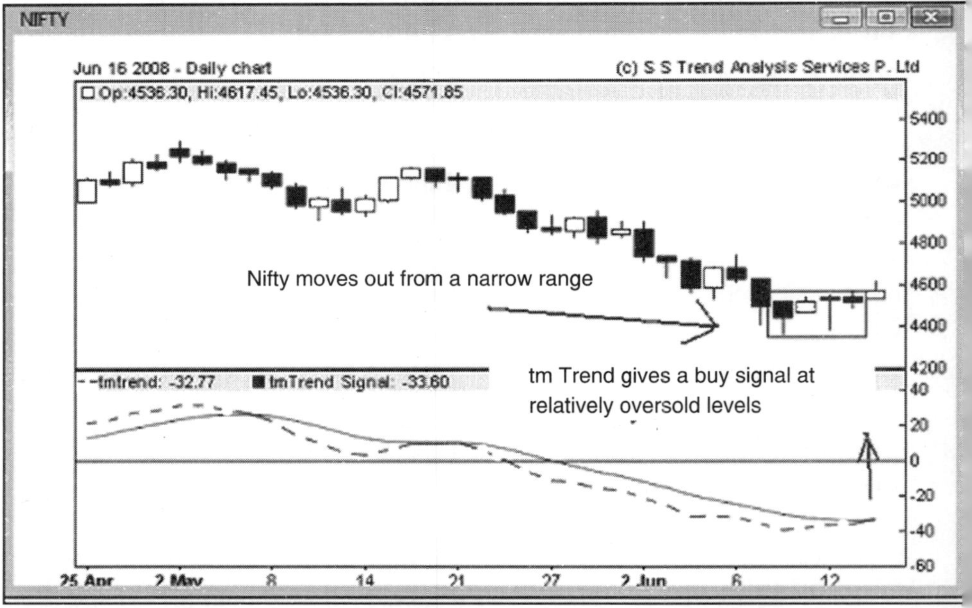

Figure 3.53: **Index in a short term uptrend.**

With the Nifty moving up from Friday's (13 June) high, the short term trend has changed to up. A gap open saw some frenzied buying in the Nifty early morning. This was not sustained, and the Index closed lower than its intra day highs. Now, this could be just a random movement or it could be a sign of weakness. We cannot say. Frankly, we should not worry about it. The trend is up, so let's go long. If the up move is not sustained, we will get stopped out.

A stop around 4,500 in June futures should be used for any long positions in the Nifty. While target setting is usually difficult, we may be looking at the Nifty touching 4,700, or higher.

The intermediate trend remains down. Therefore, the current rally does not have the force of the larger trend behind it. For this reason, it is wise to follow our stop losses.

IT, pharma, sugar, steel give the impression of up moves coming in. Real estate and banks show signs of exhaustion. There may be some relief rally possible in these two sectors but this may be a slow process, thus swing traders should look to buy, but day traders may avoid them.

19 June 2008

Resistance Before 4,700, Nifty Falls Again

Is the short term up move over? Probably yes. A move above 4,680 is required to reconfirm the up move.

The Nifty went through a dramatic decline. The decline was not so dramatic for our day trading software — Day-V, which went short at 4,625 and remained short throughout the day, covering the position at 4,565. Reliance Capital and Adlabs futures are also offered for trading in Day-V. Rel cap went short at 1,181, finally getting covered around 1,145.

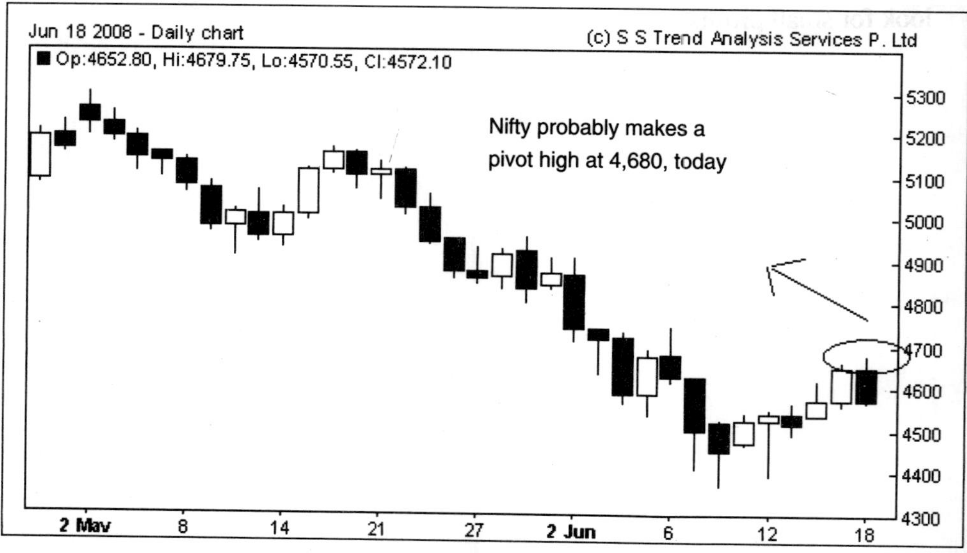

Figure 3.54: **Index falls after resistance at higher levels, look for sideways to down move, bullish above 4,680.**

Of course, disciplined trading really requires discipline. But traders can use Day-V in many innovative ways. For example, in our office, we have a structure in place every morning for the Nifty. Today morning, our set-ups were bearish, so we decided to take only sell signals in Day-V. On some days our perception is for a choppy market so we decide to avoid trading altogether. My point is: traders can use Day-V in different ways. Each method will be profitable provided you follow the method with discipline.

The Nifty may have made a pivot high today at 4,680. This will be confirmed if the Nifty remains below 4,680 tomorrow. At present, this seems likely to happen. Now, we have to assume that the brief up trend in Nifty is probably over. The up move will be reconfirmed if and when the Nifty moves above 4,680, although these levels will change over time.

What next, then? Well, the intermediate downtrend is likely to assert itself. We can expect choppy market conditions or another decline. It is difficult to say which one will actually happen.

To sum up: The Nifty up move is probably over. Use intra day charts to search for buying after sharp dips, or selling into rallies. In either case, look for small profits.

20 June 2008

More Pain for the Bulls

Nifty Falls Back to 4,500 Support

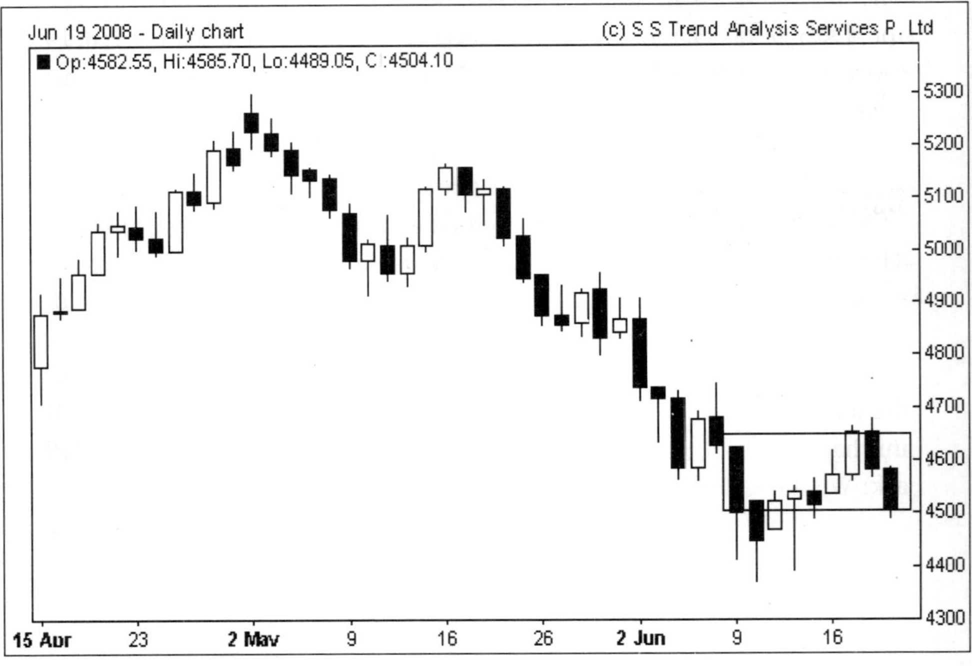

Figure 3.55: **Narrow range in Nifty between 4,500-4,650 (boxed area in the chart). A bounce from 4,500 support is possible. A big move will come when Nifty moves out of this range.**

Every time the Nifty falls to 4,400 or 4,500 support, the risk of breaking down appear large. What happens if the support breaks? Well, there may well be a free fall since there is no visible support below 4,400.

Short Term View

After two down days, the Index is probably ready for some kind of rally. Swing traders should position themselves to take advantage of an up move. Weak international markets will cancel this scenario.

The Nifty is locked in a trading range between 4,500 and 4,650. Inside a range, the market can move between bouts of optimism and pessimism. We have seen two days of pessimism. Now, it may well be the chance of the optimists. But once a trend starts, then trend following remains the best way of capturing a move. A breakout from the trading range will start a trend, so watch out for it.

Fertilizers is a small sector but remains in a bull market. The sector is a buy on dips candidate. RCom has been falling (like most other stocks). Recently, it has gone inside a narrow range with small real bodies. The stock is probably ready to make a big move.

Intermediate trend remains down. Investors may continue to avoid the market. But there are many trading opportunities. The key is to take small profits as well as small losses.

24 June 2008

Coming Soon: Bear Market Capitulation

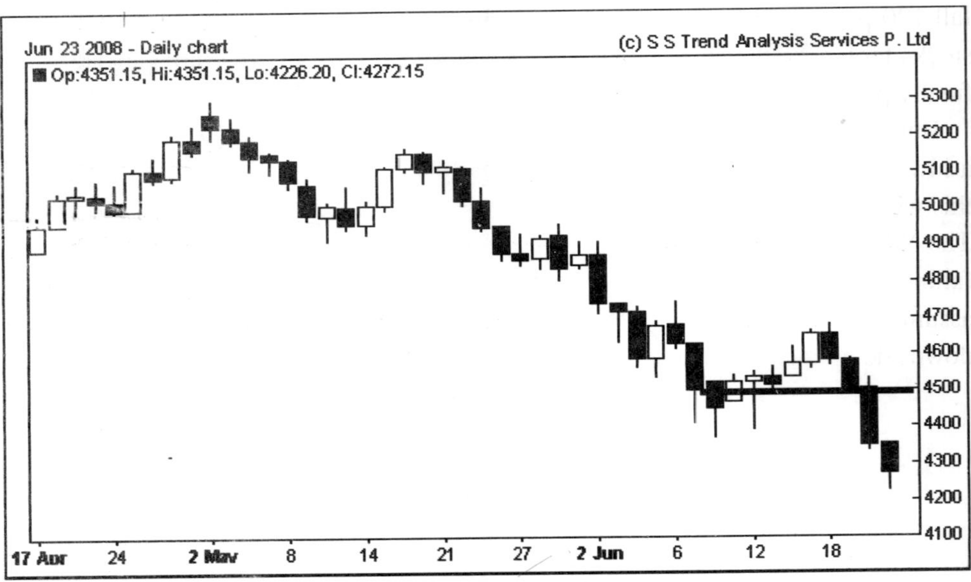

Figure 3.56: **Nifty has no significant support on the downside. Decline can stop wherever it wants. There is resistance at 4,500. A relief rally could reach the level.**

From Investopedia.com:

"Capitulation is a military term. Capitulation refers to surrendering or giving up.

"In the stock market, capitulation is associated with 'giving up' any previous gains in stock price as investors sell equities in an effort to get out of the market and into less risky investments. True capitulation involves extremely high volume and sharp declines. It usually is indicated by panic selling.

"After capitulation selling, it is thought that there are great bargains to be had. The belief is that everyone who wants to get out of a stock, for any reason (including forced selling due to margin calls), has sold. The price should then, theoretically, reverse or bounce off the lows. In other words, some investors believe that true capitulation is the sign of a bottom."

My comments:

Today, Monday, 23 June saw some signs of capitulation. The Dow was down 220 points on Friday. This seemed to be good reason for the Nifty to fall 120 points intra day, before recovering a bit. Mid caps and small cap stocks took it on the chin as they saw declines of 4% to 9%. Investors are finally panicking and selling out.

But, with the absence of support, the Nifty cannot be said to have made a low. Support comes at a broad zone between 4,200 to 3,600. Thanks to this wide zone, there is no clarity on where the Nifty could stop its decline. The Nifty will have to find out its comfort level — the point where it stops falling. This could be 4,200, or it could be 3,600 — it is anyone's guess. I assume the Nifty will go below 4,000. This assumption is made on the downside momentum that the markets are showing.

30 June 2008

Big Declines in Market as Nifty Falls 5 Percent for the Week

A bottom is not yet in place. Traders / investors must wait patiently for a base building process to begin. This has not happened yet.

Figure 3.57: **Bear market continues. Nifty support zone is between 3,600 to 4,200. Investors should wait and watch.**

We are seeing declines across all sectors, and in all categories — be it large caps, mid caps or small caps. These are signs of a bear market in progress. Such a market will end only after a period of base building. We are also likely to see a number of false rallies which will give the impression that the bear market is over. But these rallies will eventually fizzle out. Therefore, investors should watch for the first sign of a new bull market — a higher low. As already explained, the Nifty is making new lows every day, therefore as of now, there is no question of a higher low.

Inflation Expectations

Bloomberg has published an article on inflation which causes concern. For the first time in a generation, US consumers feel that their standard of living will come down due to inflation.

Lower Living Standard

"In previous cycles, consumer expectations about their financial well-being did not collapse when inflation went up," said Neal Soss, chief economist at Credit Suisse. This time around, according to the Reuters / University of Michigan Survey of Consumers, rising inflation expectations are being met with "a collapse in expectations about their own financial futures, suggesting consumers don't expect to be compensated for higher prices with higher wages,"

Credit is harder to get, and consumers are increasingly falling behind on credit card payments in addition to their interest on mortgages and auto loans.

My Notes

While these comments are meant for the American market, they will affect all of us. This means there will be a reduction in consumer spending as the common man is forced to adjust his or her budget to meet the minimum standards of living.

The last bear market was from 2001 to 2003. But the current phase is different. The 2001-2003 background was very different from today. Fearing deflation back then, many central banks were cutting interest rates. More recently, many central banks are raising rates. (As has happened in India). Therefore, this bear market may have a different behaviour.

Panic Not Yet Visible

One of the more colourful market adages has long been: "Buy when there is blood in the streets." Well, we are not quite there yet, not that every panic produces such extremes, but at current levels, the declines have been quite orderly with no signs of blood on the streets. This probably points to the conclusion that there is more downside, yet to come.

Such excessive declines usually occur in a bear market. We are in such a market now.

7 July 2008

Bear Market Continues as Share Prices See New Lows

Nifty moves below 4,000, Sensex at 13,000, both down by 35% from their highs.

Figure 3.58: **Nifty falls below 4,000; may be ready for a relief rally to 4,350.**

This week saw the Nifty go below 4,000 — a significant psychological level. The Sensex briefly moved below 13,000. We must remember that the Nifty had seen a high of 6,350 just five months ago. Since then, the Index has fallen by 35%. This is a strong bear market, not just a correction.

Nifty Watch

The Nifty made a pivot low on Wednesday at 3,850. If this low breaks, we again have a continuation of the pattern of lower lows, suggesting more weakness ahead. As the Index closed at 3,920, it is within striking distance of these lows. If by chance the Nifty does manage to move up, keeping these lows intact, then a change in trend will be assumed if the Index closes above 4,350. Between 3,850 and 4,350, trading opportunities are limited since the market may remain volatile and uncertain.

Technical traders should look at the weekly chart for the Nifty. The bull market saw the Nifty move up in a straight line advance from 2,500 to 3,600 in 2006. Week after week, the index just went up, with no correction or dip in between. Such straight line advances create a vacuum. When the market begins to move down, it encounters no significant support since such support was not created on the way up. This is the worry if the Nifty were to break below the 3,600-3,700 zone. We could then be looking at a free fall.

If 3,850 holds, we may be looking at a period of choppy market movement as Q1 results start coming in from 7 July onwards.

Gains made in the market in coming days will not signal the start of a bull market. The bear market is barely six months old. It is probably not over. Then, too, bull markets start after a prolonged period of base building, probably months or even years. Therefore, rallies should be used for short term trading — or even selling at higher levels.

Asset Allocation

Most investors have some money to invest. The critical challenge now lies in asset allocation, and particularly in moving money away from those areas where it is most vulnerable. The severity and universality of the bear market in stocks can be seen in the losses incurred by almost all momentum sectors in the stock market. Note that other than information technology and pharma, not one sector is showing positive returns. The bear has been everywhere. The biggest losers, year-to-date, have not even been the banks; real estate has taken over as the businesses most prone to falling off the ugly tree and hitting every branch on the way down.

So, What Now?

Cash was never trash, but now it is king. There is a time-honoured safe haven with a 2000+ year history of preserving wealth in real terms. It is called gold.

14 July 2008

Volatile Market Sees Ups and Downs

Closes Slightly Higher than Previous Week

The Nifty saw a large amount of volatility but finally managed to close at 4,063, up 46 points from the previous week. This is quite an achievement since the higher close came after seven successive weeks of lower closing prices.

On Friday, the final trading day of the week, inflation numbers, Q1 Infosys results and industrial production numbers for May were announced. While Infosys results were on expected lines, the industrial production numbers were a nasty surprise. At 3.8%, this is the lowest growth in six years. Inflation was at 11.89%, again the highest since 1995. The economy seems to be under pressure with high inflation and relatively low growth.

The market reflected the pessimism by falling on Friday, from an intra day high of 4,215 to an intra day low of 4,014 before closing slightly better. Clearly, the bear market is not over, it is alive and kicking.

Two different, contradictory patterns are visible in the Nifty chart.

The first is a rising flag on the daily Nifty. A flag usually comes half way in a trend. A rising flag comes in a downtrend. The flag will get confirmed if the Nifty closes below 4,000. The current leg of the downtrend started at 4,680, then touched a low of 3,850, making a total move of 830 points. From the breakdown point at 4,000, this gives a downside target of 3,170. Now, a target is just an estimate, it may or may not come about.

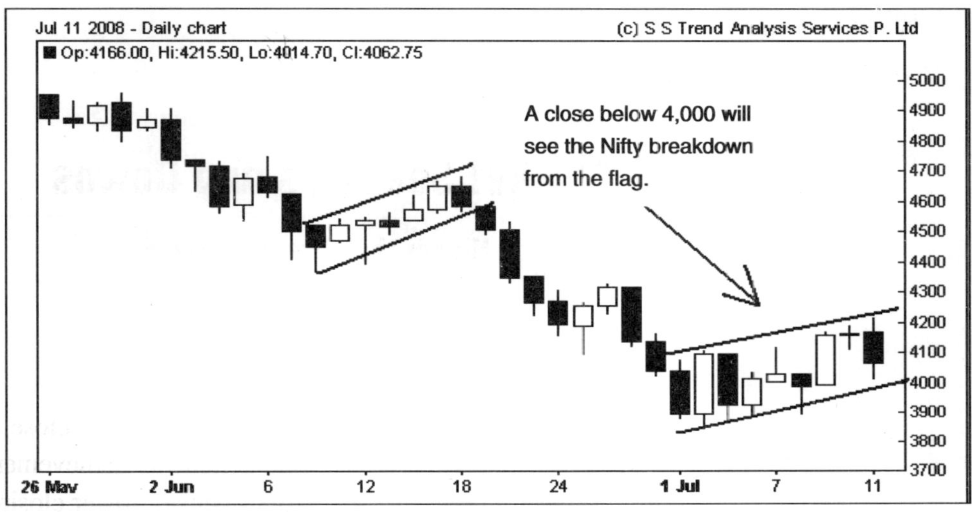

Figure 3.59: **Daily chart of Nifty; note the rising flag, a bearish pattern in a downtrend.**

The second pattern is the two-week movement in the Nifty which is holding inside a support range between 3,850 and 4,200. This suggests that the index is trying to start some kind of base building.

Figure 3.60: **Intermediate view of Nifty: The market may be trying to make a base in the support zone between 3,850-4,200.**

What is the Conclusion?

A breakdown below 4,000 will start a short term downtrend. Traders should not take long positions if this happens. A breakdown below 3,850 will reconfirm that the intermediate trend remains down. Investors can consider taking small positions while the Nifty is above 3,850. If the Nifty falls below 3,850, then do not continue with any buying, If this happens, wait for some kind of base building.

16 July 2008

Big Fall in Nifty

New Lows, No Support Close by

The Nifty continued its trending move, falling again to new lows, breaking first the 4,000 support and then 3,850 support decisively.

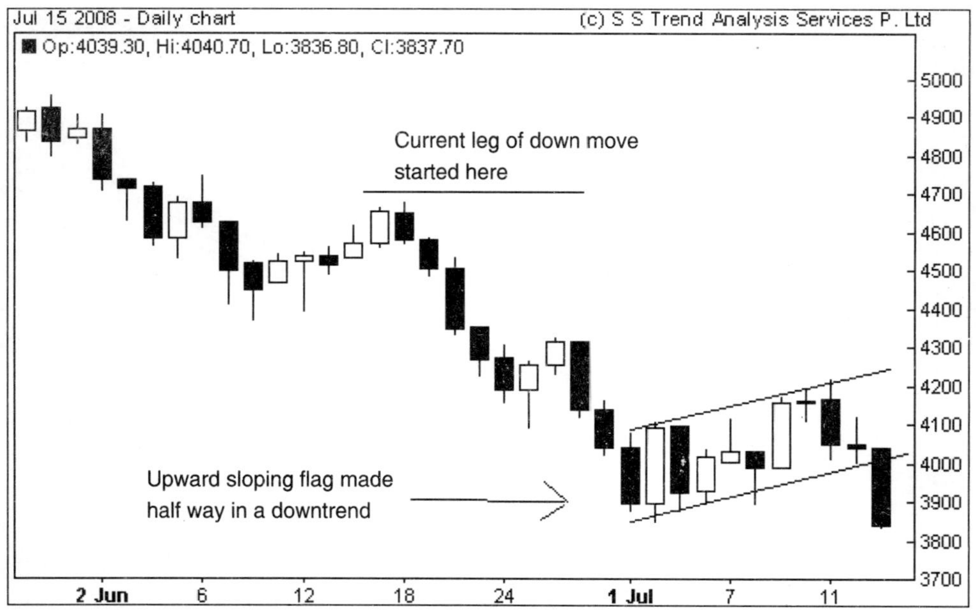

Figure 3.61: **A bearish flag in Nifty.**

Below 3,850, the Nifty has minor support at 3,600, then a free fall. The nearest support after 3,600 is at 2,600. Now, this is not to suggest that the Index will fall to 2,600. I do not know if it will. But the absence of support suggests that we do not have any measure of a point at which the Nifty may stop falling. Worrying!

The Upward Sloping Flag!

An upward sloping flag in the Nifty has broken down today. A flag is usually made half way in a decline. Earlier, we had calculated that the target for the flag comes at 3,170. Again, a target is just that — a mathematical measure. It may or may not come about. We must remember that it does often work out, so the probability is in favour of meeting the target.

18 July 2008

Ray of Hope for the Bulls as Relief Rally Picks Up Steam in International Markets

Nifty Finds Repeated Support at 3,800

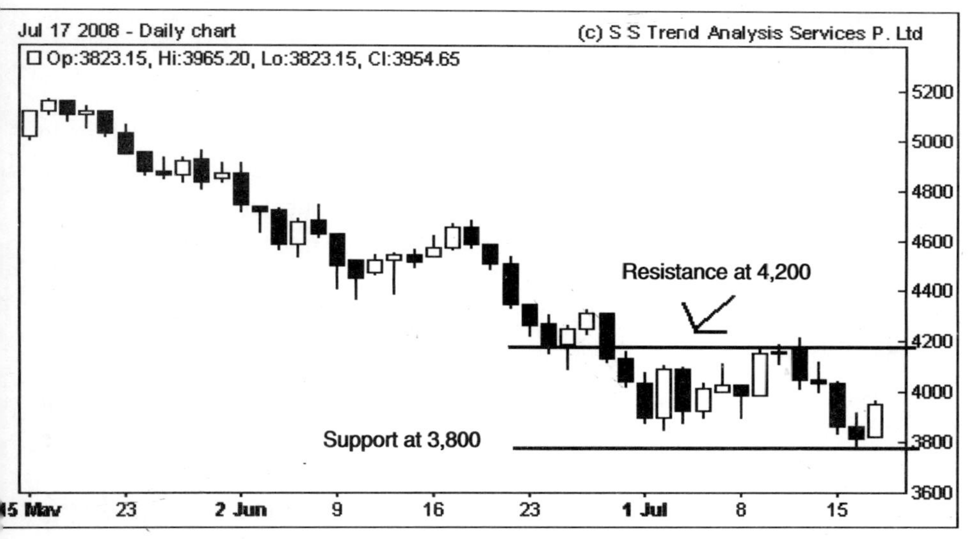

Figure 3.62: **Nifty finds support at 3,800, relief rally begins.**

So long as the Nifty remains above 3,800, dips can be used for buying. Long positions are justified with a stop below 3,800. Yet, we must remember that Indian markets face an event risk in inflation, the fate of the confidence vote and the annual monsoon blues. Thus, traders should keep volumes low and trade with stop losses.

The Nifty has been inside a trading range between 3,800 and 4,200 for over 14 trading sessions. Trading range patterns are not easy to trade, since the direction is confusing, and a trending move quickly fades away. While intra day trades are relatively easy since there may emerge at least a short term trend, on days with choppy market action, intra day trading may result in buying at the top and selling at the low. What is the option? I feel that these periods of whipsaws have to be accepted since it is not easy to predict when a trending move will begin. It is necessary to trade in smaller quantities and always keep protective stops.

Looking Ahead at the Nifty

The Nifty is at a 15-month low. Since most European markets are at 2-year lows, we are faring much better. So far this has been a bear market with very little pain — as compared to, say, the year 2000-2001 IT debacle.

But we cannot say with certainty that we have seen the end of the bear cycle. Some analysts feel that the current down move is a correction in an ongoing bull market. On this basis, they suggest that the correction may be getting closer to its end. Now, this is a matter of subjective analysis since there is no clear cut rule defining a bear market as opposed to a correction.

The index has lost over 40% of its value from its all time highs. I would classify this as a bear market. If this is really a bear move, then there may be more downside ahead, as well as a lot of time to be spent building a base. There is no way to forecast what will actually happen. Therefore, it is wise to follow our charts. Buy signals have not yet emerged on the charts.

This is fair since, till yesterday, the Nifty was making new lows. The first signs of a new bull market will come if and when the Nifty moves — and closes — above 4,200. Let us wait and watch.

23 July 2008

Nifty Rally Continues

Bear Rally or New Bull Market?

The Indian stock market continued to cheer the possibility of a win for the government in the confidence vote. As I write this, the voting has not been done, but reports suggest that the government will win this easily.

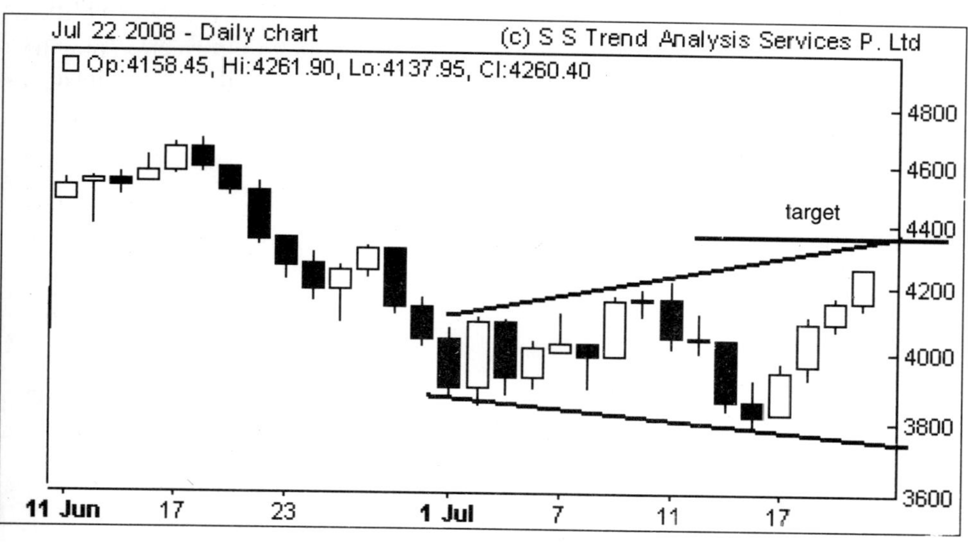

Figure 3.63: **Nifty closes above 4,200 — its previous high. The broadening pattern seen at the right hand side of the chart gives an approximate target of 4,400 where resistance should come in.**

Tuesday marks the fourth day of gains in the market, with the Nifty moving up from 3,820 to 4,260, a gain of 440 points, or almost 12% in just four trading days. This could not get better.

The short term trend remains up. The intermediate trend has become sideways today when the Nifty closed above 4,200 — the previous high. A confirmed uptrend will emerge when the Index goes through a pullback (moves down) and remains above 3,800 the last recorded low. Once we have the first pullback, investors should consider buying.

The daily chart for the Nifty has a broadening pattern which is unusual, coming as it is at the lows. The resistance line is somewhere around 4,400, maybe a little lower. The Index should see selling between 4,300-4,400.

Do Bull Markets Start with Big Bang?

The 12% rally in four days is quite a big bang for the Indian stock market. The key question is: should we consider this to be the start of a bull market. The answer seems to be: no. Bull markets start with a slow grinding process of choppy moves, repeated tests of the lows, and a complete absence of investors. None of the signs of the beginning of a bull market are available yet. We consider, then, that the current up move is a rally in a bear market.

28 July 2008

A Big Decline

Nifty Cools off, Remains Above 4,300

Figure 3.64: **Nifty remains in a bear market, below the trendline. Close above 4,540 is required for a new uptrend.**

The Nifty fell by 121 points on Friday, pushed down by bearish international markets, disappointment with Reliance results, and finally by the Bangalore serial bomb blasts.

With this decline, the Index has lost more than 200 points from Thursday's high to Friday's close. This is really good news since irrational gains have been pared down, making the market that much healthier.

At current levels, the Nifty is almost 500 points above the 3,800 lows recorded just 10 days ago. This represents a 14% gain.

Nifty Scenarios

Was the current advance a bear market rally? Here are some possible scenarios for the Nifty.

Scenario #1

As of now, it appears that the up move was part of a bear market correction. Much more time is needed for a bear market to run its course. Six months is just not enough. If this be the case, it is then quite possible that the 3,800 lows may be taken out at some point in the future.

Scenario #2

It is also possible that the Index may now move in a trading range between 4,600 on the upside and a lower support level that is yet to be defined.

Scenario #3

A remote possibility is for the Index to actually start a bull run, crossing 4,600 and touching 5,500.

Outlook for the Next Week

I assume that the Nifty is likely to face resistance above 4,400. It is possible that the 4,300 support may be broken and the Index may seek support at lower levels.

4 August 2008

Markets Continue to Rally

Dips Confirm Support

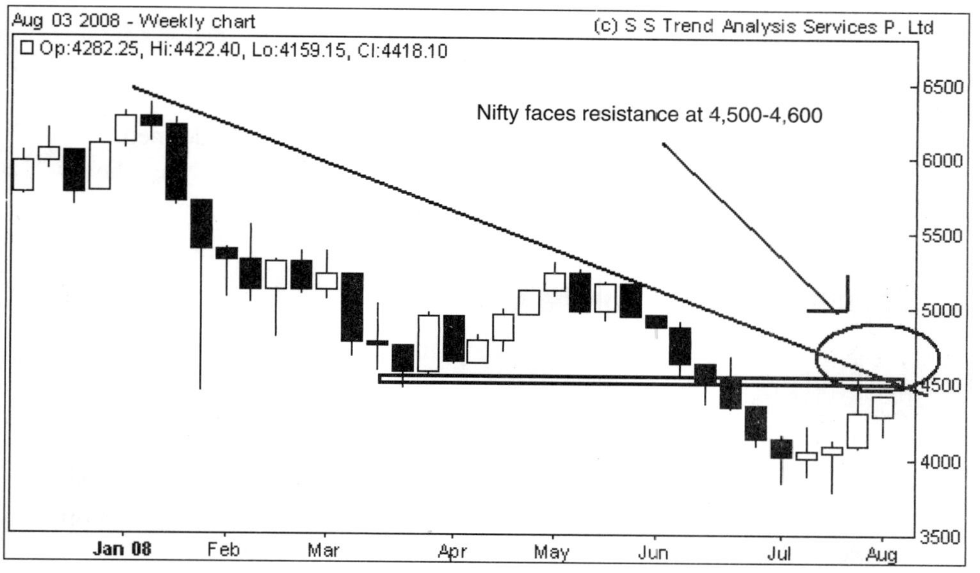

Figure 3.65: **Investors should buy small lots, traders should buy on dips.**

The stock market continued its rally during the week, with a mid-week dip providing a successful test of the lows.

The Nifty fell to 4,150 but found support there, finally closing the week at 4,418, up by 107 points over the previous week's close. This is the fourth successive week in which the index has closed higher over the previous week.

Trend

The primary (main) trend remains down. The intermediate trend is up, and the minor trend is up. It is possible for traders to take buying positions, with proper stop loss and reasonable targets.

Bullish Pattern

The Nifty has made a fairly bullish pattern with higher highs and higher lows. The Index crossed above the previous highs of 4,200, and then, 4,450. While it fell this week, it nevertheless managed to stay at 4,150, well above the previous low of 3,800.

What Can Go Wrong?

A move by the Nifty below 4,150 is almost certainly a signal that the up-trend is failing. Do not buy if this level is broken on the downside.

Possible Scenarios for the Nifty

The Nifty can easily go up to 4,550 / 4,600. This scenario will not change the bear market. Once the index reaches the 4,600 resistance, we have to watch for further moves. The market may quickly retrace after it stages a rally.

A second scenario is for the Nifty to pull back and, finally, break down below 4,150.

Both scenarios have almost equal chances of materialising.

7 August 2008

Nifty Corrects

Resistance at Higher Levels

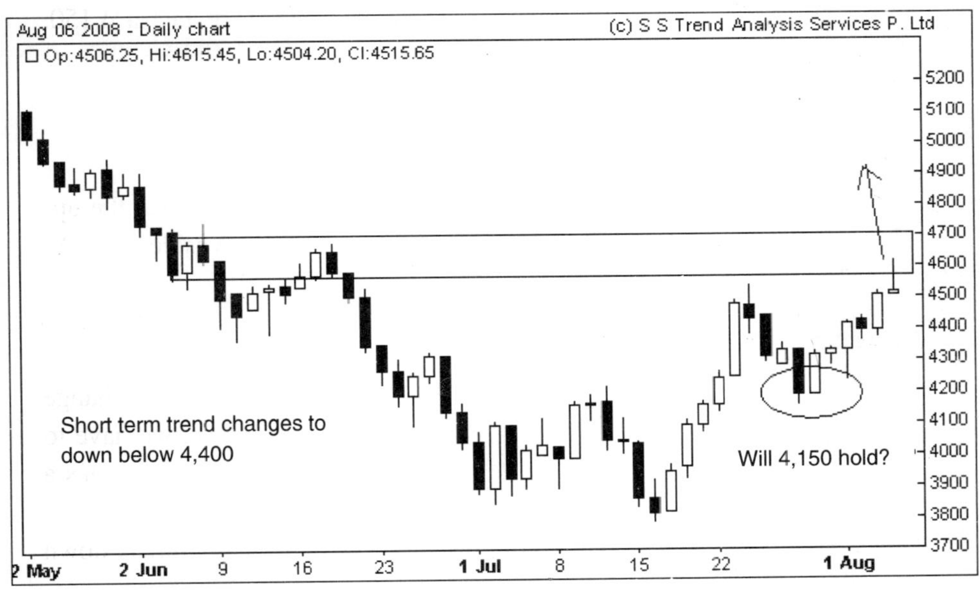

Figure 3.66: **Nifty faces resistance at 4,600-4,700. Long upper shadows tell us the bulls are exhausted.**

Strong overhead resistance at 4,600 saw the Nifty go through a painful intra day correction, finally closing at 4,515, giving up all of its intra day gains. In the process, the index also filled a gap up open — not quite bullish.

As we see a clash of two different trend flows, there remains a sense of uncertainty on the eventual outcome of this clash. The primary trend is down, while the intermediate trend is up. Soon enough, these trends will merge into a single stream. So, what will happen then? Will the primary trend change to up, or will the intermediate trend change to down?

We do not have the answers to these questions. We do know that charts will probably alert us to which of these happens.

For the intermediate trend, the 4,600 zone represents strong resistance. Surely, many old memories must have been revived as the Nifty approached 4,600. Buyers at lower levels were taking profits, while earlier buyers at 4,600 who saw the Nifty fall to 3,800, then recover, were quickly getting out at break even.

Nifty Outlook

A pivot low has been made at 4,150. While the Nifty remains above this number, the intermediate trend remains up. The minor trend changes to down if the Nifty were to close below 4,400.

Sounds confusing, doesn't it? The trader needs to know: What should I trade? All of these ifs and buts make very good reading but do not provide actionable advice to traders.

Well, we will do this again. The Nifty has seen strong resistance at the 4,600-4,700 zone, where such resistance was expected.

The trader has two courses of action, both of which will prove to be correct provided she exercises prudent money management.

First, go with the primary trend. This is a bear market. The strong resistance encountered by the Nifty at predetermined resistance zones tells us that the bulls are exhausted. Day traders can go short below 4,500, while swing traders should sell below 4,400. An initial stop loss should be somewhere above today's high — 4,616.

Second, remain with the intermediate trend, which is presently up. Day traders should buy the first signs of strength with stops below that day's low. Swing traders should buy before close of trade if the day is closing strong, or, buy above the high of the previous day. Stops will be below 4,400. A minor downtrend starts below 4,400, thus long positions are not advised once a down move starts.

If the trade goes in your favour, so far so good. If you find yourself in the wrong direction, the stops will ensure that your losses are manageable. You will be ready for another trade.

With some thought, you can develop another trading plan. All such plans will be successful if you know when to get out if you are wrong.

12 August 2008

Market in Sustained Up Move

Nifty Inside Resistance Zone

Figure 3.67: **Nifty breaks out from a bullish head and shoulder pattern, giving a target of 5,200. The trend is up, stay with long positions.**

The stock market continued to be in a firmly bullish mode, moving up on a gap up, closing almost a 100 points above Friday's close, at 4,625.

Traders should go with market flow. This is my favourite theme for short term trading.

A question arises: What exactly is market flow?

Answer: It is momentum . . . .

If momentum is on the side of the bulls, then we should try to be long. If momentum is favouring the bears, then either stay short or stay away.

Currently, we do not need a rocket scientist to tell us that momentum favours the bulls. A quick look at the end of day chart for the Nifty will tell us that prices are going up, with a classic bullish pattern of higher highs and higher lows.

Traders should then look to buy on dips, breakouts. There will come a point when this buy trade will result in a loss. That will be the first sign that the buyers are getting exhausted. This has not happened yet.

We have referred to a zone of resistance between 4,600 and 4,700 in the Nifty. This zone still exists. A close above 4,600 is the first sign that the Nifty is gathering enough strength to move up. Such a close has happened today. The Nifty should close above 4,600 for another two days to give a confirmation that the resistance zone has been crossed.

A close above 4,600 is required when the Nifty continues to trade inside the resistance zone between 4,600 and 4,700. If the index moves above 4,700, then there is a confirmed breakout.

13 August 2008

Nifty Faces Heavy Weather at 4,600, Retraces

Figure 3.68: **Nifty is locked in a narrow range (boxed area in the chart). 4,500 is support, while 4,600 has become resistance. A move above 4,500 or below 4,500 should give a trading opportunity.**

The resistance at 4,600-4,700 proved to be real resistance. The Index could not sustain these higher levels, and fell to close below 4,600. The reason for today's decline was poor industrial production numbers and, more particularly, low growth numbers in the infrastructure sector. While the reason was good enough, the Index did not have the strength to overcome such pessimism.

A narrow range in the Nifty between 4,500 and 4,600 seems to have developed in the past five trading sessions. This small range is not going to last for many days. Soon enough, there will be a breakdown below 4,500 or a breakout above 4,600. This should happen in the next few days.

Traders should wait for this range to break out. Patience!

18 August 2008

Nifty Records First Weekly Decline after Five Weeks of Rallies

The market is facing strong resistance at higher levels. After a 22 percent rise in just one month, a correction is likely.

Figure 3.69: **Nifty is in a trading range between 4,200 and 4,600.**

The technical picture for the Nifty is like this:

Primary trend: Down. This remains a bear market.

Intermediate trend: Up. This seems to be a bear rally, although the trend has been tradable.

Now, at 4,600 Nifty, there is significant resistance. The market has tried to cross this resistance three times but failed. A new bullish move will take place only when the Nifty crosses above 4,600 decisively. The Index should close above this level for three successive days. This has not happened yet.

It appears that the intermediate trend is in danger since bulls seems to be losing control.

Minor trend: This is down, although this trend can change quickly. The Nifty was range bound between 4,500 and 4,600 for six trading days. It is unusual for the Index to remain in such a narrow range for so long. On Thursday, 14 August, this range broke down on the downside, thus signalling weakness in the market.

What Lies Ahead?

The bear market seems to be continuing. It is possible that there may be a significant low made at 3,800 in the Nifty. The market could remain in a trading range between 3,800 and 4,600 for many months. Now the definition of the range is rather subjective with some analysts probably identifying different levels. The basic concept, however, is that there is likely to be range bound movement. In such a scenario, buying should be done only on substantial dips.

For the Nifty, there is support at different levels. First support comes in at 4,400. If this support breaks, then we should look for 4,250. If that, too, breaks, then look for 4,100.

On the upside, there remains resistance at 4,600. With the breakdown of the 4,500-4,600 range, resistance also comes in at 4,500. Worries of many kinds.

Traders should consider the environment apart from technical factors. For the Indian market, the environment is not good for the bulls. Inflation continues to move up, there is political uncertainty, industrial production growth rate has fallen a lot and crude prices are moving up again. In such a difficult scenario, the first priority should be preservation of capital.

20 August 2008

Market Decline Continues

World Markets Caught in Pessimism

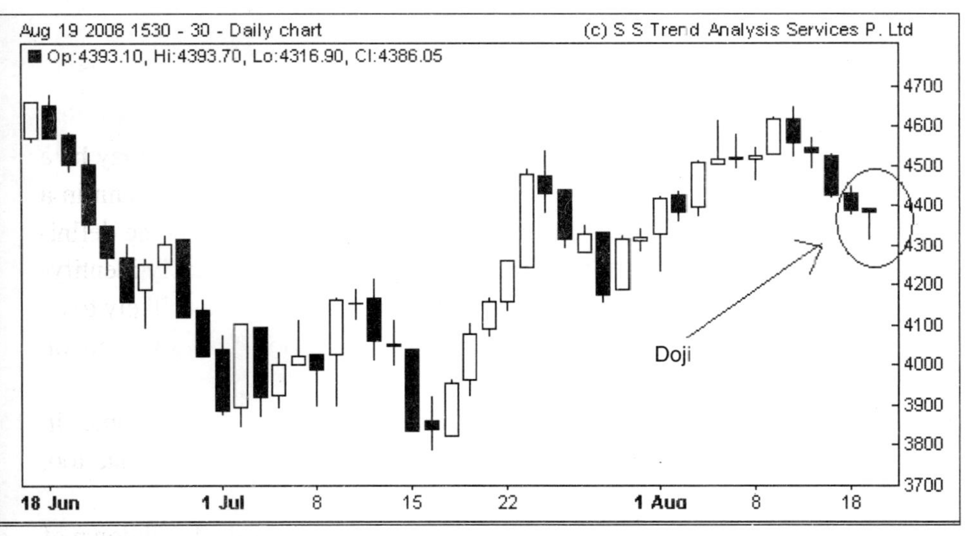

Figure 3.70: **Nifty may have seen a short term low with a long legged Doji. Buying is suggested if world markets remain steady.**

Short Term

The Nifty fell again today, the fifth day of declines and lower close. With today's fall, which saw an intra day low of 4,316, Nifty has come close to a projected target of 4,300-4,190. Our analysis suggests a rally from this target zone which may reach 4,400-4,450 in the time zone August 25-27.

Quite often, we will find support emerging at the most unlikely locations — but the fact is that these areas of support have been identified using un-conventional methods and they do well.

After a blazing rally from 3,790 to 4,650, the Index has retraced 320 points, almost 38% of the rally. This is a normal retracement. The intermediate trend is assumed to be up, even after this correction.

But the scenario may change if we assume that the intermediate trend is complete, with the primary decline asserting itself.

For the intermediate term, our software projections are quite pessimistic.

A target of 4,600 has been achieved. The next move is expected to be down, with a possible target of 4,000, and a time target of first week of September.

Now, targets are just that — numbers which have worked in the past, but may or may not be accurate this time.

Then, a short term up swing and an intermediate decline is the scenario that works out. Traders should then buy in anticipation of a small up move, then look to take profits at higher levels. Signs of weakness after a rally should be used to sell.

As usual, please use stops to protect your positions. Also what we have discussed are possible scenarios and not trading suggestions. You should use technical tools to determine actual entry and exit levels.

22 August 2008

Big Decline in the Market

Nifty Breaks Down from a Trading Range

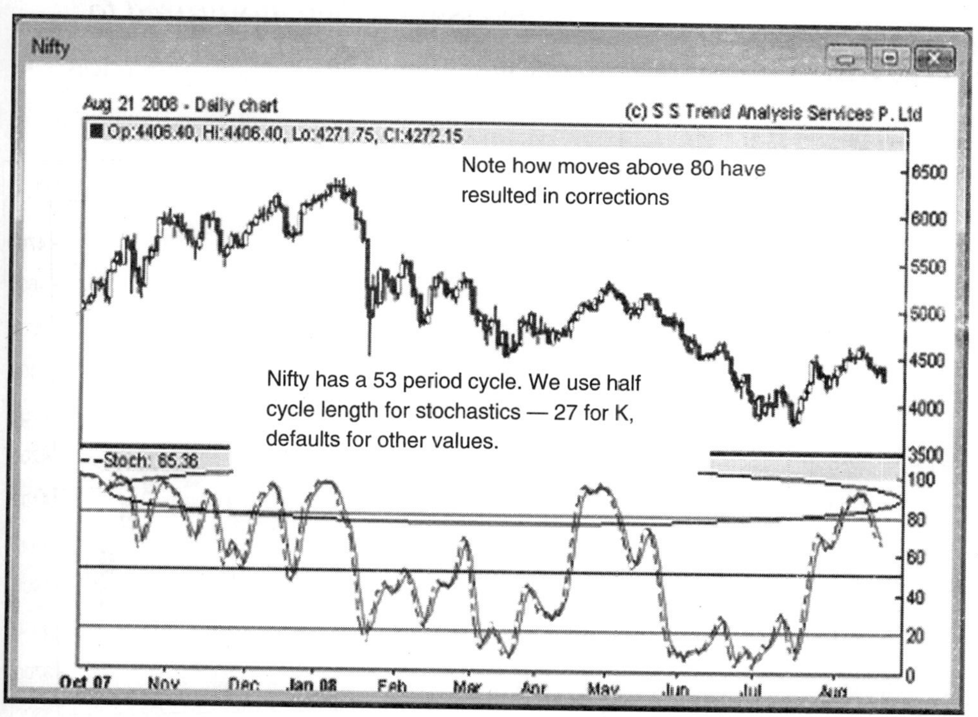

Figure 3.71: **Daily chart of the Nifty with a 27- period stochastic.**

The Nifty fell out of a narrow trading range, delighting to short term traders by offering a one-sided move and closing at the lows of the day. Traders go through a series of whipsaws and losses for such trend days.

For the Nifty, every decline brings the Index closer to a "normal" correction, removing the excesses of the earlier 22% rally in just one month.

We assume that the intermediate trend is now sideways. The up move is done with. Then, with the primary trend down and the short term down, the momentum favours selling. At some point, this selling will also be over done, like the buying earlier was. Traders should trade with an open mind. We are not bulls or bears, we are traders.

Given on the next page is a daily chart for the Nifty with a 27-period stochastic*. Why 27? The Nifty seems to be responding to a 53-period cycle**. So, we use a half cycle length for stochastic, which gives us 27. In the chart, note how a move above 80 by the stochastic was invariably followed by declines. This happened earlier also in periods not shown in the chart. With stochastic at 65.36, there is probably more room for prices to go down.

---

* Stochastics is a technical indicator that measures momentum. A rising stochastics suggests bulls are strong, while a falling number suggests bears are strong.

** The lookback length of momentum and trend indicators should be half of the cycle length currently valid for the security. The valid cycle length is difficult to identify and changes rather quickly. Yet, using a fast fourier transform, some kind of cycle length can be obtained, half of which should be used as the lookback period.

28 August 2008

Market is Still Inside a Narrow Range

Look for Big Move Soon

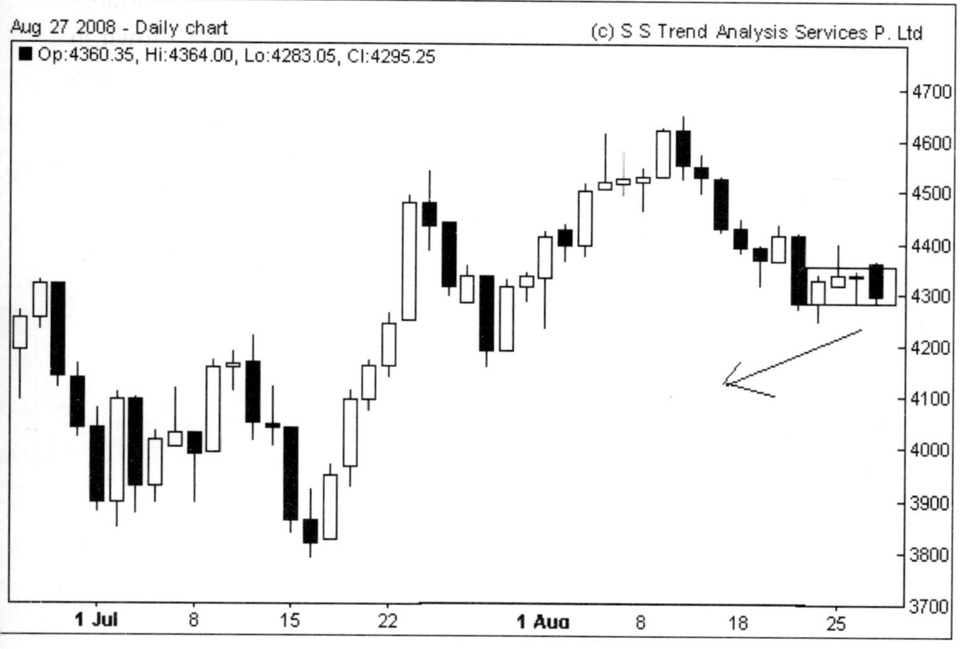

Figure 3.72: **Nifty is locked in a narrow range.**

The Nifty remained locked inside this extremely narrow range, between 4,340 and 4,280, for the fourth day running.

It is quite unusual for the Index to move in such narrow ranges. A big strong move is coming. Though the direction of this move is yet unknown.

29 August 2008

Nifty Breaks Down from Narrow Range

Touches 4,200

Figure 3.73: **After correcting 50% of its previous up move, the Nifty is now in a support zone.**

There is support for Nifty in the 4,120-4,220 area where the market could find some kind of buying coming in.

- If 4,120 support breaks, the Nifty is probably heading down to test 3,800 again.
- If this support zone holds, then look for a rally to 4,280 initially, then, maybe, 4,400.

Let the market tell us where it wants to go.

2 September 2008

Nifty in a Trading Range

Offers Many Trading Opportunities

As the index continues to move in a narrow band, there appear to be opportunities for buying on break-outs and selling on breakdowns.

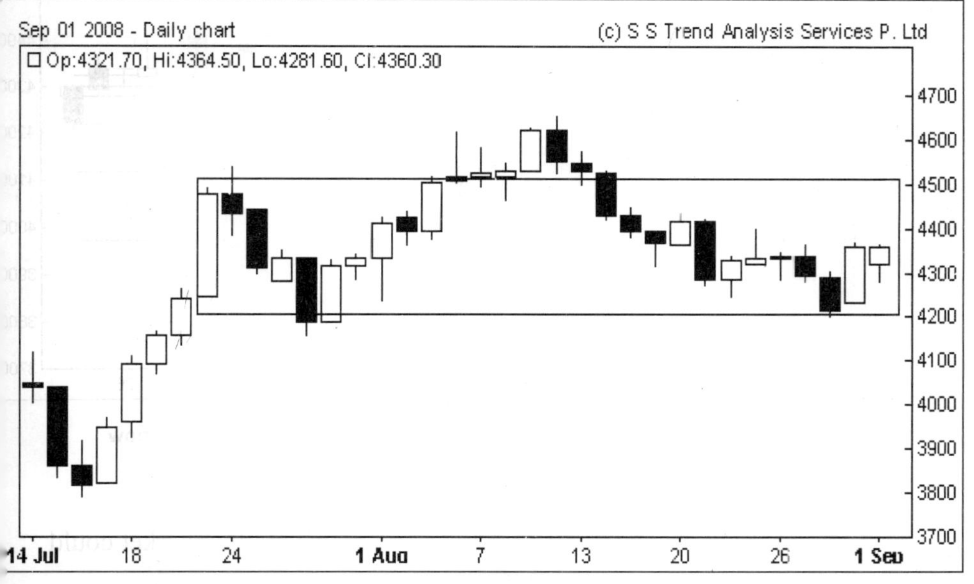

Figure 3.74: **This trading range in the Nifty lies between 4,500 and 4,200. A smaller range has resistance at 4,360. Buy above 4,360.**

The Nifty has two distinct trading zones. The first is a larger range, between 4,200 and 4,500. A move out of this range will offer a significant trend.

The second range is between 4,360 and 4,200. This is the range which can easily be broken any time. If this happens, traders should go long, with proper stops.

In spite of small daily ranges, volatility continues to be at the higher end. Currently the 10-day historical volatility is 85% of "normal" long term 100-day volatility. I say that this is at the higher end, because a low volatility situation develops when current short term volatility is 50% or less than long term volatility. Therefore, it is possible that the market may continue to move in a narrow range for a longer period.

The trading idea from this information is to accept that a strong trend may not emerge soon. Trading should be focused on small profits.

12 September 2008

Nifty Declines

Index Breaks Down from Minor Trading Range

Figure 3.75: **Nifty is still in a trading range with strong support at 4,200-4,250. Look for bounce from here. If 4,200 breaks, avoid further buying.**

The Nifty fell again, erasing all the gains from Monday's rally and, in fact, losing some. With today's decline, the Nifty has broken down from a minor trading range between 4,400 and 4,500. Purely as a technical number, the pattern target for this breakdown was 4,300 — a target that has been touched today, in fact crossed on the downside.

The Index had recorded a low of 4,200 on 28 August 2008. Using different parameters, there is a trading range between 4,250 and 4,650. Thus, there is significant support between 4,200 and 4,250. Consider this as a band of support. The market is now coming close to a test of this support range.

The key question is: Will this support band hold? Will there be a bounce from this level?

The answer is: The market is in a trading range. We expected the market to face resistance when it reached towards 4,650. In the same way, we should expect the market to provide support when the Index comes close to the support area. (It already is close.)

The risk: It is always possible that the market may finally decide to move out of this trading range by falling below the 4,200-4,250 support zone. This is the risk in taking a long position in anticipation of support. But the same risk exists when we anticipate that resistance will hold and sell near the resistance.

Consider buying when there are signs of strength coming in. As the Nifty is close to its support zone, this is a low risk area for a short term trade.

16 September 2008

Big Decline in the Nifty as American Financial Markets Get into Trouble

The bankruptcy of Lehman Brothers has made big waves in the financial markets worldwide. This has caused the Indian markets to fall big time; in fact, the Indian market also faced the issues of the Delhi bomb blast. Together, the two events have caused substantial decline in equities.

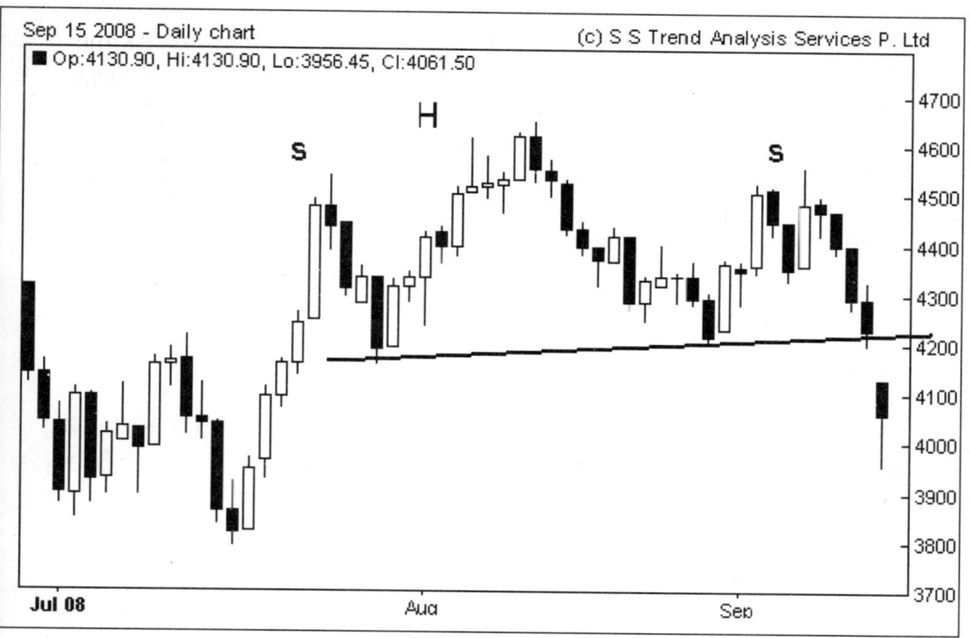

Figure 3.76: **Nifty breaks down from the trading range, confirms bearish head and shoulder pattern, looks towards 3,800.**

Should You Buy Now?

This is what I wrote in the blog www.indiatechnicals.blogspot.com today morning at 8:57 A.M.

There is a temptation to buy. After all, how much lower can it get? Remember, this is dangerous thinking. What stops the Nifty from breaking below 3,800, and finally reaching 3,200 or even 2,650? I am not suggesting this will happen. My point is: never go against the market. If this market is ready to move up, then there will be signs: support will emerge, momentum will slowly change in favour of the bulls, etc. The correct way to think is this: At 4,000 levels, the market is attractive, therefore I will buy whenever there are signs of favourable momentum.

Any given level is NOT a buying or selling opportunity. Appropriate market action at that level creates the opportunity.

Patience, then!

Can the Market Go Down Further?

Unfortunately, yes!

It does appear that the bear market is alive and kicking. If we are in a bear market, then the most likely course for stocks is to go down. How much downside is possible cannot be predicted. The very fact that more downside is possible should alert us to think of the unimaginable.

Reduction of Risk

Why did the institutions refuse to buy Lehman? Because they found too much risk. Why is the US Fed nationalizing Fannie and Freddie? To reduce the risk of default. The underlying theme is: lessen your risk. Then, if large institutions are reducing risk, why should we increase our risk?

The worst is not over because the extent of damage to the Western financial system is yet unknown. Bill Gross, head of Pimco, said that we may be seeing a "destructive financial tsunami".

Investing

For investors, it is not possible to exactly time the market, therefore, buy in small lots.

If you are looking to invest, you may plan to put in 10% of your planned investments. Then, add if there is a decline. Do not add on rallies.

For selection of securities, focus only on blue chips. Forget about momentum stocks. Generally, avoid stocks that are into some kind of financial engineering, like Sterlite, Tata Motors, Hindalco. Here is an illustrative list which includes large caps and mid caps but is still all blue chips: Reliance, State Bank, Tech Mahindra, ONGC, Cairn, Nag Fert.

22 September 2008

Nifty Has Made an Intermediate Low

A Bullish Bounce Back is Possible

Figure 3.77: **The weekly chart of Nifty shows Nifty is still trading range bound. Resistance comes near 4,600.**

The market has bounced up from significant support found at 3,800 for the Nifty.

After a round of terrible news, the market has moved up on the back of news that the American and European regulators may take some action to prevent further damage to financial markets.

This news has brought some cheer to the markets.

We remain in a bear market. But even bear markets will have intermediate rallies. We are seeing such a rally in the market now. Resistance comes in around 4,200 (a level which has been broken on Friday), and, then at 4,500. Finally resistance comes in at 4,650. If the Nifty were to move above 4,650, the primary trend should change from down to up.

On the downside, the Nifty has found significant support at 3,800. Again, on Thursday, the Index found similar support.

For investors, dips remain buying opportunities. For traders, volatile markets are not easy to trade. The trader should develop a view on the market, then trade only in the direction of that view.

CASH is KING, but INVEST wisely to grow your cash.

Blue chip stocks and gold may be proper opportunities.

25 September 2008

Subdued Trading

FNO Expiration Tomorrow, Market May Give a Trending Move

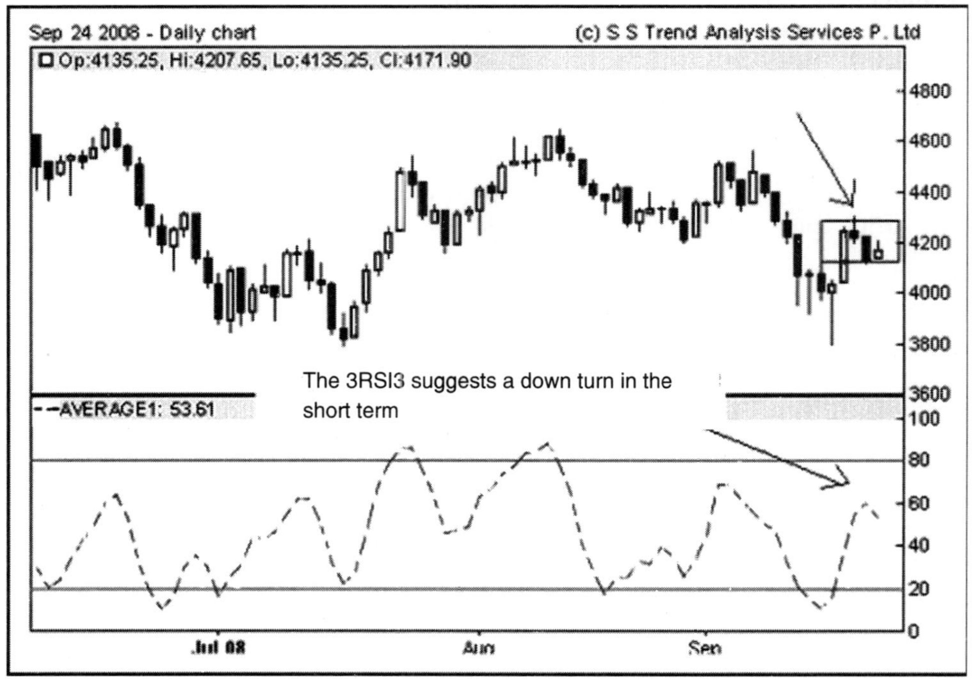

Figure 3.78: **The Nifty is in a small trading range between 4,300-4,140.**

The Nifty remained in a narrow range today. The Index has now defined a small range between 4,140 and 4,300 in which it has spent the best part of four days. A move out of this range should give a trending, tradable move.

While it is anybody's guess as to the direction of the breakout, a short term indicator on the Nifty does suggest a down move. This is the 3RSI3.

The 3RSI3 is a 3-period moving average of a 3-period RSI. This indicator will often catch short term cyclical turns.

Summary

The Nifty is again inside a narrow trading range between 4,140 and 4,300. There is a buy with a stop below 4,140. Go short on a breakdown.

The index continues to remain inside a larger trading range between 4,650 and 3,800. We remain in a bear market. There is some possibility of a minor or intermediate up move. Buy on dips.

1 October 2008

Dramatic Reversal in Nifty

Short Term Up Move May Have Started

The up move may continue. Resistance comes in around 4,150-4,200. Once again, 3,800 has proved to be support.

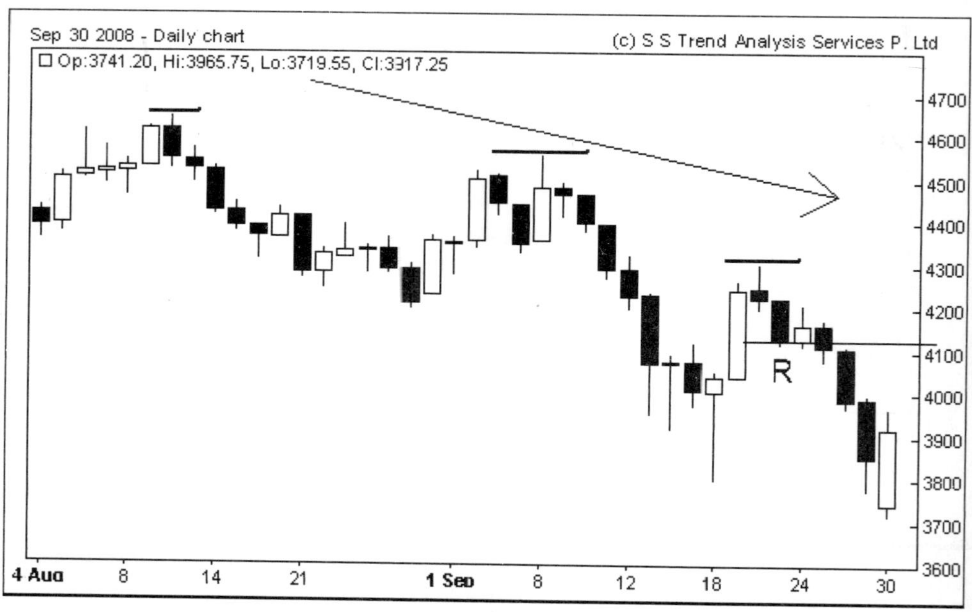

Figure 3.79: **Oversold Nifty bounces back, looks for relief rally. Resistance at 4,125 and support at 3,800.**

The markets can, and do, surprise us. After the worst ever decline in the US markets, India opened just a wee bit lower, then started its way up, finally ending higher, yes, higher, by 67 points.

Is this the start of a bull market?

Unfortunately, no. We saw the Nifty fall day by day even when the American markets were going up. I suspect all sellers were exhausted. Today, may, simply be a relief rally. Also, bear market rallies are sharp and sudden. Today's up move has all the marks of a bear rally.

Bear markets do not end with a big bang.

Bear markets end when sellers are exhausted as well as buyers. Bull markets start, almost by stealth. People have forgotten about the stock market. Then one fine morning, they realize that markets have been slowly but steadily going up for many days. We have not reached this state of affairs, yet.

So, what's going to happen?

I feel that the down move has a long way to go, at least in terms of time spent. We may see sharp and sudden rallies, as well intermediate up moves, but the bear market is likely to stay with us.

Investors should wait patiently. This is not the correct time to invest. Those with less patience can buy blue chips with the full understanding that there is likely to be more pain ahead.

Traders should try to use intra day moves for trading. Swing trading is a good idea, but requires overnight positions. There is risk as well as reward in overnight exposure. If you are comfortable, then go ahead and take it.

7 October 2008

Probably the Worst Part of the Bear Market

Soon, We Should See Light at the End of the Tunnel

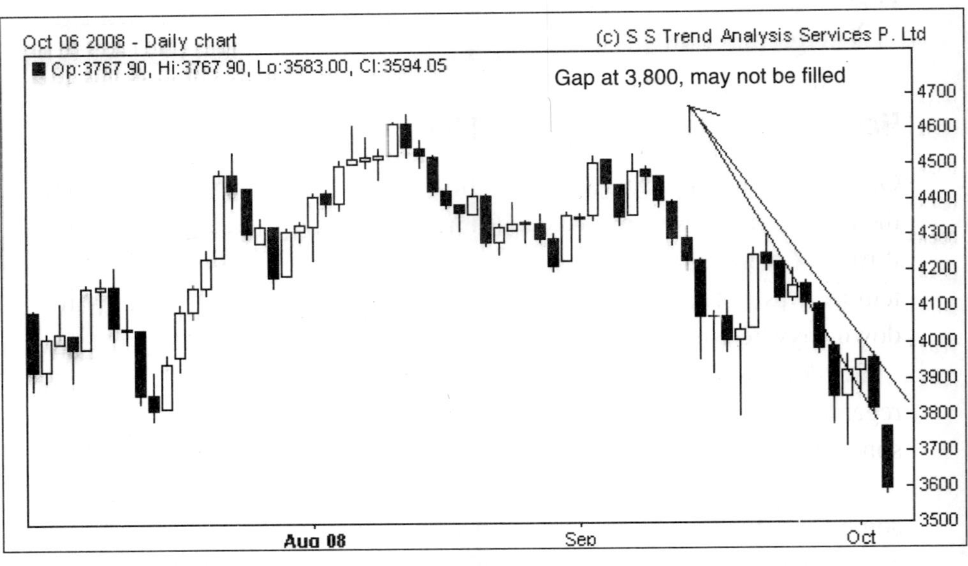

Figure 3.80: **New lows in Nifty. Support comes around 3,600 which is also the current level.**

While there is widespread panic, we should remember that equities will never become zero. The panic will subside, soon enough. A bear market will not end with a bang. We will probably see many months, or even years, of range bound movement.

It will take time to heal.

"We now believe recessions in the US and the UK will be deeper and longer than previously forecast," said Larry Hatheway, an economist at UBS in London. "For the first time, we also anticipate recession in the euro zone."

Who did it?

This time, the financial services industry has caused the catastrophe.

Investors are finally waking up to the notion that it isn't just the US financial system that is in trouble, but that pretty much every advanced economy (save Japan, although Canada has yet to produce any bad headlines) has a banking system in not-so-good health. And economies that may indeed have sound banks will nevertheless be pulled down by the large number of institutions in their trading partners that are afflicted.

You are not alone.

Hedge Funds Lose Money in 2008

Oh, how the mighty have stumbled. In a market where everyone is feeling the heat, even the well-respected, historical top performers are now finding it rough out there. Numerous iconic hedge funds have found out that September was not kind to them. Most have lost money in 2008, they are down anywhere from 10% to 50%.

So, don't feel so bad if your portfolio is underwater because even those regarded as "some of the best in the game" are finding this market troublesome. No one is invincible in this environment.

Overall, though, this has been the worst year for hedge funds in quite some time. Even some of the historically brightest managers in the game are stumbling a bit. And, undoubtedly, such struggles will lead to investor redemptions and continued deleveraging.

A hedge fund provides some basic assumptions going forward:

- Risks to the global economy and financial markets remain very high, and have escalated with recent government policy response fumbles. Sometimes, panic can be quite self-fulfilling or circular.
- Events of the year have increased stress on the hedge fund industry as well. Fund flows, general stress in financial markets, and regulatory changes are all adding to the evolutionary pressures on the industry.

> Ultimately, we do think that the hedge fund industry model is likely to be tested and re-shaped in ways that may be quite meaningful.

Danger levels are clearly extremely high. However, it is also true that dislocation has created profit opportunities that are the best I have seen in my 18-year career. Danger has created severe dislocation — but just as in prior "danger" periods (the Asian crisis, 1998, and 1990), these moments of chaos are often followed by periods of extraordinary return. We see this in our markets and in our portfolio — even when factoring in high degrees of pessimism, select opportunities are truly remarkable. Put simply, markets are a train wreck and there is substantial opportunity to profit handsomely from dislocation.

13 October 2008

Recession, Depression, Asset Destruction

It's Not Good News

As the Nifty closed at 3,277 and the Sensex at 10,527, there is a sea of pessimism all around in the financial world. Unfortunately, it is slowly affecting the broad economy. There seems to be a sense that America and Europe are already in a period of recession. The only question is: How severe will this recession be? Some analysts suggest that the next few years may see a recession, or even a depression. Most analysts are agreeing on the fact that the next few years will see asset destruction.

Risk of Severe Global Depression

On 9 October, Roubini warned of a global systemic financial meltdown and a severe global depression:

> "The US and advanced economies" financial system is now headed towards a near-term systemic financial meltdown . . . .
>
> And in a world where there is a glut and excess capacity of goods while aggregate demand is falling soon enough we will start to worry about deflation, debt deflation, liquidity traps . . . .
>
> At this point severe damage is done and one cannot rule out a systemic collapse and a global depression."

My Views

India remains on a growth path. Yet, world events will affect us. We could expect a slowdown in India. Investors should understand that cash is king. Investments should be made with the utmost care.

Dividend Makes the Day

Ask your broker for a list of high yield stocks. These stocks should also be owned by honest and fair managements. If you get a yield of 10% or more, then you may consider investing in such stocks. Please remember that the reason to invest will be dividend. The price of the stocks may continue to fall. But, so long as you get 10% or more, you can invest and easily wait for better times.

Why is a Bottom Not Visible?

In the past few years, during the roaring bull market, buying off the lows has led to further strength and buying, as value-oriented investors leaped at opportunities. Thus far, in the current phase of market decline, bounces in market (such as we saw last week) have been selling opportunities and rallies have been quite temporary. We won't really know when we've bottomed until we've seen a reversal off price lows that doesn't invite renewed selling.

With new lows made regularly, the test of lows has not taken place.

What may happen next?

It seems the market is getting ready to either:

(a) Complete this capitulation and reverse upwards very hard, or
(b) Enter into a long process of base building which could last for many months, or even years.

We know that the stock market will never become zero. This fact is an advantage since at some point stock prices will touch the floor. At the floor level, price damage to stocks will be minimum. But, time can still remain a big factor. There is a strong possibility that the market may continue to drift sideways. Fortunately, this sideways phase will at least ensure that the process of price damage will be over.

A Look at the Nifty

The Nifty at 3,277 is at two-year lows. This is not so terrible as the accompanying chart will tell you. In 2003, the Index was at 920 in April. Since then, despite all of the chaos, the market has managed a respectable 350% gain till date in five years. That is impressive.

Figure 3.81: **Nifty at two-year lows but still has attractive returns to offer, even after the current decline. From 920 in 2003, it was at 3,277 on 10 October 2008, a gain of 350%.**

For the technical traders, there is no significant support below 3,800. The next level of support comes in at 2,000. I am not suggesting that the level of 2,000 will be reached. Far from it. My point is that the traders have no way of saying where this decline will stop. In the absence of technical support, the Nifty will have to stop wherever it wants. This could be anywhere between 2,000 and 3,277 where it stands today.

Traders should avoid trading in increased volatility. Investors must wait for a base building process to start. This process will be the first signal that the bear market is over. Have patience!

16 October 2008

Big Decline Again

Nifty Continues in Bear Grip

A resistance zone between 3,500 and 3,600 has provided a low risk buying opportunity. Buy only if the Nifty closes above this zone, that is, above 3,600.

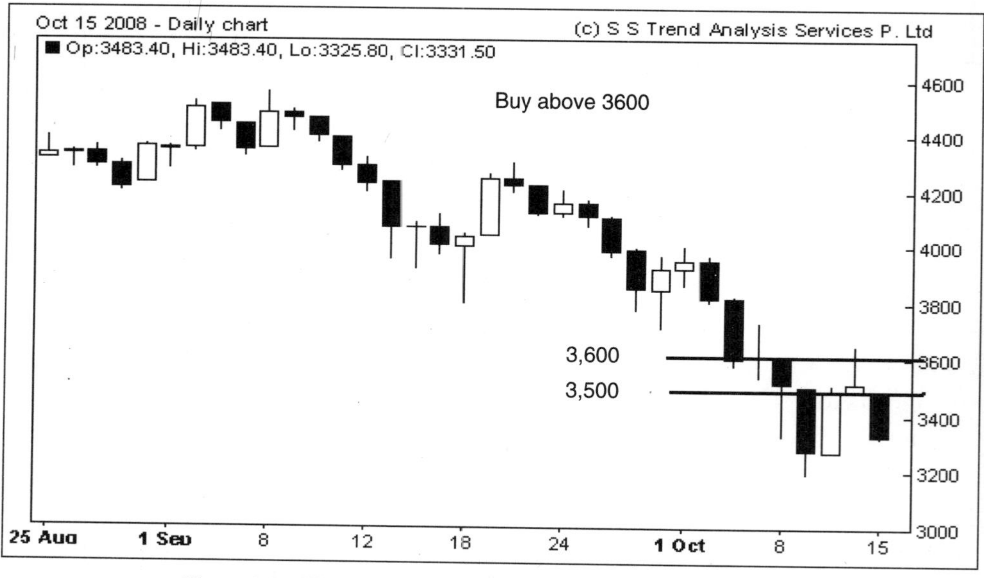

Figure 3.82: **Nifty faces resistance between 3,500 and 3,600.**

Buying is suggested if and when the Nifty closes above 3,600. This is good news since the buy level has come down from 4,000 to 3,600. As usual, these levels will change over time.

The trend remains down. Downside momentum is so strong that even one day of up move is not being sustained. After the Nifty moved up on Monday, the next day saw a decline, and the day after — today has seen the Nifty fall by 190 points. That's a lot!

20 October 2008

Big Decline in Nifty, Sensex

Figure 3.83: **Nifty' 2002-2003 low lasted for 10 months.**

The possible good news may be that market may be ready for at least a short term capitulation. The massive decline on Friday, 17 October, suggests that almost everyone who wishes to sell is selling.

The bad news, of course, is that the market is showing no respite from selling. Momentum is completely on the side of the bears. Even the smallest rally fizzles out in a day. The concept of "oversold" is no longer valid.

How Does a Bear Market End?

Nifty 2002-2003

Earlier, the Nifty went into a bear market from the year 2000. This lasted for three years. The end of the bear market was in the form of a trading range (base) which lasted for 10 months. Figure 3.83 shows it all.

Base Building is Essential

The point to understand is that a bear market does not end in one day. There is a base building process which takes many months. The time taken to build a base may vary from 3 months to 10 months. But the consolidation process is required to signal the end of any bear market.

Q. Market has fallen so much, Why should I wait, let me buy now?

A. As just explained, the bear market will not end because we are willing to buy. The market will end when all the sellers have sold. This process takes time. Therefore, early buying can result in:

(a) Paying higher prices because stock price levels may continue to fall,
(b) Require a lot of patience since the markets may continue to fall, then consolidate, and
(c) Buying the wrong stocks.

Every new bull market starts will new favourite sectors. This becomes evident in the early stages of a bull market. Buying early could result in your owning the wrong stocks in the wrong sectors.

The correct way to enter the market is to wait for signs of bottoming out. Patience!

Q. I already own shares, I want to know when the market will come back to my levels.

A. The market may or may not oblige you by reaching your pre determined levels. If you have mid caps or small caps, look for a method to switch to blue chips. If your lot size is large enough to equal the F&O lot size, then try to sell calls against your holdings. Do not try to overtrade and "recover".

Nifty Watch

The S&P Nifty has fallen to its lowest in 27 months. The Index is touching the psychological level of 3,000. It is not easy to say if this level will hold, but it may provide a short term respite.

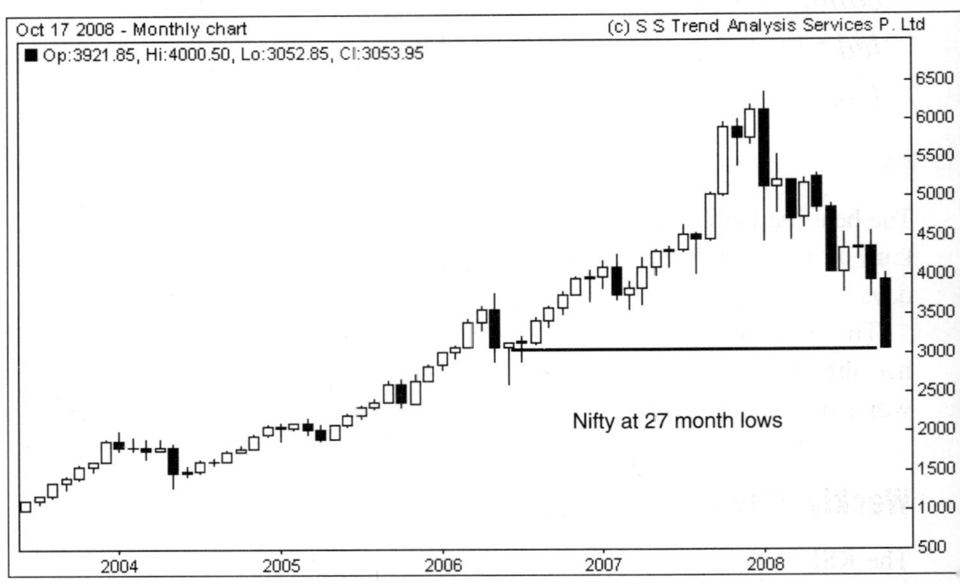

Figure 3.84: **Nifty reaches the psychological level of 3,000. Bear market continues. Buy only after consolidation.**

Volatility is at extremely high levels. Traders should trade with low volumes while such volatile conditions exist. Support for the Nifty comes in at 3,000, while resistance comes in at 3,300. Please note that the Nifty does not have significant support after breaking down from 3,800. The Index can now stop wherever it wants.

23 October 2008

Back to the Bears, Nifty Falls Again

Closes at New Lows

So much for the rally! After a few days of relative calm, suddenly, the Asian markets got the jitters. This led to steep declines in the Nikkei, then to the Asian Contagion, finally to new lows in India.

The bear market is alive and kicking. We expected that there will be some kind of a relief rally. There was a small rally, but it was just a couple of days.

The Nifty fell again today, by 170 points. This is a lot since the Nifty has already halved itself. Unfortunately, it does appear that things will get worse before they get better.

Weekly Nifty

The RSI on the weekly Nifty is currently at 22.5. This is the lowest level since 2002. In the period 2001-2002, the RSI fell below 25. This was a sign of weakness. It took the market two years of sideways movement before the new bull market started.

Figure 3.85: **On Nifty's weekly chart, the RSI fell to 25 in 2001-2002. The market remained in range for two years after that. The RSI is again below 25. Thus bear market is not going away in a hurry.**

It is difficult to say how much time this one will take. But the bear market is not going to end quickly, that much seems evident.

Bloomberg Reports on China

At the heart of the crisis that toppled Lehman Brothers Holdings Inc. is an out-of-control system built on debt. At the heart of China's problems is frantic development that also cuts corners to meet over ambitious targets.

Roth Capital Partners says Chinese growth will slow to about 8 per cent in the fourth quarter and 6.5 per cent in 2009.

My Notes

While a slowdown in China will not mean end of the world, it is likely to cause enormous pain throughout the economic environment. Not good news!

27 October 2008

This Bear Market is Different

Figure 3.86: **Nifty comes close to a support zone between 1,800-2,500. There is minor support at 2,500 and significant support between 1,800-2,200.**

In the good old days, analysts came on CNBC and said "This bull market will last forever, this time it is different". I was always skeptical about this explanation — "it is different." It never was different — greed was in control every time there were bull market excesses.

Now, ten weeks into the relentless selling that is going on, I sometimes think — "This bear market is different". There are no rallies, no pullbacks, just selling. The Nikkei falls 11% because Sony disappointed. India falls 14% because the Nikkei falls. Europe falls because S&P futures are locked in a limit on Globex, then surprise! — the Dow and S&P lose just 4% each, while the rest of the world loses 8% to 14%.

On Friday, the so called "Black Friday" — I thought, the Nifty is at 2,500, very close to a strong support base between 1,800 and 2,500. On CNBC, I said at 3:15 P.M. — "Those with spare money not required for next five years may like to invest 5 per cent in the market."

First, I practise very conservative asset allocation. From July 2007 onwards, my allocation for equities was cut slowly till it became 30% of total portfolio. Therefore, I do feel financial pain, but the pain is probably manageable.

Now about this bear market. A 400-point decline (Nifty not Sensex) appears to be "irrational pessimism." That was my first reaction.

Now, after a restless night, I am not so sure.

What is "deleveraging"? How will the worldwide credit crisis affect us? How much impact will a worldwide recession have on India? What happens if "hot money" continues to flee?

Finally, let us face it; the middle class investor is devastated. Her investment of ₹ 100 has become ₹ 20. The first time investor has lost all her capital and, therefore, will not re-enter this market for the next five years.

Then, there are fundamental changes in world economic and social order. Nationalization is again in favour. Croney capitalism (crooked capitalists in alliance with the powerful) has caused worldwide havoc. How much damage has been done? Will a repair job swing the other way — too much control?

Now, for the good part. If you note, almost all the issues I have outlined relate to financial engineering. This bull market was created by financials, and the bear market will see the end of financial services as we know them. That's fine. Maybe the economic order is resilient, manufacturing and services are fine, and will grow once the system is purged of these horrible financial wizards.

So, what is the answer? Er. . . what was the question ?

The question could be: When will this bear market be over? The answer should be:

> The Nifty is now at levels where it will find significant chart support. There is a lot of support between 1,800 and 2,500. This means that we may see the end of this leg of the bear market between 1,800 and 2,500. This process may take its own time but there will be many opportunities for investors in the near future.

31 October 2008

Who Can Say When This Bear Market Will End?

What I can tell you is that bear markets typically end while the business cycle is still suffering. Why does this happen? Because the stock market is discounting events three to six months in advance.

Near a Pivot Point

Jesse Livermore said in 1940:

> "Whenever I have had the patience to wait for the market to arrive at what I call a 'Pivotal Point' before I started to trade; I have always made money in my operations".

The Need for Bear Markets

Bear markets are necessary to help deflate the overvalued price / earnings ratios and overpriced shares in times of extreme exuberance. Bear markets create widespread negativity, overwhelming pessimism, fear, uncertainty and a total lack of confidence among investors. Cash exits the stock market as people panic like sheep and prices start to adjust back to reasonable levels, paving the way to new opportunities around the corner.

3 November 2008

Nifty Ends October with Record Losses

Experts on the Market

Everyone is an expert when it comes to the market, or at least a sure-shot fortune teller. Everyone seems to think they know what is supposed to happen, especially if you hear the experts on TV or read the business newspapers. The end result is — the "experts" probably create a lot of confusion in your thinking.

Questions in your mind: Is the bear market over? Is it too early to buy? Should we wait on the sidelines?

Answer: We should let the market tell us what it wants to do.

Significant Up Move Begins with Reversal and Follow Through Day

William O'Neil, developer of the CANSLIM investing method says:

> "All major bull markets started with a reversal and then a follow-through within the next four to ten trading days."

What is a follow through day?

The follow through day occurs when the index records a gain of at least 3% with above average volume.

Investors and traders should wait for a follow through day next week. If such a trading day comes about, it will be a signal for a new up move.

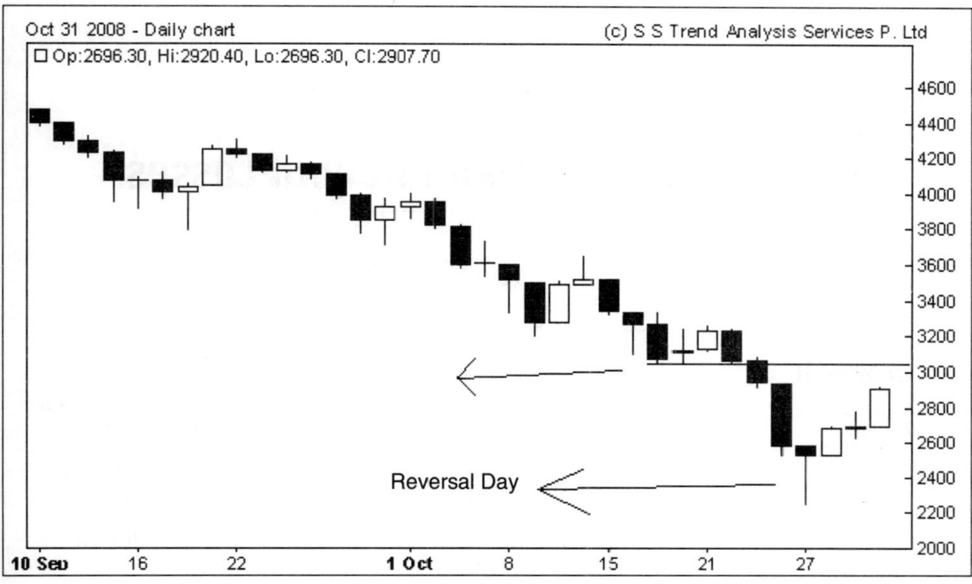

Figure 3.87: **Nifty's daily chart indicates strong resistance around 3,025.**

Option and Day Trading — The Best Strategies During a Financial Crisis

Today we are experiencing an unprecedented global financial meltdown that is scary. The world's leaders are meeting to determine how to handle it. By not risking any long term positions, we are not committed to any direction, and even hold long and short positions on the same futures at the same time.

The importance that volatility plays in options and day trading should not be underestimated. In fact, it is the key factor which drives how much premium can be charged / received when purchasing / writing options and selecting stocks for intra day trading. Low volatility makes for a difficult environment to write options and capture premium in a risk adverse manner.

See that we get some high volatility market condition almost every day. Maybe your strategy is to stand aside with cash and exploit the huge swings in stock market volatility, and capturing only no-brainer portions of each swing in any direction on any pair we are monitoring. So what is the best trading strategy for today's condition?

Be a day trader! Open and close position intra day, avoid aiming for high targets and just hunt for small amount of pips, say 20 to 30 points a day is the best strategy for today. The more points you aim for, the more risk you'll get! But future day trading will requires an additional investment of time as well as money and, sure, it will cost you extra to open a trade daily.

By aiming 20 to 30 pips on each trade, you'll easily fill this target as compared to a trader who aims for 100 pips. But although it is easy to reach 20 or 30 pips, just do two or three trades per day. Don't try scalping by entering the market many times per day, it's the sure way to losses. Do one trade per day even if the market is on your side, set your exit channel 20 or 30 pips, always use stop loss, look for the best time for trade and, most important, keep discipline in following the rules.

Summary

A sustained uptrend is possible if the Nifty sees a follow through after a reversal day that occurred on 27 October. The Nifty is in an intermediate uptrend. This uptrend will be strengthened if the Nifty were to close above 3,000. There is considerable resistance at higher levels, therefore traders and investors should take profits wherever possible.

4 November 2008

Nifty Touches 3,000

May Face Significant Resistance at Current Levels

On the back of a rate cut in India, cheerful markets abroad, the Nifty rallied to close above 3,000, up 175 points. The Sensex also closed above the 10,000 mark.

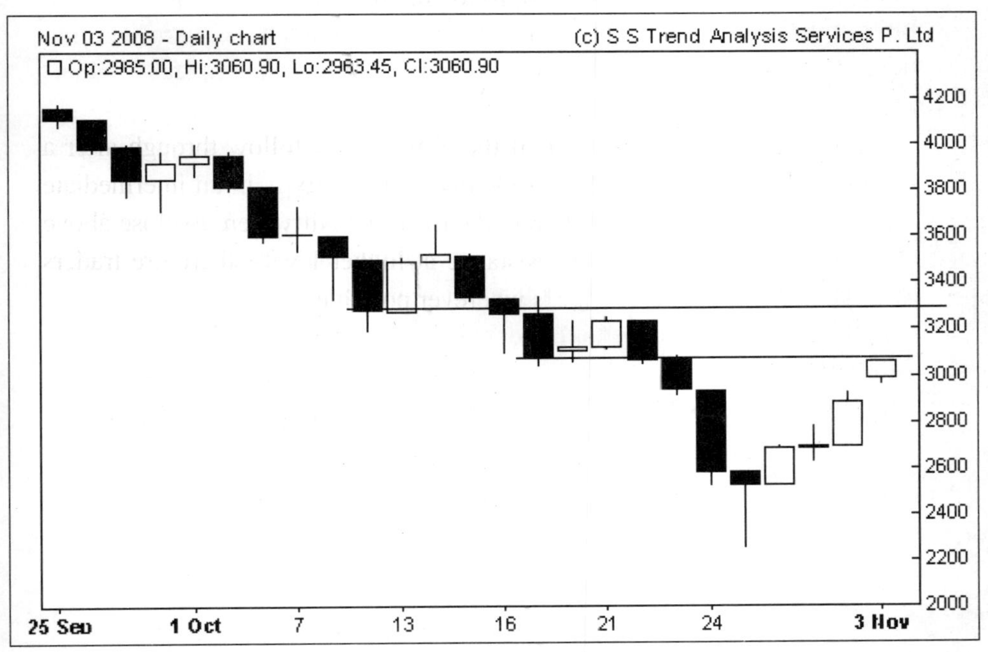

Figure 3.88: **Nifty's short term trend is up but it faces strong resistance at 3,000-3,050 and then again at 3,250-3,300.**

Happy Days are Back Again?

The Nifty has seen the fourth successive day of gains. Does this signal a return to the momentum days?

The answer lies in what we mean by "better days". For many "momentum" stocks, their previous all-time highs will never come back. Owners of such stocks should plan for switching to better quality blue chips.

For newcomers, first time investors, traders and existing investors with funds, it is possible that there will be investment opportunities. The one-sided bear market has hopefully come to an end.

The Nifty

The market is reaching short-term overbought conditions that over the last many years have led to at least short-term pullbacks. Whether it is able to rally in the face of such conditions or whether it pulls back sharply in the next few days could be a telling sign of strength or weakness, and whether a character change could be in order.

In any case, a test of strength is imminent. This will involve a dip or a decline and potential support emerging at lower levels.

The Nifty has strong resistance first at 3,000, then at 3,250-3,300. A move above 3,000 can be bought into, expecting some short term gains. If there is a breakdown below 3,000, short term traders can look for selling opportunities although position traders should book profits and simply step aside.

Support for the Nifty will come quickly, at 2,900, and then at 2,700.

6 November 2008

Nifty Resistance Holds, Markets Decline

Actually, this is good news. After many days of almost free-for-all movement, classical chart resistance seems to work. This should also mean that chart support levels will also be respected.

For weeks altogether, the market has moved almost like a drunken elephant, without any clear direction. It does appear that, finally, the market is adjusting to the new reality of lower prices, cooling down, and accepting the "normal" support and resistance levels.

There is strong resistance in the 3,200 area. Today, the resistance held, with the Nifty closing below 3,000, losing almost 250 points from its intra day high. That is a lot, almost 8%.

Too Much Volatility

The market continues to exhibit far too much volatility preventing any kind of low risk trading.

Increased volatility is not a sign of base building which is essential for a bull market to start. My point is: the first signs of a new bull market will emerge when volatility falls. This has not happened yet.

Figure 3.89: **Nifty's dip to a support level offers buying opportunities. Support comes near 2,700.**

The Nifty

The index, closing below 3,000 is not a catastrophic event. The market has moved up 50% from its lows of 2,252, in just 8 days. This could not be sustained. Today's decline should be taken as a correction. I assume that the intermediate trend remains intact, although volatile markets can do anything, anytime.

Support for the Nifty will come in a range between 2,700 and 2,800. If this support does not hold, then we have to step aside and let the market decide where it wants to go. If the support holds, then this should be a dip, which is a buying opportunity.

Why this column is still looking at buying?

Because there are no signs that the up move is over. Today's decline is considered a correction. As usual, the markets decide, and we can go wrong.

10 November 2008

Market Remains Steady

Likely to Move Inside a Trading Range

After a week of volatile movements, the Nifty closed at 2,973, a gain of almost 100 points for the week (previous week close: 2,885). The Nifty has thus recorded a second consecutive week of gains.

Analysis of the Indian Market

Worries

Volatility Remains High

Intra day volatility remains extremely high, with the Index moving in wide swings during the trading day. On Thursday, 6 November, the Nifty moved up 5% in one hour and 20 minutes, then fell a similar percentage in just 25 minutes, making a 10% move in two hours. This is a cause for concern, since high volatility is usually a sign of bear markets.

Risks to Exports

As the world slows down, there are chances of a slowdown in exports. This has already happened as the new foreign trade numbers suggest a significant downturn in export growth.

Adverse Impact on Cost of Capital from Capital Outflow and FX Weakness

FII selling has been continuing. The share of foreign ownership in Indian companies is at a five-year low, at 18.6%. The weakness of the rupee and capital outflows will adversely affect market sentiment.

Hit from Financial Market Instability

The world wide instability in financial markets is going to last for a year or even two years. There is little desire to take risk. There will be negative impact of the financial crisis on Indian markets.

Optimism

Markets are Discounting All Bad News

The market has been anticipating the economic downturn and earnings downgrades. Indeed, the Nifty and Sensex have declined far ahead of earning declines. Therefore, the markets may well be discounting bad news which is likely to come in. To that extent, the markets could prove resilient if and when the actual earnings downgrades happen. The point then is: maybe, the markets are discounting the future, and the worst is where we are now.

Summary

India would now appear to be in an excellent position to attract money flows since, for the most part, it does not have the credit problems which are plaguing Western economies. However, this process will unfold gradually as investors get their confidence back. The process of deleveraging is too fresh an experience for investors to rush back into markets and it will take for support to be built.

The market is likely to remain in a broad trading range between 2,500 and 3,500 for some months. Investors and traders can now buy on dips and take profits wherever possible. This may become a market where trading profits will come. This is good news.

Closer Look at the Nifty

There is strong support for the Nifty in the 2,700-2,800 range. If the Nifty were to close below this range, we can again expect a free fall to 2,000, or even to 1,800.

Figure 3.90: **Nifty in a trading range; support above 2,800 and strong resistance between 3,200 and 3,250.**

A rally should see resistance first around 3,200, and then around 3,500. The approach should be to buy on dips and exit whenever there is a sudden, sharp up move. The trading range market is likely to see selling on every rise.

14 November 2008

Nifty Breaks Down from Trading Range

Figure 3.91: **Nifty breaks down from a trading range and could move to 2,600 or even lower.**

After spending seven trading days inside a range, the Nifty broke down to close at 2,854, below the 2,900 support.

A breakdown from the range has fairly bearish implications. We are looking at a pattern target of 2,600 for the move. But the eventual decline may be more as momentum continues to favour the bears.

Who is Selling?

Trapped investors, tired investors, short term bulls who want to get out . . . a variety of different reasons for selling exist.

What Should Investors Do?

Do not buy on declines since the lows of this bear market may be further down.

What Should Traders Do?

Go short on rallies. If the intermediate trend turns up, then swing traders can also buy for a short term trade. Currently, the intermediate trend is down.

19 November 2008

Downtrend Continues, Expect Lower Level

Figure 3.92: **Nifty's daily chart shows a downside breakout from the range 3,200-2,900. Pattern objective is near 2,600.**

Nifty Watch

Intermediate as well as short term trend is down. Traders should trade with least volume. Any kind of buying is not suggested as the market is very volatile.

Support may come between 2,500 and 2,600. Buying can be considered after getting visible and clear support.

20 November 2008

Choppy Market with Down Bias

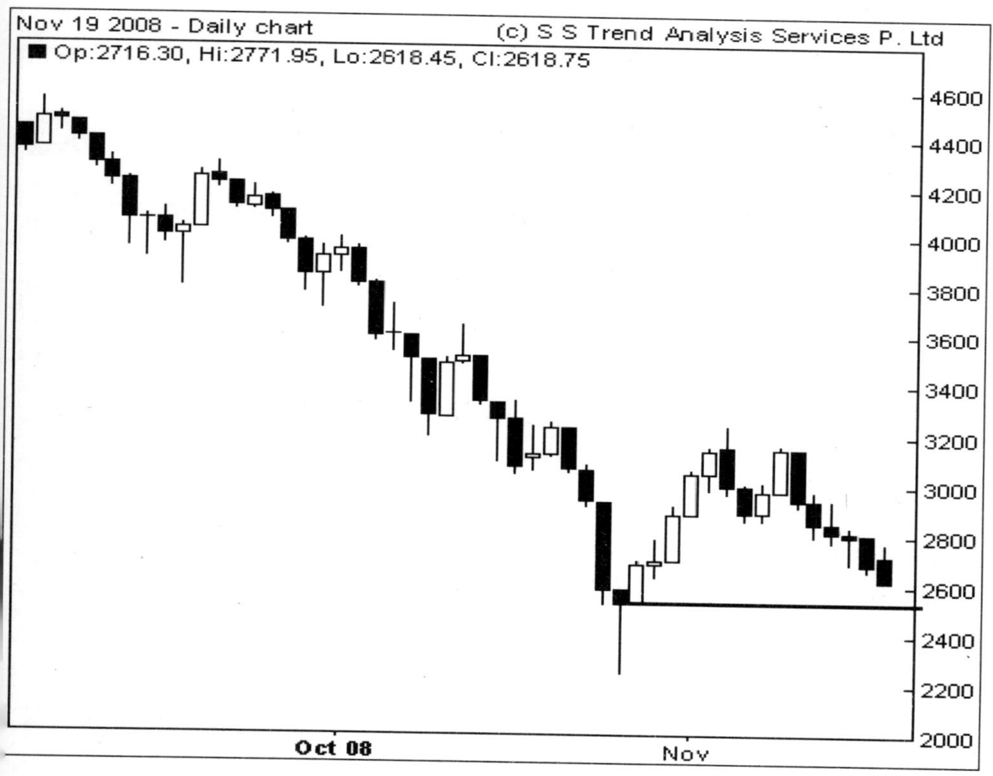

Figure 3.93: **Nifty daily. Test of closing low around 2,525. No buying is suggested.**

The world markets are volatile, directionless, confusing to traders. Yesterday, the Dow was trading minus 150, then suddenly, a last-hour rally saw it move up by 300 points. What is such a market movement telling us? **Volatility inside a bear market is not bullish.** The message may well be: that there is more downside.

Why? Because a bull market starts when the markets literally go to sleep. Volatility falls dramatically, the daily, weekly, monthly ranges contract. People forget that the stock market exists. An increase in volatility, such as we are witnessing now, is giving quite the opposite message.

The Nifty closed near to the 2,525 close made in October. Is this a test of the lows? It may well be, although the momentum suggests that this is a bear market rather than a friendly "test". Any rally in the Nifty will face resistance at 2,900. If and when the Nifty closes above 2,900, the next resistance is at 3,200. A new bull market should start if the Nifty were to close above 3,200. This seems like a tall order, as of now.

Inside such a strong down move, the wise trade is to go with the flow, which is down. Any up move will be corrective in nature, and, corrections cannot be easily traded.

A close below 2,525 will take the Nifty into new closing lows for this bear market. That is a sign of more downside. It is possible to assume that the Nifty may eventually touch 2,000, or go even lower. There is no rush to buy. Wait patiently.

What to Do with Existing Investments?

What should I do with my investments? Many market participants have asked this question. Here is my view:

Investment in shares is part of your total investment planning. You may have a plan that goes like this:

50% of liquid funds to be invested in shares (this should be reduced to 40% when the market is in a strong bull grip; it should increase to 60% when you perceive the market is in a bear grip).

Now, we assume that the current market scenario may well be called a strong bear grip. Having a plan makes the decision process easy. If your current investments in shares are more than 60% of your liquid assets, then you have to bring it down to 60%. You need to sell on rallies. On the other hand, if your investment is less than 60%, then you can add whenever there is a panic decline.

This is about asset allocation. The percentages given here are only indicative. You should modify them to suit your own needs.

Now, many participants purchased shares for making a quick profit. They are stuck with these shares which have suddenly become a long term investment. Trading must always have stop losses. If you still own these shares, then clearly you did not follow the stop loss rules. If you are one of these traders, ask yourself: What do you do when you make a mistake? You should seek the answer to this question. Each trader will get an answer that suits his / her mental attitudes.

21 November 2008

Bear Market Continues

Nifty, Sensex May Go Below October Lows

The Nifty fell to 2,500 before recovering a bit to close above 2,500. Compared to most world markets, the Nifty did better, actually losing less. I am not sure if this is any consolation to investors who have seen almost 80% of their capital vanish.

The Test Has Come

When the Nifty closed at 2,525 on 27 October 2008, and then subsequently rallied, there was a sense that the Index will fall again for a "test". That event has now come about with the Nifty falling again to 2,503 today.

How will this test unfold?

First, the index should hold the 2,500 lows. This will happen if the Nifty does not close below 2,500.

Second, slowly, steadily, the Nifty needs to rally and eventually cross 3,240, the pivot high made after the 27 October decline. This could happen fast, or it could take its own time. That's not a problem. In fact, the more time it takes, the better.

What do you do while the "test" goes on?

First, we need to understand that this is a bear market. Momentum clearly favours more downside.

Now, with this understanding, traders may buy when there is a buy signal on intra day charts. Keep a stop, plan to take profits if there is a move in your favour.

Going short is more difficult although the trend favours short sellers. The difficulty lies in keeping wide stops. If you go short with tight stops, chances are you will be stopped out. Consider going short after a short term rally that lasts 2 to 3 days. Will such an event occur? The answer is yes, sooner or later.

Nifty Watch

A breakdown in the Index may occur below 2,500, probably leading to another free fall all the way to 2,200. A rally will face resistance at 2,600, then 2,700, then 2,900. At this point, the Nifty faces significant resistance at 2,900, although these levels will change with time.

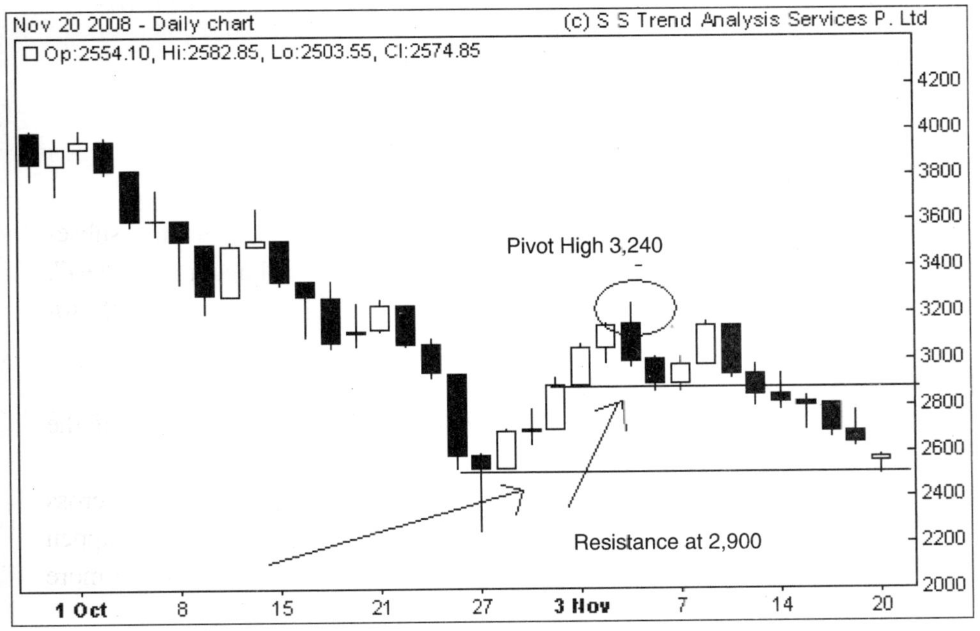

Figure 3.94: **Free fall if Nifty breaks 2,500. Wait for new patterns after significant decline.**

Does Technical Analysis Work?

The answer is yes. Recently, the Nifty was inside a trading range between 2,900 and 3,200. I had suggested that the Nifty will have a target of 2,600 if the 2,900 support breaks. The support did break, and today's Nifty low was 2,503. The issue is: Can you trade on my analysis? The answer is no. Trading is finally an activity that requires confidence. You have to develop your own rules. You can use inputs (example: my analysis) to clarify your rules, but the eventual decision should be yours.

The financial system is so mind-bogglingly complex that very few, even those with far deeper backgrounds than ours, fully understand it.

The global economy is likely to show the scars of this crisis for several years. Stocks are very reasonable buys for brave value managers willing to be early. History warns, though, that new lows are more likely than not.

24 November 2008

The Markets Have a Terrible Week

The Nifty fell this week. The index saw seven consecutive down days before a relief rally raised prices on Friday.

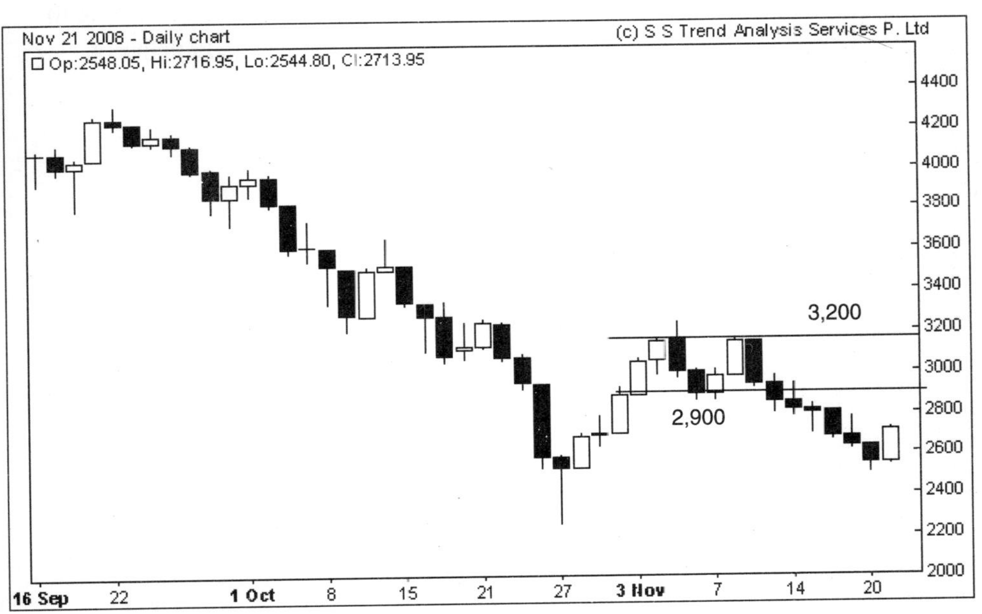

Figure 3.95: **Buying on dips is possible after volatile declines. There is support at 2,500; avoid buying below 2500. Any relief rally will face resistance at 2,900, and then again 3,200.**

The Nifty is likely to touch 2,200 again. The market is in a bear phase with lower lows being made regularly. There is strong resistance around 2,900 in the Nifty. If this level is crossed, then we can expect another round of resistance at 3,200. On the downside, 2,500 offers some support. A breakdown from 2,500 could see the Nifty in a free fall.

The Bear Market in Context

We do not know what the market will do in the future. There are people much smarter than we are who claim to know that. What we do know is what it has done. Every time the Indian markets have gone through a bear cycle, they have taken between 3 months to 12 months to develop a base. A new bull market has started only after such base building. So, why should this time be different? As the markets make new lows, day by day, with a lot of volatility, the process of base building has not started. This means investors need to have lot of patience while waiting for the bear market to end and a new basing process to begin.

Why is the Rupee Falling?

The answer is: the rupee is not falling, it is the US dollar which is rising. Thanks to the strength of the dollar, all other currencies are getting devalued against the dollar. So, why is the dollar rising?

Two reasons: First, The US trade deficit is dropping slowly due to:

(a) Fall in crude prices, and
(b) Decline in imports as American consumers cut back on buying.

It means that a lot fewer dollars are now going into the world economy. Second, demand for dollars is rising as the world seeks a safe haven in the current global recession.

Thus, it should not be a surprise that the dollar is rising. The dollar rally may be temporary. The US will face a serious problem in 2009. Tax revenues are going to take a very serious fall. Capital gains taxes will contribute nothing in 2009. And income taxes will drop as unemployment expenses rise. The perceived need for government stimulus will be offset by the problem of funding the deficit. Traders expect even more volatility in the currency and interest-rate markets next year.

How Does it Affect Indian Markets?

Volatility in international currency and interest-rate markets is not good news. The Indian economy can suffer unpredictable consequences from such volatility, including another round of FII outflows. Therefore, it is too early to say that the bear market in India, as well in the world has come to an end.

This, too, shall pass. At some point we will hit a bottom. Just as irrational exuberance led us into foolish actions, we are now becoming too pessimistic. The pendulum will swing. Minsky taught us that stability breeds instability. The more stable things are, the more comfortable we are with taking risk, which ultimately creates the conditions for a normal business cycle recession. This time we took on a whole lot more risk than usual and are facing a deeper recession. But the opposite is true as well. Instability will breed stability. We will adjust to the new environment by becoming more conservative. And that new conservative environment will bring about a new stability, albeit at lower levels. But it will be a level from which we can begin to grow once again. It has been this way since the first traders began trading thousands of years ago.

The Potential for a Large Stock Market Rally

We could see a very large rally as value buyers enter the market while short sellers begin to cover their positions. For traders, this will be a chance to make some money. I think it will be a bear market rally as the recession will still be in full swing, and we could see a pullback when surplus money gets fully deployed. But it will be fun while it lasts.

2 December 2008

Decline Once Again

Lower Levels Likely

Figure 3.96: **Nifty weakens again. This could be a bearish flag which will be confirmed if Nifty closes below 2,700 on Tuesday.**

Nifty Watch

The Nifty closed at 2,686.05, down 69.05 points, lower by -2.51%.

An outside day was made today. This pattern is made at the top of a minor rally. It is likely to be a reversal pattern. The coming days should see a decline in prices.

The long term trend is down with the 200-day average falling. The intermediate trend is down with the 50-day average falling. The short-term trend is up with the 8-day average rising.

The Bank Nifty closed at 4,128.45, down 162.70 points, lower by 3.79%. The CNX IT closed at 2,423.75, down 26.20 points, lower by 1.07%.

Sector Watch

The CNXIT continues to outperform. In today's context, this means that the CNXIT fell the least.

Nifty Patterns

The minor rally in the Nifty saw a move that came close to the 2,900 resistance (today's high was 2,832). As expected, the 2,900 zone did act as resistance, with the Nifty giving up all the gains made in the previous two days.

The small rally in the Index looks more like a rising wedge / rising flag. Such patterns come half way in a trend. The down move was 600 points, from 3,200 to 2,600. A breakdown at 2,700 now gives us a target of 2,100 approximately. Targets are just that, estimates of what may happen. They do not assure any outcome. But we do get a roadmap.

What can go wrong? If the Nifty were to close above 2,900 we will have to look at the scenario once again. Till then, we assume the down trend is intact.

4 December 2008

Markets Remain Inside Narrow Range

For the tenth day, the Nifty remained inside a narrow range between 2,550 and 2,750.

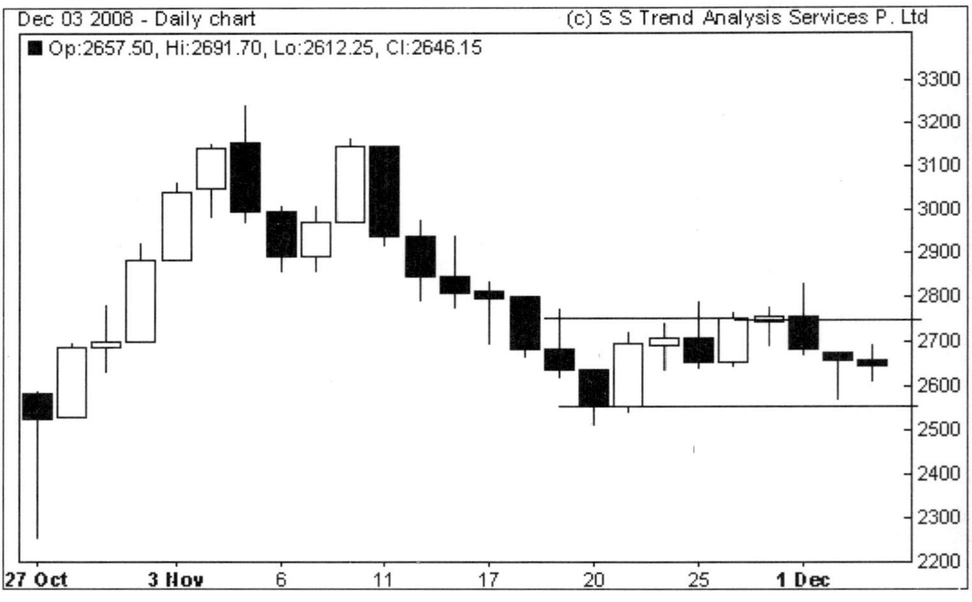

Figure 3.97: **Nifty remains in a trading range between 2,555 to 2,755. Wait for breakout / breakdown.**

A move out of this range is likely to give us a trending move. Then, a close above 2,755 is a signal to buy. Below 2,555, we should expect lower levels. Inside this range, there are few opportunities for trading.

Investors and position traders ask the question: Is it time to buy? The answer is: we do not have any patterns yet that suggest a base building process has been completed. Now it is quite possible that the current move in the Nifty between 2,250 and 3,250 may be part of a basing process. We will know this only when the Index moves above 3,250. We will get some early warning. A move above the current trading range will represent such a warning. Till we do have convincing proof of bottoming out, it is wise to stay away. You can nibble at stocks that you like — blue chips only. But, if you have spare cash, keep it spare.

5 December 2008

Nifty Sees a Breakout

Maybe Looking at Higher Levels

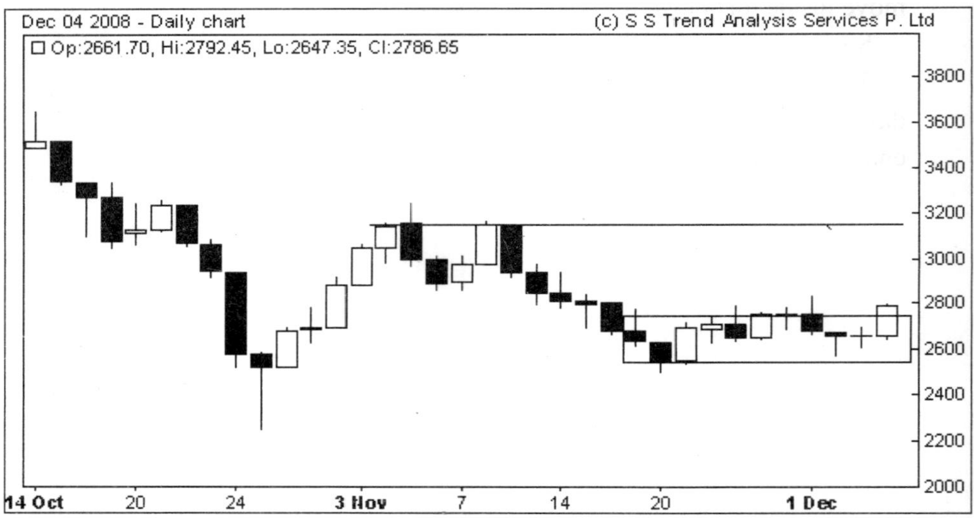

Figure 3.98: **Nifty breaks out of its trading range, closes above 2,750 resistance. A subsequent close below today's low 2,647 will cancel the breakout.**

One of the nice things about technical trading is flexibility. Rather than tell the market what it should do, technical traders follow the market. While this is difficult to do, in the long run, it pays money.

The Nifty was in a trading range between 2,555 and 2,755. A close above 2,755 today was a clear signal that the Index is breaking out from the range. The target for this breakout is 2,950. Traders should be long at close of trade today. What is the stop loss? It is 2,647, i.e. today's low, or, 2,555 the support line of the trading range. The two stops are for different trader profiles. The closer stop is for the swing trader, while the wider stop is for the position trader.

Is This the Start of the Bull Market?

Not really. It is possible that the Nifty may see a strong bear rally, reach 3,200, and then start a drift down to 2,000. I, of course, cannot say that this will happen, but there is a strong probability, so who knows?

We should also be open to the possibility that the Nifty may be building a base at current levels that is between 2,500 and 3,200. The Index could move inside this range for many weeks, or even months.

So, how do we trade?

The trading range breakout tells us to go long. Search for dips on intra day charts. Buy with proper stops. Maybe we will get a traditional year end rally; have fun!

11 December 2008

Rally is On!

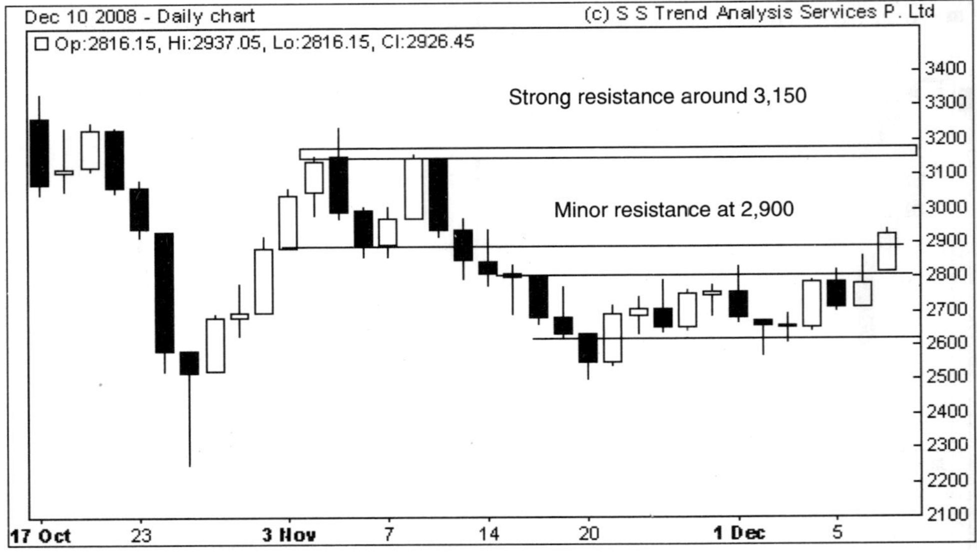

Figure 3.99: **Nifty's daily chart shows the up move continuing, may reach 3,150.**

After many days, the Nifty saw a one-sided move, rallying right from the open to close at the highs of the day.

The up move of the Index from its breakout around 2,750 suggests that a minimum target of 2,950 is expected for this breakout. It is possible that the minimum may be exceeded. It is also possible that the rally may quickly fizzle out, although strong momentum favours the bulls.

The strategy should be to buy on dips. Position traders should hold on to long positions, since there may well be more upside. Swing traders should plan to exit after a Range Expansion day. (Today was such a day for many "momentum" stocks).

15 December 2008

Market Rally in Danger of Facing Resistance

Figure 3.100: **A possible negative divergence in Nifty, RSI higher but price lower. Look out for a down move.**

After strong rallies till Thursday, the market faced strong resistance around 2,900. An intermediate uptrend started from 2,500. The move has taken the Nifty to a high of 2,935 approx. Around 2,900 there exists a lot of resistance which is likely to act as a barrier to any further rise. The Nifty now has two different options:

1. Go through a dip or consolidation before it can cross 2,900 decisively, or,
2. Fail to cross the 2,900 barrier and eventually resume its down move.

The Nifty closed at 2,921, i.e. almost at the point of resistance. The Index saw a good week for the bulls, gaining 200 points, almost 7% in a week that saw most world markets close with losses.

Support for the Nifty comes in at 2,800, while resistance comes first at 2,900 and then at 3,150.

The CNXIT Index has been falling even as the broad market rallies. The top IT stock — Infosys — has a bearish head and shoulders pattern in its monthly chart. This suggests lower levels ahead. Investors may avoid IT for some time.

Bear Rally or New Bull Market?

The answer is not easy to find. The correct approach is to go with the trend. Currently, the intermediate trend is up. This trend will change if and when the Nifty closes below 2,800. Buy on dips while the Nifty remains above 2,800.

The minor trend is sideways. On Friday, the Nifty moved through a lot of volatility, moving below 2,860 where the minor trend changed to down. The Nifty then rallied to close above 2,860. The minor trend is therefore sideways, or confusing.

Investors Must Be Prepared to Wait

This bear market may not vanish quickly. While there will be value in many stocks, investors should be prepared to wait. It is likely that earnings setback may, in fact, cause re-ratings of stocks.

Indian Industrial Output Falls for the First Time Since 1993

According to Bloomberg, "India's industrial production unexpectedly fell for the first time in 15 years, putting pressure on policy makers to add to interest rate and tax cuts to shield the weakening economy from a global recession.

"China's industrial production growth is likely to drop to 5 percent in November, the weakest pace since Bloomberg data began in 1999, according to the government. Production in South Korea declined for the first time in 13 months in October."

Are We Getting Decoupled?

On Friday, world markets were falling anywhere between 3% to 5% while the Nifty actually held its own. Does this mean that the Indian market is going to get decoupled, and not getting affected by world trends? The answer seems to be no. The market is not decoupled. If world markets perform poorly, Indian markets are likely to follow them although they may become divergent for a few days.

World Wide Economic Conditions Worsening

Currently, most evidence indicates that the global recession is still deepening. A rally in the stock markets does suggest that markets are trying to look forward to a recovery though it's not yet clear when this might happen. But if news continues to remain pessimistic, then the rally will fizzle out.

This seems to be a real danger with markets falling on Friday given the news that auto bailout plans in the USA have failed.

Summary

Given the uncertainty over corporate profits, investors need to be selective. They should not assume that the bear market is over. Instead, they should look to buy stocks where at least some kind of base building is evident. Many stocks will come in such a list in the next few months. Investors should wait for a bottoming out process.

18 December 2008

Finally, a Correction?

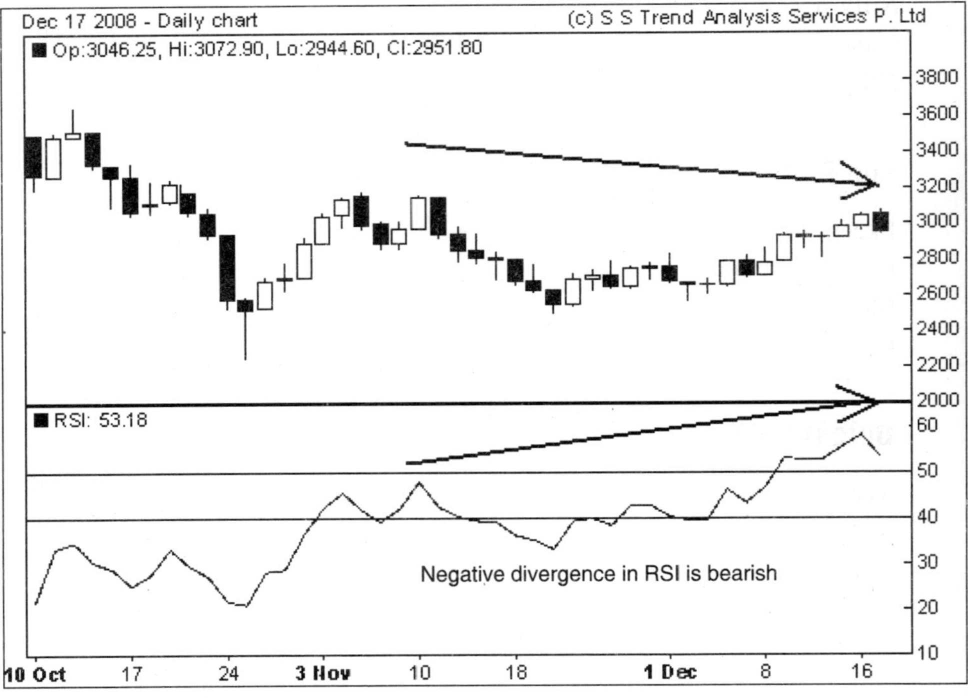

Figure 3.101: **Nifty falls, has support at 2,900, 2750.**

The headline assumes that today's market decline is just a correction in an up move, rather than the start of a new bear trend. Why?

With the market moving in one direction — up, over the past week, it was not really a surprise to see a day of large down move. First, we are in a bear market so declines should come easily. Second, the market was quite "overbought" and this fact has been highlighted over the last three days in this letter.

Today, the negative divergence visible in the RSI was confirmed when the RSI made a top by moving lower. We have a confirmed pattern of higher highs in the RSI but lower highs in price. This is a negative divergence, suggesting a dip or a consolidation (see the chart).

If the pattern works out, then we should expect the Nifty to move down to 2,450. There is a big if, since the market does its own thing.

Today's high at 3,073 also has some significance. Assuming that the Nifty does not go above this number tomorrow, the 3,073 level will become a pivot high. Then, a reaffirmation of the up move will require the Nifty to close above 3,073.

The Public is Missing

I keep thinking that most of the current activity is from institutional investors; the public is still "not even looking" at their brokerage accounts. Most will enter at the top of this rally, at which point we should be getting out?

Quickly, About the Nifty

The Index is in an intermediate uptrend. The trend will change to down if and when the Nifty closes below the minor low at 2,812. The minor uptrend will change to down if the Nifty closes below the support defined at 2,945.

23 December 2008

Get Ready

Big Move Coming

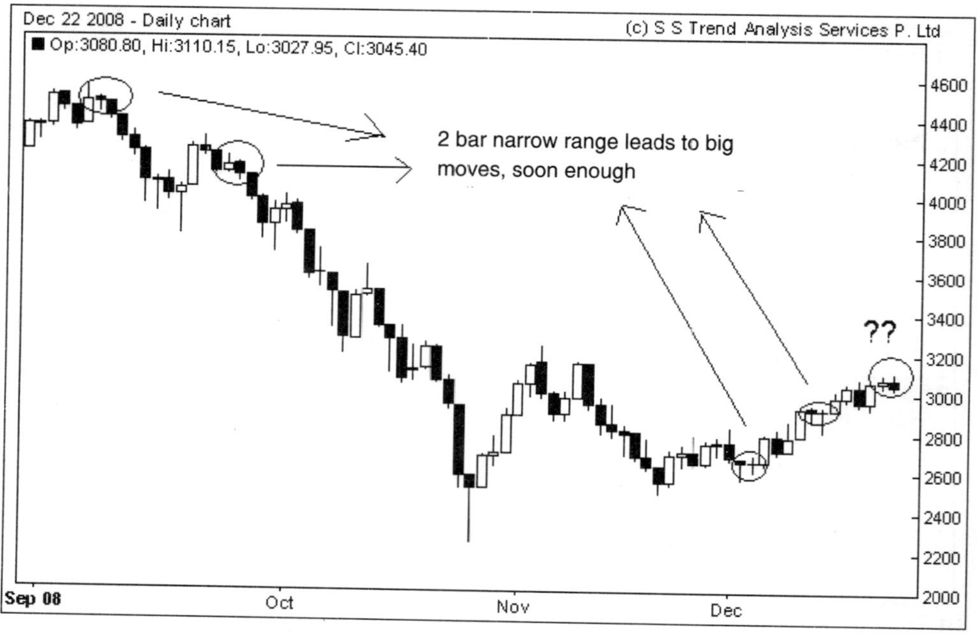

Figure 3.102: **Nifty's daily chart.**

For the second successive day, the Nifty remained in a narrow range. Two days of narrow bars are a signal for a big move coming soon. See the chart for what happens after narrow range bars. Note how the market moves decisively in one direction or the other.

The Nifty has almost touched the 3,150-3,200 resistance zone. When the market comes close to a significant resistance number, there are two options:

1. The market will cross the resistance and move up to the next level (3,800 approximately). This process takes its own time. It is not an immediate move, but it often works out, slowly.
2. The market tries to cross the resistance. Eventually, it fails to do so. Then prices begin a slow descent. Prices should then touch support levels (2,750 in this case).

Figure 3.103: **RSI gives a bearish signal — prices lower but RSI higher. Nifty faces resistance as RSI reaches 60.**

The move above 3,150 or below 3,000 (closing beyond these levels) will probably justify a new position. Watch the markets, and go with the flow.

24 December 2008

Nifty Breaks Down Below Narrow Range Bars

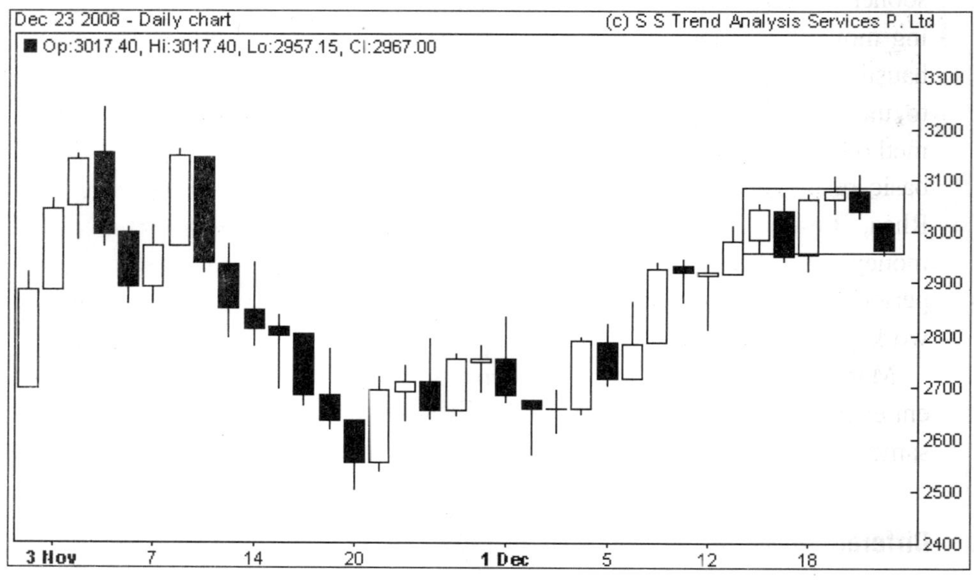

Figure 3.104: **Nifty ranged in a box. A close below 2,950 will see the index break down.**

The Nifty closed at 2,967, below the lows of the last two days which had narrow range bars. This is the beginning of a short-term down move. I will assume that the intermediate trend changes to down if the Nifty closes below 2,950. This has not happened yet.

Traders should go long either on intra day signals, or on a close above 3,150. If you are short today, the stops should be the close of yesterday, i.e. around 3,045.

Given below is a brief note on my ideas of how a trend will end.

How Does a Trend End?

How does a trend come to an end? This interesting question must be answered. After all, traders and investors are advised to exit when they perceive that the trend is facing a reversal. But what qualifies as a reversal? Are reversal signals different for day traders, swing traders, position traders and investors? This note will try to answer these questions.

Trend is defined as a move of prices in any one direction. Prices keep on moving in one direction (up or down) offering opportunities for gains to people who participate in the move with the trend. At some point, sooner or later, all good things must come to an end. So also with a trending move. Technical analysis provides many ways of identifying the exhaustion of a trend. Some of the methods are difficult, almost impossible to understand, leave alone follow. The simplest, easiest to understand methods are also the ones that will survive different types of markets. The basic rules were defined by Charles Dow, then elaborated by Hamilton, Rhea, Edwards and Maggie, and, finally by David Fuller (fullermoney.com). My own ideas on trend exhaustion have been formed over a period of time, based mainly on my perception of the markets and the work of the masters.

Markets are dynamic, therefore signs of trend exhaustion will be different every time a trend comes to an end. But the broad patterns will be the same. After all, crowd psychology does not change.

Different Ways for the End of an Uptrend

Distribution

After a sustained up move, momentum starts falling. Prices still go up, but at a slower pace. There are visible signs of a consolidation at current levels. Since the trend is up, it is assumed that the market will resume its up move after the consolidation is over. But either through a large down day, or through a series of narrow range bars, prices eventually break down from the consolidation. This is a sign that the trend has reversed.

Trend Reversal

The uptrend is defined as a series of higher highs and higher lows. After every up thrust, there is a brief corrective dip and prices then move up crossing the previous high. Usually, the dip will stop above the previous low. Eventually, after a dip, prices move up (as before) but fail to cross the previous high. Then a subsequent dip pushes prices lower than the previous low. A pattern of lower highs and lower lows is established, thus reversing the uptrend.

Inverted V

While everyone is enjoying the up move, prices suddenly fall, almost like a crash. If the price fall goes below a significant support level, then it is assumed that the uptrend has come to an end. The difficult part is to define the "significant support level".

Different Ways for the End of a Downtrend

Accumulation

After a sustained down move, momentum starts falling. Prices still go down, but at a slower pace. There are visible signs of a consolidation at current levels. Since the trend is down, it is assumed that the market will resume its down move after the consolidation is over. But either through a large up day, or through a series of narrow range bars, prices eventually break out upward from the consolidation. This is a sign that the trend has reversed.

Trend Reversal

The downtrend is defined as a series of lower highs and lower lows. After every down move, there is a brief corrective rally and prices then move down below the previous low. Usually, the rally will stop below the previous low. Eventually, after a rally, prices move down (as before) but fail to cross the previous low. Then a subsequent rally pushes prices higher than the previous high. A pattern of higher highs and higher lows is established thus reversing the downtrend.

The V

While everyone is staying away from the market which seems to be in a bear grip, prices suddenly rise, almost like a sudden thunderbolt on a sunny day. If the price rise goes above a significant resistance level, then it is assumed that the downtrend has come to an end. The difficult part is to define the "significant resistance level".

These simple, easy to understand ideas are valid on all time frames and for all types of trading and investing.

29 December 2008

Who was to Blame for 2008?

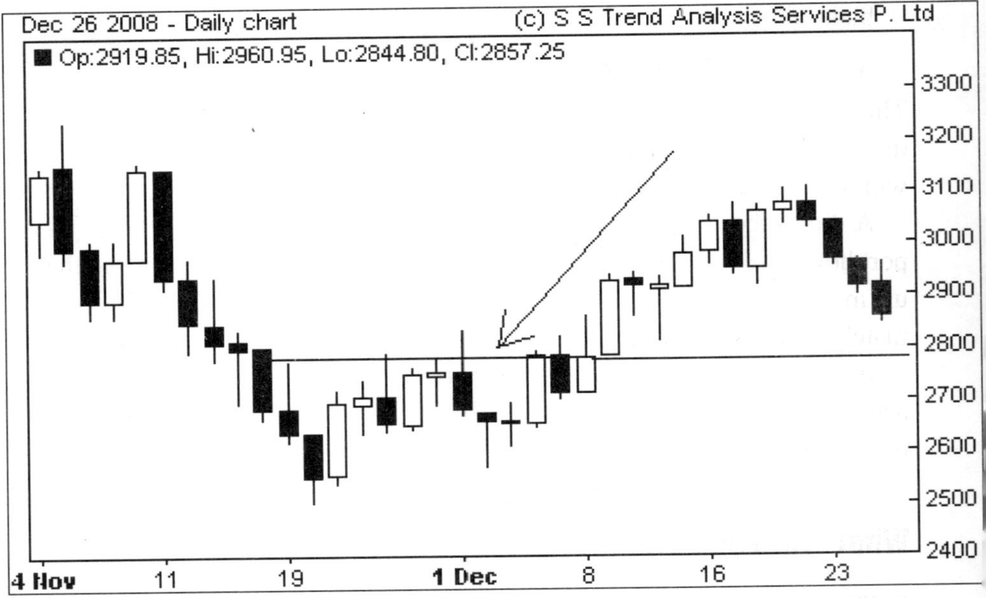

Figure 3.105: **Nifty's daily chart shows support coming around 2,785. Below 2,785, look for weakness.**

As the year 2008 comes to a close, investors must be feeling a sense of betrayal. At current levels, the Nifty has fallen 3,500 points from its January 2008 highs. That is a decline of 55%. This is the average decline. Most mid cap and small cap stocks have lost even more.

Who should be blamed for this large destruction in wealth?

- **The Super Rich.** Their greed knew no bounds. The government has given them a free run in the capital markets. They took full advantage of this freedom and manipulated markets to their benefit.

- **Investment Bankers, Brokers, Analysts.** These people believed every single word uttered by the super rich. They passed on these words as their own opinion to innocent investors. As the bubble burst, investors who listened to these people were badly hurt.
- **Government Authorities.** Leverage kills investors. Despite knowing this fact, the authorities encouraged the use of devastating leverage in the futures and options market which destroyed the average investor.
- **Investors.** You took unacceptable risks. You believed in people who were out to take your money. Surely, you have to share some of the blame.

After five weeks of rallies, the Nifty started a process of correction. This correction could be a dip in the up move. Or, it could be the continuation of the bear market. We have to wait for the market to tell us what it will do. Will we see lower levels again?

A dip in the Nifty should find support around 2,785-2,750. If this support holds, we assume that the Nifty has gone through a correction and the up move will resume. If the market fails to hold 2,785-2,750 (approximately), then the bear market is likely to continue.

In any case, the market may go through a three-week period of subdued activity. This will ensure that the market takes some rest and is ready to move one way or the other when the earnings start coming in mid-January.

What Will 2009 Bring for Us?

It appears that the recession / depression in the Western world (USA and Europe) may continue, or even get worse. The markets are, therefore, likely to face resistance around 3,800. A rally to this level is possible some time next year. The downside risk continues to exist, with the Nifty going for a test of the 2,200 lows made in October 2008. A really severe bear market could see the Nifty at 2,000, or even lower. These are only possibilities. The market will finally decide what it wants to do.

12 January 2009

Markets Stunned by Satyam Missile

Is anybody safe? Investors who put their hard earned money in the hands of large businessmen can be wiped off in a minute. The Satyam episode proves this.

How should you protect yourself?

1. **Stay with Blue Chips.** Avoid running after momentum stocks. Even if you get lower returns, stay with the best.
2. **Diversify.** Do not put all your eggs in one basket. Diversify your investments into different sectors and different companies. Never risk more than 15% of your capital in any one company, and more than 20% in any one sector.
3. **Avoid the "Averaging" Trap.** If you get caught in a wrong trade or investment, accept the loss and walk away. Never average and buy more.
4. **Remember That Trading is a Numbers Game.** If your trading ideas are sensible, you will make money in the long run. Do not be worried by small setbacks. You manage these setbacks by cutting your losses.
5. **Always Let Your Profits Run.**

Market View

The Nifty remains inside a trading range and needs to close above 3,150 for a bullish breakout. Since the primary trend is down, anything below 3,150 qualifies as a downtrend. The market, then, is in a downtrend. This downtrend will become stronger if the Index closes below 2,800. A close below 2,800 will mean a breakdown from the trading range.

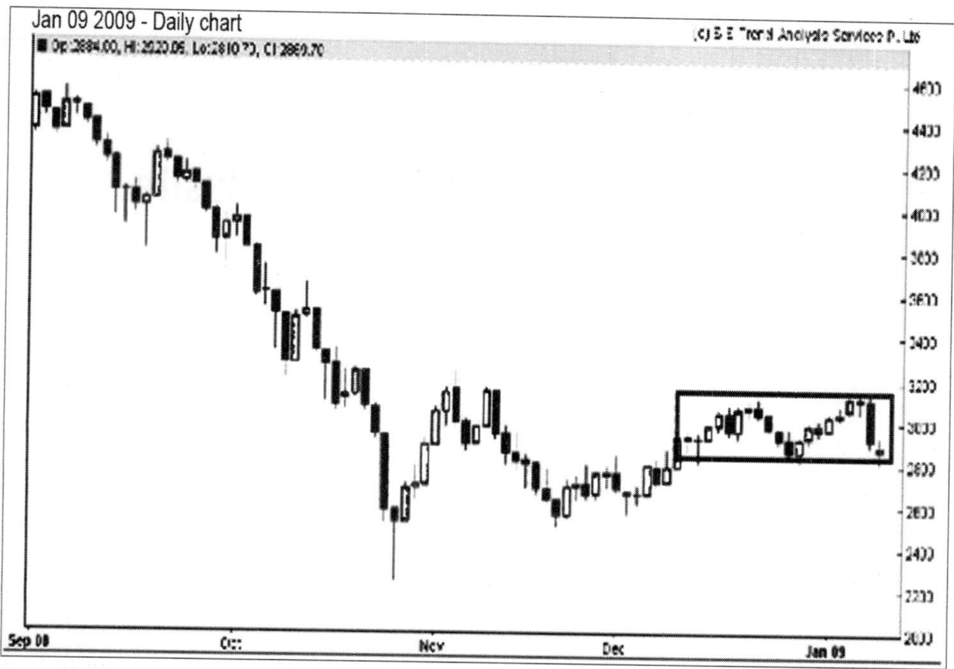

Figure 3.106: **Nifty's daily chart shows that the market remains in trading range. Deep downtrend possible below 2,800. Avoid buying during earnings season.**

With the trend now down again, investors should stay away. Buying on dips is no longer a good idea. It is wise to let the earnings season finish off. A review of the markets should be taken after this is over.

14 January 2009

Market Choppy, Remains Weak

After a 450-point decline in the Nifty, the market may see a relief rally any time. But this would be a rally in a bear market. Traders can catch some part of the up move if possible, but investors should stay away

Figure 3.107: **Nifty breaks down from a trading range; may be looking at 2,450-2500. Strong resistance at 2,800 then at 3,000.**

The Index has broken down from a trading range, giving a target of 2,450. Since we are in a bear market, the targets may well be exceeded on the downside. Resistance comes in around 2,800. Any rally will face significant resistance at these levels. If the Nifty does manage to breakout higher, the next level of resistance is at 3,000. Since we are in a downtrend, there is no visible support. There is minor support around 2,700, and then at 2,500.

Infosys saw a 4 percent gain after it announced results. The long term chart (monthly) of Infosys is suggesting a significant breakdown with a target of approximately ₹ 800. Today, the stock moved up from ₹ 1,130 to ₹ 1,230. If and when there is resistance in stock prices, the share will offer a short selling opportunity.

Reliance continues to fall. Again, here too, the long-term charts are suggesting a major breakdown.

All in all, we may be looking at difficult times ahead.

The time for buying will come later.

We are witnessing a sharp and rapid downtrend. Chances are that we will see waterfall declines, meaning big down moves in succession. Once the down move ends, a period of consolidation is likely. The markets will surely move up after this entire process is done with. That will be the time to buy. When will this happen? Maybe by the end of January or maybe, later, in February. Investors should wait patiently for this process to be completed and buying opportunities to emerge.

"Frightening Global Downturn: The UK faces terrible times It is clear that the UK economy is facing a very serious recession, and the downturn is deepening at an alarming pace," said a BCC report based on a survey of almost 6,000 firms which employ 680,000 people.

"Due to the global economic downturn, there is less demand abroad for German goods, such as cars and machine tools. Germany is heavily reliant on exports, which saw their largest fall in November since reunification in 1990.

"Japan's current account surplus narrowed for a ninth month in November as exports slumped by a record in the wake of the global recession.

"In a dismal prelude to the earnings season, Alcoa Inc. reported a quarterly loss of $1.19 billion Monday, days after the aluminium giant announced cuts due to sinking prices and demand for the metal."

19 January 2009

Intermediate Downtrend, Again!

The Nifty has broken down from a trading range to close at 2,800. We have an intermediate downtrend in effect.

Figure 3.108: **Nifty is in a large trading range between 3,150 and 2,500.**

Resistance should come in around 3,000. Before, 3,000, there is minor resistance at 2,875. Support comes in at 2,700, then again at 2,500. We have the chances of another trading range developing between 2,500 and 3,000. This also means that there is downside potential for the Index to fall again to 2,500.

Is there a possibility of a new bull market starting in the next few days?

The answer is no. A bear market ends with a lot of base building and a fall in volatility. This has not happened yet. Thus, we have to assume that the bear market may continue for a long period of time. Within the down trend, there will be rallies, but these are likely to be trading rallies rather than investment opportunities.

Investors Should Buy — and Then Sell

What is trading? It is when you both buy and sell. Now, if the investor is willing to sell his shares then he becomes a trader. This enables him to survive in a bear market and, actually, make some money in the process.

Opportunities for Trading

Infosys, and the fertilizer and sugar sectors offer opportunities for trading. Look for dips, buy, and sell on a rally. Do not worry if prices go higher after you sell. You are trading, so small profits are acceptable.

Outlook for the Next Few Days

The market may remain in a trading range. Around 3,000, look to sell or exit positions. A dip of 200 points is a buying opportunity. Do not overstay in the market.

28 January 2009

A Bit of Sunshine

After four days of down moves, there was a small bit of sunshine today as the Nifty rallied.

Figure 3.109: **Nifty likely to see significant resistance around 2,830-2,850.**

Depending on how the American markets move, the Nifty may well enjoy some more gains until it reaches significant resistance between 2,830 and 2,850 (see chart). This means there is at least one more opportunity possible for buying on dips, maybe tomorrow or the day after.

The Bank Nifty has gone into a narrows range today suggesting a breakout either tomorrow or the day after. Traders may like to buy a breakout above 4,215 and sell below 4,115. Keep a stop on the other side.

The Nifty remains in an intermediate downtrend. This is my chart reading, based on a continuing pattern of lower highs and lower lows.

6 February 2009

More Confusion as Market in Indecision

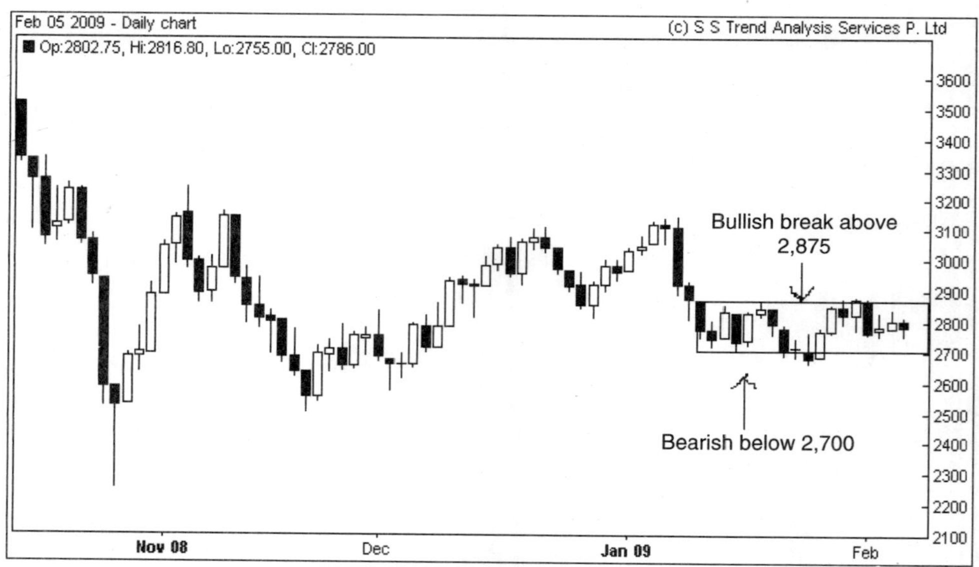

Figure 3.110: **Nifty in trading range for the last 18 days.**

A trading range is difficult to trade. The trading difficulties arise when we wish to search for trades inside the range. The best, perhaps the only, trades come when prices breakout of the trading range. Now here is our problem. We want to trade but opportunities are missing since the index remains locked in a range.

The solution then is to focus on individual shares and let the index be. Of course, we are watching the Nifty every day. Before we look at individual stocks, here is brief picture of the Nifty.

The Nifty is inside a trading range between 2,875 and 2,700.

Wait patiently for a range breakout. Buy above 2,875 and sell below 2,700.

An option trade is possible. Buy 2,700 put, buy 2,900 call.

Be prepared for losses if the Nifty remains in trading range throughout February. This is the risk.

9 February 2009

Market Locked in Narrow Trading Range

Traders should wait for clear signs of breakdown / breakout.

Figure 3.111: **Nifty still finding her way! 2,875 and 2,700 continued to act as strong resistance and support.**

The Nifty has been trading in a tight range for the last 19 trading days. Because the primary trend of the market is down, there is a stronger chance that this range may eventually result in a breakdown. Various indicators are suggesting that Nifty is getting ready for a big move. The move could be up or down.* A close above 2,875 should be bullish while a close

* Decline in 14 period Average True Range, Fall in 10/100 Historical Volatility Ratio below 0.5.

below 2,700 is certainly bearish. A breakdown below 2,700 will mean a target of 2,450 and maybe even lower. The point then is that a trader should not try to buy any dips below 2,700. An upside breakout could see the Nifty at 3,000+. There is significant resistance at 3,150 and the Index is unlikely to be able to cross this level easily.

What should the trader do?

Above 2,875 Nifty, buy for small gains. Below 2,700 either go short or stay away. Inside the trading range, buy dips for 30-40 point profit.

17 February 2009

Market Sees a Breakdown

After a four-day consolidation, the market finally moved out of the consolidation, taking the interim budget as a trigger. A trigger is just a reason for the market to do what it intended to do anyway.

Figure 3.112: **Nifty breaches the support level of 2,835.**

Always Go with the Trend

So far, the short-term trend was up. Now, with the Nifty moving below 2,835, this trend has changed to sideways. Long positions should be closed since the Index has violated a significant support level.

Has the Downtrend Resumed?

Not really. The Nifty was inside a trading range between 2,700 to 2,875 and this trading range probably continues with different boundaries — 2,950 to 2,760.

Looking at a Scenario

The market is moving inside a range although the range is probably wider than the one we are tracking. The real range may well be 2,500 to 3,200. Maybe, the Index will move inside this larger range for months altogether, before deciding on a trending move. The next move could be down to 1,800 or up to 3,800. All of this is just to build possible scenarios for the Index.

If This is a Trading Range, How Should I Trade?

The nice thing about a range is the fact that there are opportunities on both sides, the long side as well as the short side. In a few days time, most stocks will reach support areas. This will be a time to buy for small up moves. Traders may consider going short on rallies. Going short will no longer be easy, though. I suspect that the best part of the bear market is behind us. Every rally now will raise the question: "Is this the real 'bull' move?" Thus, short selling may remain rather difficult from now on.

The Nifty

While the Nifty remains inside a trading range (2,760-2,950), it is difficult to trade since we have already seen two failed breakout moves. First, the Nifty fell below 2,700 to 2,635 but rallied back inside the range without reaching its downside target. Now, the Index broke out above 2,875, went to 2,950 but has retreated back into the range. Therefore, it seems that using oscillators to identify extreme conditions may be the more profitable way. This means using tm Stock, or RSI, CCI, stochastics, or some such method.

24 February 2009

Markets Slide

Entering an Intermediate Downtrend

Figure 3.113: **Daily chart of Nifty shows that the index could drift around 2,600 level.**

On daily charts, the Nifty is still looking to find its way. It has got resistance at 2,800 and support at 2,740. This is a very narrow range and it is unlikely to be sustained for more than one day.

If 2,740 breaks down, one can expect the level of 2,600. On the other side, if Nifty has to rally from here it needs to fill a gap and go above 2,850. If Nifty succeeds in moving above 2,850, we can expect that downside could get over at least for the short term.

Figure 3.114: **Weekly chart of Nifty.**

On weekly charts, Nifty has strong support at 2,600. If Nifty closes below 2,740 one could expect to see the 2,600 level.

Short Term Trading Strategy

- If Nifty rallies, go short with a stop loss above 2,850.
- If Nifty breaks down below 2,740 one can go short with an approximate target of 2,600.

6 March 2009

A Market Without Buyers

Declines Continue

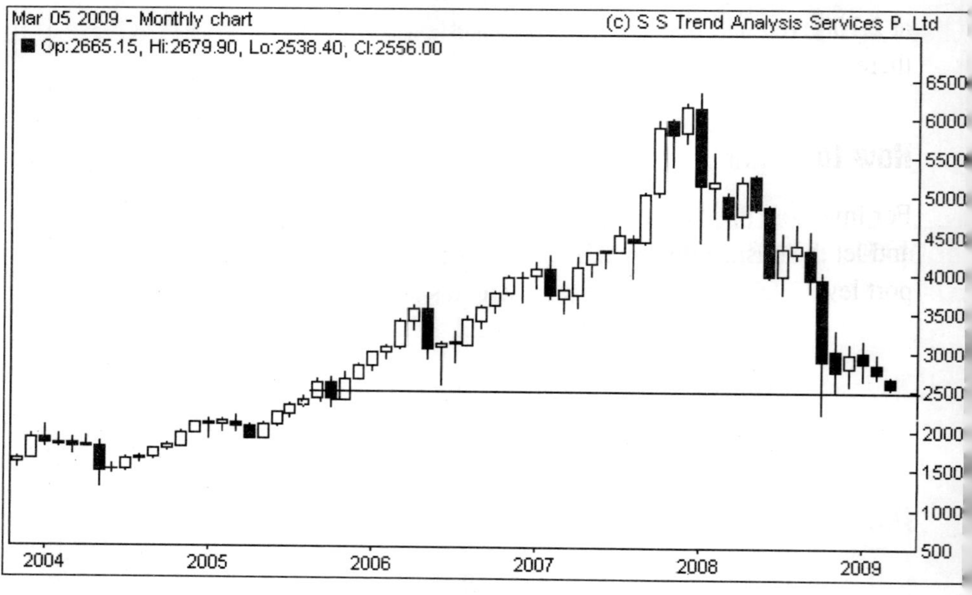

Figure 3.115: **Monthly chart of Nifty shows support at 2,500.**

Levels to Watch

The Nifty ignored all possible upbeat cues (higher US markets, rate cut in India) to close at its lowest level since 20 November 2008. But that's the good news. The Sensex has closed at its lowest level since November 2005. The Sensex, then, is lower on a closing basis than the October 2008 lows. The fact that the Sensex has broken below its earlier lows is not good news. Sooner or later, it is possible that the Nifty may follow the Sensex. Based on this premise, it is fair to suggest that worst is not over for the Nifty.

The possible targets for the Nifty are in a range between 1,800 and 2,000. How did we arrive at these magical numbers? Below 2,500, the Nifty could see a free fall as there is no support at all. The next support is a range between 1,800 (the high of year 2000) and 2,000 (the high of January 2004 before the election correction).

Nifty has minor support at 2,500. If it fails to hold out these levels, then we might see a free fall in Nifty. If we do see a rally, then there is resistance all the way up; first at 2,600, then at 2,650, and significant resistance at 2,700. We will discuss the resistance levels above 2,700 when we reach there.

How to Trade

For investors this is not the time to go long. Investors should wait patiently and let the dust settle down. Brave-hearted traders can buy Nifty at its support level (2,500) for a relief rally with a strict stop loss.

9 March 2009

Markets End Week with Large Losses, Small Rebound

The first four days of the week saw significant losses in the Sensex and the Nifty. Friday saw some kind of a relief rally.

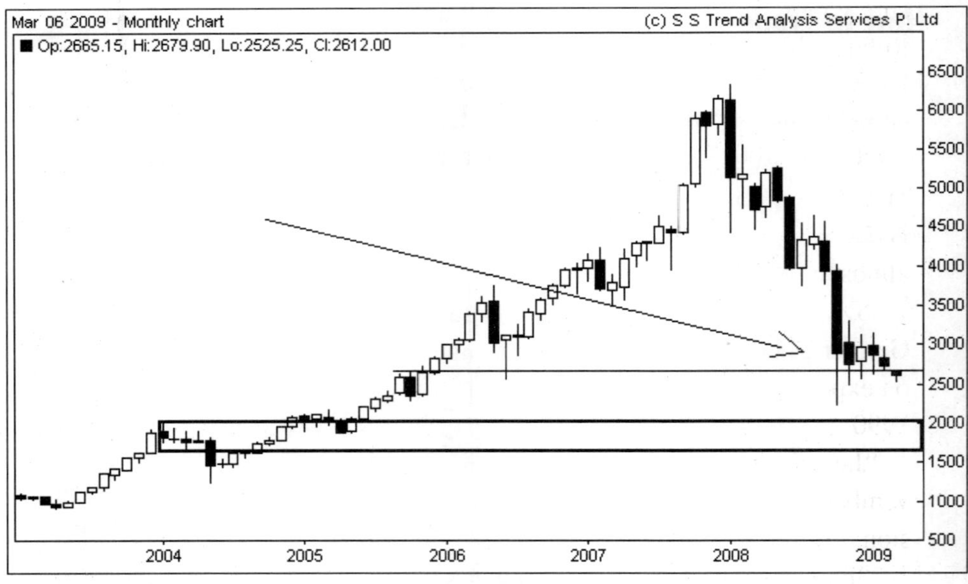

Figure 3.116: **Nifty breaks down on its monthly chart. Support area for Nifty lies between 1,800-2,000.**

The Nifty has significant support around 2,500. This support can hold for a while. It does appear that another sharp decline could see the Index breaking down below this support. Below 2,500, we have a free fall, maybe all the way down to 2,000. Support for the Nifty comes in a zone between 1,800 and 2,000. The scenario, then, is not bullish. At least, not yet. In the heavyweights, banks can see more declines. Reliance, NTPC, Bharti Airtel can also see lower levels. The IT sector may remain an out-performer. Investors should wait patiently for signs of consolidation before considering any new buying. Traders should go for short-term trading, selling on rallies and buying on dips.

16 March 2009

Bulls Back in Action

Figure 3.117: **Weekly chart of Nifty shows the index bouncing from its support level of 2,500.**

The Nifty has broken out of a four-day consolidation between 2,580 and 2,620. This breakout suggests that the short-term trend is now up. A close above 2,800 is required to change the intermediate trend, which remains down as of now.

Traders should either step aside, or buy on dips. Conservative traders can consider buying if and when the intermediate trend changes to up. This will happen when the Nifty closes above 2,800.

Technically Bullish

On the weekly chart, a positive divergence between the Nifty and the 14-period RSI is now visible. The RSI is at 39.47, almost touching 40. I consider a move above 40 as a low risk buy signal — with proper stops. Many of these moves eventually end up in failure. Therefore, there is no way to suggest that the RSI signal will be a success. But traders may wish to take a buy on dips strategy. At worst, if the market falls, there will be small losses, and of course, non-participation in the decline.

Future Shock

Here are some scenarios:

Well, the Nifty could confound everyone by continuing to move up, quickly, reaching 3,500. All talk of 2,000 will then vanish as our friends will start talking of "fundamentally sound" companies and economy. Then, just before the election process starts, the markets could weaken, finally reaching 1,800 which, by then, everyone may have forgotten about.

Or, the market could do what everyone is suggesting — see a failure in the current rally, then fall below 2,500, and finally bottom out around the 1,800-2,000 levels.

Finally, the market could continue to drift between 2,550 and 2,800 .

Which scenario will work out? That is an answer only a fortune teller can give. My point is: depending on your trading profile, follow the market momentum. By going through a process of scenario building, we are not taken aback or shocked by what the market does. And, markets are unpredictable.

20 March 2009

Market at Crossroads?

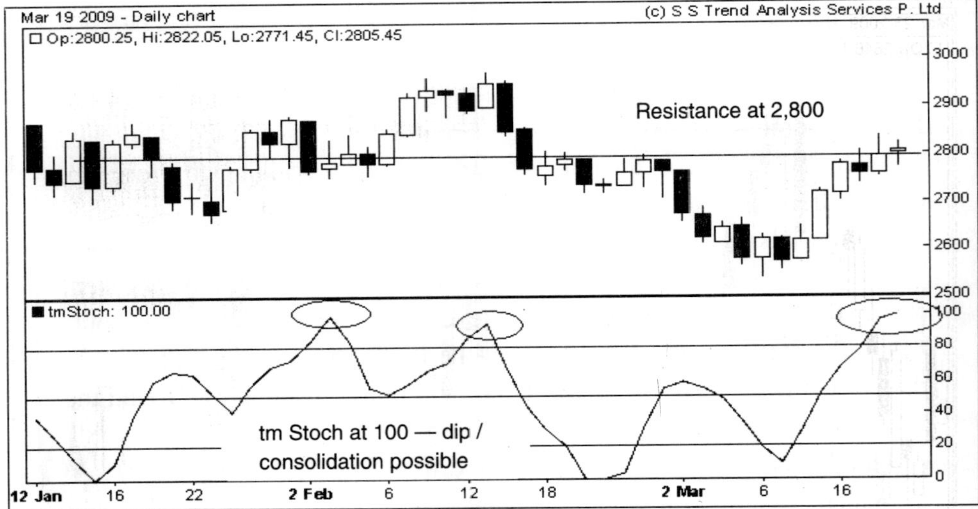

Figure 3.118: **Narrow range, Doji today. Careful please, Nifty at resistance. Buy only on a dip.**

The Nifty has moved about like a drunken elephant for the past two days. Yesterday it remained up for most part of the day, then fell in the last hour. Today, it moved up, fell sharply, then rallied again in the last hour. While our analysis can easily go wrong, bull markets are built on foundations of stability, not on such erratic moves.

The Nifty closed above 2,800. But the close was marked by a Doji, a narrow range day. Both these patterns coming after a sustained up move do not inspire confidence. If the Nifty were to trade above today's high of 2,825, then there will be a strong probability that a genuine up move has started. This is easy to determine tomorrow, so keep watching.

Support for the Nifty comes in at 2,760, while there is resistance at 2,825. The long term trend does not change every day. It is a bear market.

24 March 2009

A Grand Rally

Figure 3.119: **Nifty breaks out from an inverse head and shoulders pattern.**

The Nifty provided bulls with a big gift, a 140-point rally in the market. This is almost 5%, and should, therefore, count as one of the few "mother of all rallies" we have seen.

Directional Days

The Nifty broke through its 2,800 resistance with a big gap up. The Index then never looked back, moving up steadily throughout the day, gaining almost 80 points from its open. This means anyone buying in the morning, or later was amply rewarded by the market. Such moves are called directional days when the market moves in one direction. These days are different from gap days since after a gap up or down, the market may not have any follow through during the day. A directional day is an affirmation of strength (or weakness, if the market continues down).

When directional days appear as part of a bull run, they tell us that there is more upside left and bulls are in control. But when they appear inside what is till now a bear market, their message is probably — here is a good day, enjoy it.

Nifty Outlook

This rally started from 2,540, crossing resistance levels at 2,700, then 2,800 and is now standing at the 2,950 resistance. After 2,950, we have bigger resistance at 3,150. There is a large trading range between 2,550 and 3,150. The Nifty will need to cross the 3,150 levels to begin a new bull market. Will this happen? Now, that is anybody's guess!

Traders should go with the momentum, which is clearly up.

Investors are advised to stay away since the idea should be to buy on dips. A rally that has moved up 15% is no longer a dip.

If investors took some trading positions they need to protect these positions by keep a trailing stop. Identify the low of the past three days and keep it as your stop. If your stock moves up dramatically in one day (like Rel Cap did today), then keep your stop below the low of the latest trading day.

26 March 2009

Market in a Range

Trend is Sideways, Not Down

Figure 3.120: **Non-stop rally brings Nifty near the top of the trading range (3,150). Traders should remain buyers on dips.**

The Nifty moved in a trading range today, alternating between bouts of up and down moves. The net result was a gain as the index did manage to close fairly higher.

A close above the recent pivot high of 3,016 will tell us that the trend remains up. The worry is the same as on earlier occasions: the market has moved up fast.

Short term support for the index is at 2,950. Resistance for the Nifty comes in at 3,016.

Above 3,016, we can expect the bulls to take charge again. The Nifty is well on its way to touch 3,150, which is the upper band of the trading range between 2,550 and 3,150.

How Do You Trade? Go Long on Dips

Should you invest? Much as it disappoints readers, investment must wait for a decline.

30 March 2009

A Great Show

Figure 3.121: **Daily chart of Nifty. If Nifty breaks 3,150-3,200, the next target could be around 3,400-50.**

With a non-stop straight line rally from the 2,540 lows in the Nifty, the stock market has moved up more than 20% in about three weeks. With this rally, the market has erased the memories of the Satyam debacle of January.

Figure 3.122: **Nifty's daily chart shows classic example of a bear market rally.**

Has a Bull Market Started?

Quite possibly. But the confirmation will come only after a correction. The correction (this will be a downtrend) should obviously only be a retracement of the up move from 2,540 to whatever top is made. Roughly, if a correction stops above 2,800, then the chances will be stronger that the bear market has come to an end.

Emerging Markets Rally

Hong Kong's benchmark Hang Seng Index has advanced 14.5 per cent this month, the most since October 2007. Templeton Asset Management Ltd.'s Mark Mobius said earlier this week that a "bull-market" rally in developing-nation equities has begun.

(*Source:* Fullermoney.com]

How Much Higher Can the Market Go?

Again, the market has its own mind. A high probability scenario is a fast galloping rally to 3,400. This will take the Nifty above the 3,150-3,250 resistance. A breakout above this resistance will suck in most wavering investors and traders who may buy above 3,250, hoping to ride on till the next resistance which is at 3,850. Smart money wants to sell at the highest price, but not wait for a sudden crash. Thus, we may well see the market top out before the 3,850 resistance. We selected 3,400 as a possible target because of a confluence of different technical methods at that point. (Please see chart)

Will the Market Breakout of the 3,150-3,250 Resistance?

Again, this is only a probability. Given the strength of the upside momentum, it seems quite likely that the Nifty will take out this resistance.

> With all the talk of "depression", we know that markets discounted a great deal of very bad economic news. Even some of the bears have said that this was an overreaction. We know that a small but powerful group of short sellers, operating in concert with their investment bankers, formed a very aggressive cabal of bear raiders. Others rode on their coattails. Yesterday's short sellers are among today's buyers. We also know that there is a great deal of investment cash on the sidelines, waiting for a signal.
>
> (*Source:* Fullermoney.com]

Will Nifty Fall to 2,000?

With every passing day it becomes that much difficult for the Nifty to decline to 2,000. But a bear market rally can quickly fizzle out and a new downtrend can make lower lows all the way down to 2,000. Therefore, we have to wait for correction (please see above) to say with some conviction that 2,000 will not come again.

> The global equity rebound in March that sent the Standard & Poor's 500 Index to its best monthly advance in 17 years is a "bear-market rally" and US Treasury yields will "remain relatively low" as investors flock

> to the safest assets, Roubini said. Treasury Secretary Timothy Geithner's new plan to remove toxic debt from financial companies won't be enough for insolvent banks, he said.
>
> (*Source:* Fullermoney.com)

Should I Invest Now?

No. Investing should be done only on dips. There will be many opportunities to buy if this is really a new bull market. Ideally, you should wait for the next correction.

> Markets are much more volatile than the underlying fundamentals, for a very human reason. Think of the market as a drama, which is produced by fundamental economic factors but acted out by a crowd of investors. Crowds are manic / depressive. Consequently they become too optimistic on the way up and too pessimistic on the way down.
>
> (*Source:* Fullermoney.com)

How Do I Trade?

Go with the flow of market. Trend is up, so buy on dips.

1 April 2009

Nifty Probably Near an Intermediate Top

A Correction was Coming, Anyway

Given the sheer power of the Nifty's gains, having increased 23% off the March 6 lows in what has to be a sharp, quick bull market move within the context of an overall bear market, the Indian stock market was probably ripe for a correction.

Is this a Correction in an Uptrend?

Since the primary trend is bearish, we will assume that the intermediate uptrend is coming to an end. The process may take some time as stocks go through distribution. But we should be clear in our analysis that we are seeing the end of this up move.

The current down move is a part of topping out process and at some point we can expect another downtrend.

Should We Initiate Short Positions?

The process of distribution will see choppy market conditions with sudden, sharp rallies as well as declines. Day traders and swing traders should consider short positions whenever set-ups are available. Position traders should not initiate long-term short positions because we cannot say with certainty that a top is in place.

Should We Buy if Nifty Breaks Out Above 3,150?

If there is an immediate breakout we should not buy because market is already over extended. If this breakout happens after a downside correction, then buying should be considered.

What Should Be the Present Trading Strategy?

As we are in a choppy market, this provides opportunity for traders to trade on both long and short side. Traders can buy on dips and sell on rallies by using different indicators, like RSI with period 3.

Use RSI-3 with extreme values 90 and 10. Whenever RSI reaches 90, traders can consider short positions and when RSI dips to 10 traders can go long.

This indicator provides some big moves in choppy markets and the best part is this indicator can be used for both swing and intra day trading.

What are Strength and Weakness? How Can These Be Identified?

Strength and weakness are associated with support and resistance.

Markets will reach support, then hold it. Often, prices will touch resistance, then fail to cross it. The reverse can also happen; e.g. when the market touches support, then breaks down to move lower, or touches resistance and then breaks out to move higher:

- Strength is support holding out, not getting broken on the downside.
- Weakness is resistance holding out and not getting broken on the upside.

Let us consider an example. An intra day trader is waiting to buy on signs of strength. The market is falling. He waits patiently. At some point, the decline stops and a trading range develops. The trading range is support. If prices move up from the range, this will be a sign of strength. The range also allows the trader to execute a low risk trade since a breakdown from the range is a clear signal that the trade is not working out.

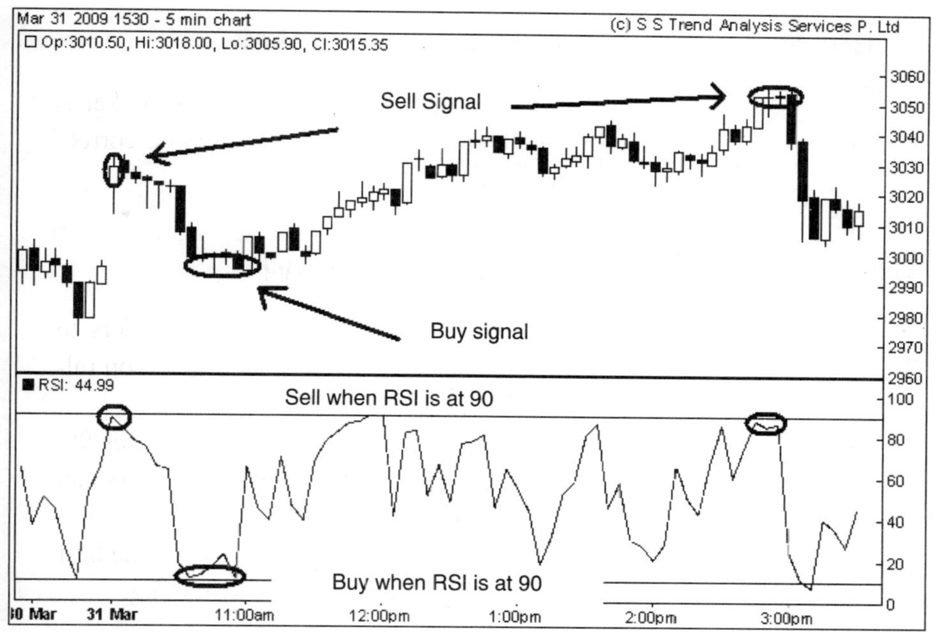

Figure 3.123: **5-minute chart of Nifty for 31 March 2009.**

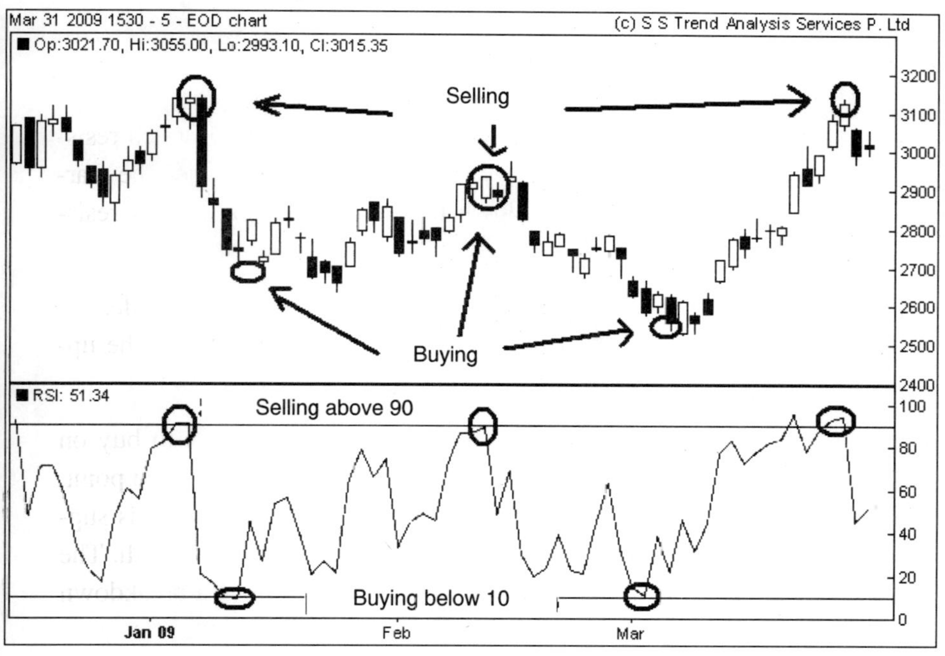

Figure 3.124: **Daily chart of Nifty for 31 March 2009.**

How do you identify a support in the making? The answer is "momentum". As prices decline, momentum is on the side of the bears. At some point, the decline stops. Now the bears do not have the benefit of momentum. This fall in downside momentum is the first sign that there may be support coming in. It could easily be just a pause before a new down move begins. That's not easy to predict. For, equally, it could also slowly lead to a trading range, then an upside breakout from the range. When this happens, the message is: there is support. This is a sign of strength.

9 April 2009

Bulls Get It Right!

A 100-point gap down, then a scorching rally that adds 90 points of gains to the Nifty tells us that the bulls are here in full strength.

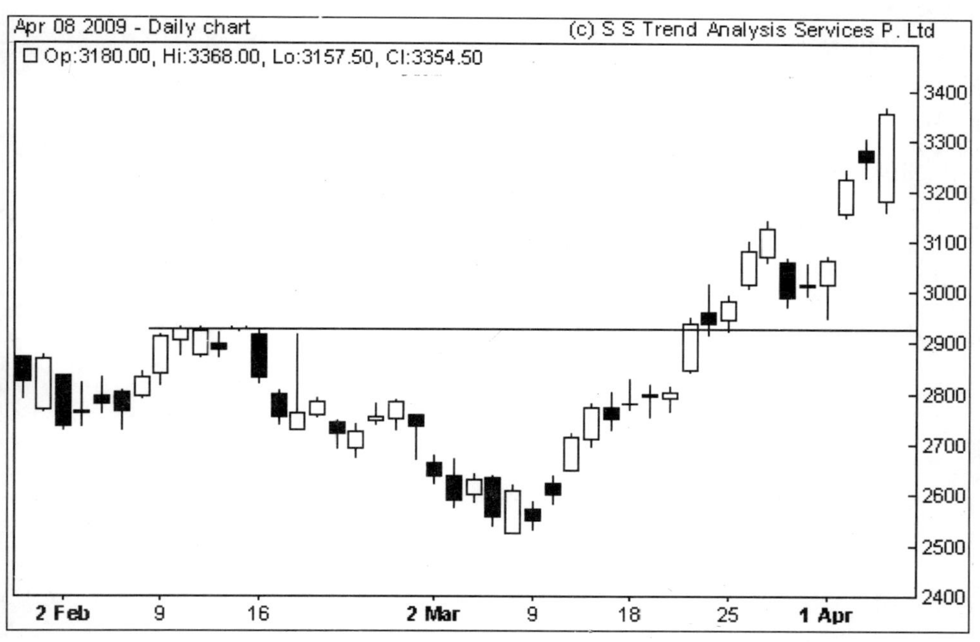

Figure 3.125: **Bulls take a strong grip on Nifty. Breakout above 2,935 provides the spark to bulls. Traders should buy on dips.**

Buy on Dips

While there will come a time when this rally will stall, that time has not come yet.

How to Detect a Change in Trend?

A word of warning to traders and investors; you must ride the trend. The trend is up. If and when there is a change of trend, you should exit immediately by taking whatever small losses there may be. How will you know that the trend has changed?

Step 1. Understand Your Time Frame

- Investors / position traders: track your stocks in the daily chart.
- Swing Traders: track your positions on a 60-minute chart.

Step 2

Use a 13-period weighted moving average to track your stocks. If the price closes below this average, take this as a warning sign. Lighten up!

16 April 2009

What's a Bear Market?

Does Anyone Remember?

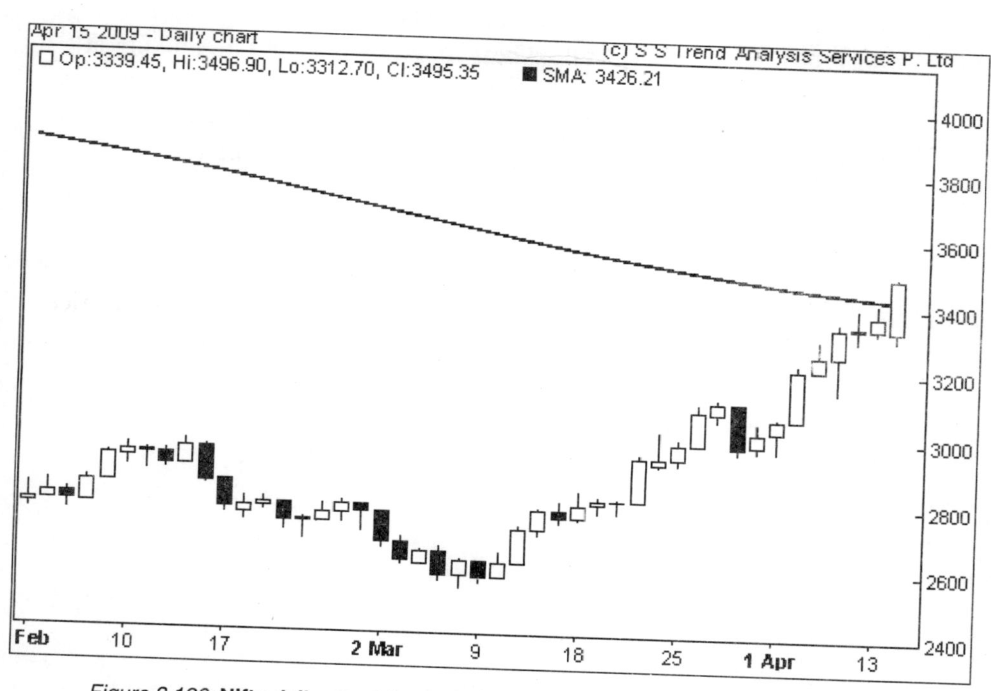

Figure 3.126: **Nifty daily chart for 15 April 2009. Nifty closes above its 200-DMA. Traders should buy on dips with appropriate stop and loss.**

The Nifty continues its up move, gaining points every day. With today's close at 3,484.15 the Index has closed above its 200-day moving average — a sign of a bull market. The Nifty is up 37.16% from its lows made on 6 March, exactly 40 days, i.e. about 6 weeks, ago.

Looking at the 37.16% Gains

In the history of the Nifty, from 1990 onwards, such gains have only come once earlier — in 1992 at the time of the Harshad Mehta bull run. In 1992, after these gains the market crashed. Not a good sign!

Has the Bull Run Started?

Well, the Nifty has crossed above its 200-day moving average. It is also 37.16% above its lows. These are signs of strength. But such gains have been recorded earlier in American bear markets. So, one never knows.

Instead of thinking about bull or bear moves, we should be looking at the current trend. And the current trend is up. That's what we should be looking at.

Traders should look to go long at every dip. The bulls are in control, until proved otherwise.

20 April 2009

Stocks Advance Week Over Week

Infosys Results Disappoint

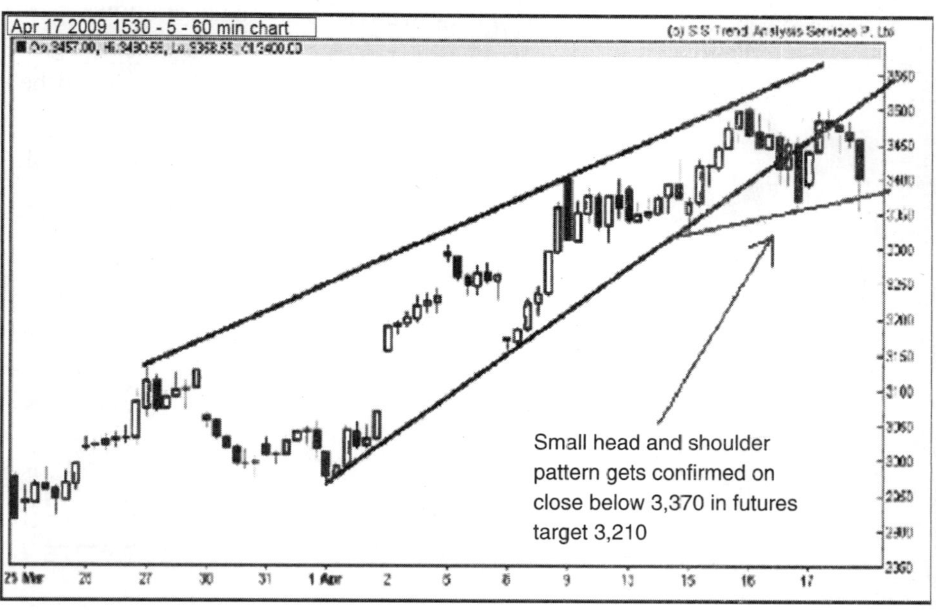

Figure 3.127: **Nifty near month futures — A rising wedge breaks down. The 60-minute chart suggests weakness, turns bullish above 3,510.**

The Nifty (close: 3,384, previous week: 3,342) and Sensex (close: 11,023, previous week: 10,803) continued their gains over the previous week. On Wednesday, IT bellweather Infosys reported its results and suggested that the coming year 2009-2010 will be difficult with profits actually moving lower. The market did react by keeping Infosys share prices low, but the broad market (other sectors) were not affected.

Market Slow Down Seen, At Least in the Short Term

The 60-minute chart for Nifty futures suggests a topping out pattern forming. A rising wedge, which is the sign of a top, has been made and prices have broken down from it. A small bearish head and shoulder pattern is also visible. The pattern gets confirmed on an hourly close below 3,360. Once confirmed, it gives a target of 3,210 on the downside. Both these patterns are cancelled if the futures were to trade above 3,510. A chart for the S&P 500 60-minute also shows similar patterns.

The Longer Term View

Figure 3.128: **The weekly chart shows Nifty trading above its range of 2,700-3,100; indicating continuing strength on a weekly basis. Long upper shadows at the end of week indicates lot of resistance at 3,500 levels.**

A sharp unprecedented rally in the Nifty has seen gains of 29.2% over six weeks. Such a percentage gain has never been recorded in the S&P Nifty since its origin in 1994.

Such gains were recorded in 1992 and 1993 — before the NSE started its operations. I say this since pre-NSE the stock market was manipulated and illiquid, and FIIs were also not present in the market then. Thus, comparisons may not be accurate. Be that as it may, in 1992 back to back gains were seen for many weeks (this was the Harshad Mehta bull run), then a new bear market started.

In 1993, 17 December marked a record breaking six week gain. This was the recovery after the 1992-1993 bear market. This seems similar to what we may be seeing now. Accordingly, let us examine the 1993-1994 bull market in some more detail.

The market bottomed out at 599 in April 1993. A new rally started which took the Nifty to 1,070 on 17 December 1993 which also recorded a six week gain of 29.99%. From this level, the Nifty took 10 months to top out at 1,385 in September 1994. The subsequent bear market took the Nifty down to 813 and the Nifty moved in a trading range between 800 and 1,250 for the next 4 years.

Summary: What Does All This Mean?

The current up move is not like the 1992 Harshad Mehta bull market. It is a strong bounce after a bear run, just like the 1993 move was. We can expect some more gains, either now or after a correction, and thereafter probably a long, protracted trading range.

Nifty Views

The Index has support around 3,150. A correction can easily bring down the Index to this level. Rallies should face resistance at 3,500, where the 200-day moving average now stands. A breakout above 3,500 may see another move to 3,800-3,900.

Alternately, the Nifty may drift down, and the trend turns sideways until the 3,500 resistance holds.

Traders should trade with an open mind, taking appropriate long as well as short positions. Earlier, for the past few weeks we had suggested that short positions should be avoided. Now, both long and short positions may be considered.

Investors must wait for a correction before planning new buying. Take profits on your existing positions, at least partially.

Short Term View

In the last few trading sessions the market witnessed high volatility and faced stiff resistance at the 3,500 level which indicates that this might be time to take some profits and wait for the market to either correct or consolidate.

Traders should not build aggressive short positions; instead, shorts should be made for small profits and with strict stop loss as the market's intermediate trend is up.

Investors should hold on to their positions as Nifty is trading above the 3,100 level.

22 April 2009

Range Bound Nifty

Wait for the Big Move

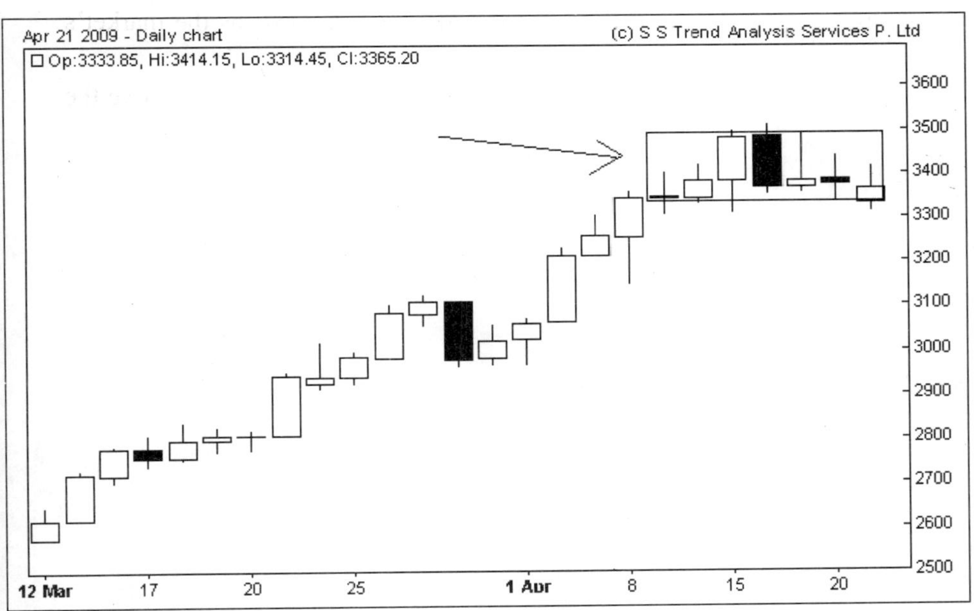

Figure 3.129: **The daily chart of 21 April 2009 shows Nifty in a trading range between 3,350 and 3,500. A move out of this range should provide a trend, wait patiently.**

The Nifty has now spent seven days inside a trading range between 3,350 and 3,500. This is in the nature of the Index. The Nifty goes through this process of expansion and contraction, regularly. After a big thrusting move beyond the 3,150 resistance level to 3,500, we now have the Index taking rest, moving inside a trading range. A move out of this range should be expected soon enough.

A close below 3,350 will tell us that the Nifty is ready for a correction. This down move should then go to 3,150 at the least. A close above 3,500, on the other hand, would suggest strength with more upside possible. We should then be looking at 3,800.

Nifty Support and Resistance

We have mentioned that Nifty has support at 3,350 and resistance at 3,500. For tomorrow's day trades we should expect support at 3,310 and resistance at 3,420.

24 April 2009

Suddenly, the Nifty Wakes Up from Slumber, Pushes Ahead!

Figure 3.130: **The head and shoulder pattern gave a false signal. Close above the shoulder line gives bullish signals.**

While we were apprehensive of a correction or a dip, the market has its own mind. We must listen to the voice of the market, which decides how the markets will move.

Today's big rally certainly tells us that the Nifty is not going down. But, more than this, a bearish head and shoulder pattern identified earlier on 60-minute charts is now to be accepted as a failure. The Nifty has closed above the right shoulder, on an hourly basis, and we have a failure of the bearish pattern. The failure is also a bullish sign of a market that is not going down.

What is the Nifty Doing?

Short Term Outlook

The Index remains in a range between 3,350 and 3,500, today's big move notwithstanding. A close above 3,500 is going to tell us about more upside. A close below 3,350 should have been bearish, but yesterday's close below this level turned out to be a one-day dip. Maybe a second close below 3,350, if it comes about, will be bearish. The short-term outlook, then, is to wait for a breakout on either side.

Intermediate Outlook

The current nine-day range may well become a substitute for a correction. Investors are advised to buy on a close above 3,500. This remains a high risk opportunity, so keep volume low.

Summary

Any rally that comes in now may take the Nifty to 3,800, or even higher. We cannot predict it. But the rally is possible going to be the last of the bull's efforts.

Traders should go with the momentum. Buy above 3,500. Investors should also buy above 3,500, but in lower volumes.

28 April 2009

Nifty Remains Steady Amidst Declines

Maintains Leadership Among World Markets

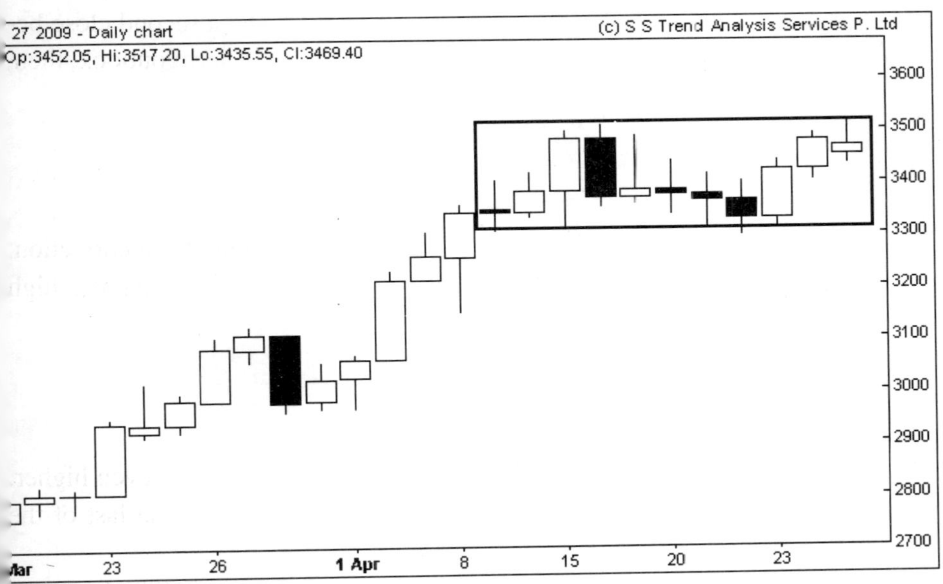

Figure 3.131: **Nifty daily chart shows 11 days in a trading range. Nifty is getting ready for big move. Direction unknown! Close above 3,500 is bullish; below 3,350 is bearish.**

The Nifty continued to show strength today while most world markets fell, including Asia, Europe and the US futures. Is this a sign of resilience, as our TV headings tell us, or is it a temporary disconnect?

My view is that India is almost fully coupled with the international markets. If for some time we move up while the world moves down, this is a short term disconnect. Sooner or later, our markets will move in tandem with world markets. If world markets continue to go up, we will do so. If world markets begin a correction, we will follow them; if not today, then a bit later.

Nifty Watch

Once the Nifty closes above 3,500, there is an opportunity to go long. An immediate target will be 3,650, and probably higher, as the market tends to overshoot when it breaks out in the direction of the trend. In the unlikely event of the Nifty drifting down to close below 3,350, look for a decline to 3,150 or thereabouts.

Afterword

Often, small events lead to the creation of history. This trading range broke on the upside, and went on to 4,500 in just three weeks, a gain of 30%, and finally reached 6,350 in 18 months. The message is: when a pattern comes, it is wise to trade it, and let the market give us the rewards.

Chapter 4

Real-Time Trading

Some Examples

FOR TRADERS AS WELL AS INVESTORS, CLASSICAL CHART ANALYSIS offers opportunities to enter or exit the markets at turning points. My newsletter analyses the markets based on chart patterns.

Trading consists of two parts — analysis and execution. The analysis identifies trading signals based on consistent methods of technical trading. Once these signals are identified, the trader must then begin the process of executing these signals, which require:

1. Converting the analysis into actionable ideas – when to buy, what kind of stops to use, what will be the trailing stop or profit target, volume of trading, and
2. Actually taking the trade by entering these actionable ideas into the trading system, which is the stock market.

The newsletter provides the analysis. The trader or investor does the execution. Each person has his or her own risk appetite. One trader may like to buy options when the newsletter gives a buy signal. Another trader prefers to buy selected stocks when the buy signal comes. A third trader uses the signals to day trade in the direction of the signal. Each trader or investor will have different ways of using the newsletter advice. The advice helps the trader by doing the hard work of analysis, as well as highlighting trading opportunities in the ongoing market scenario.

In the pages that follow, I have picked some examples from among the newsletters featured in Chapter 3 to explain how traders could use the analysis contained in them, and have also highlighted what actually happened in the market subsequently.

14 September 2007

Nifty Closes Higher, Getting Ready for Breakout

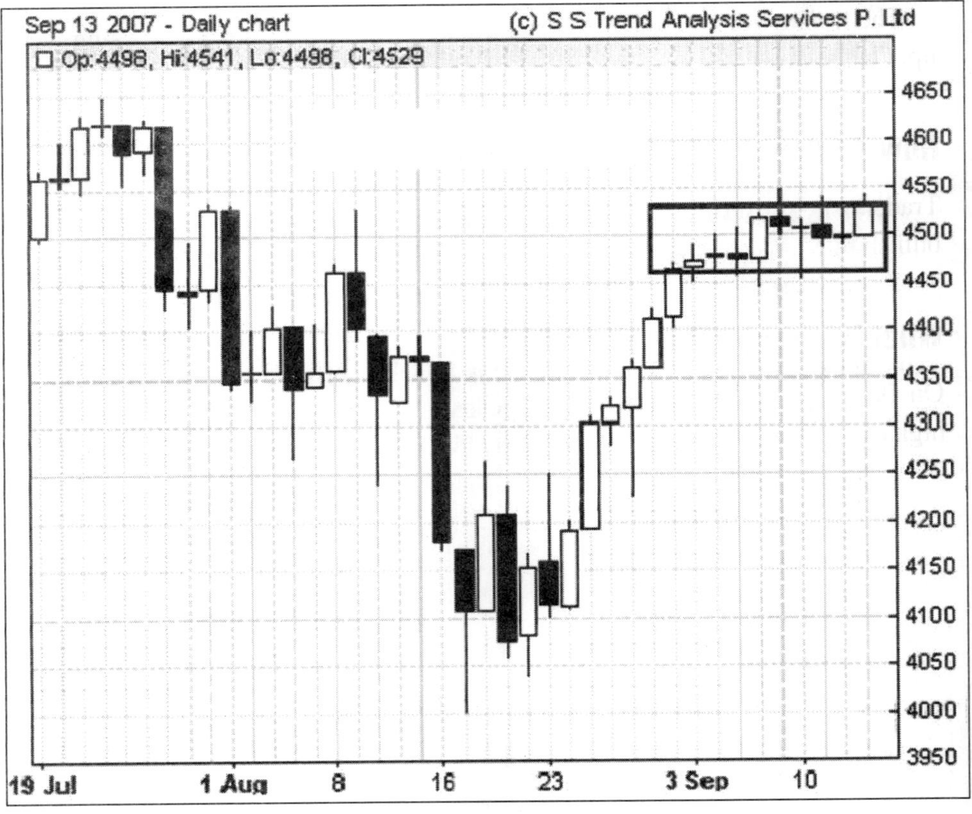

Figure 4.1: **Nifty on the verge of breakout from a trading range (boxed area in the chart).**

The CNX Nifty index closed higher today. Buyers came in from the start of trading. The market is in the top part of the trading range. Any close above current levels would reconfirm the current uptrend from the beginning of the month and forecast additional gains, while a move below new support in the 4,500 area would forecast a return to the recent lows in the 4,470 area. The primary uptrend is alive and well. The Sensex is within striking distance of its all time highs, while the Nifty needs just 100 points more to reach record levels again.

The short term trend remains up. Traders need to worry if the Nifty were to move below 4,470. Till then, buy on dips.

The trading range in the Nifty continues. It is on the verge of breaking up. On the downside, a close below 4,470 will be bearish.

How Traders Can Use this Analysis

Traders should set up their trading to go long, stay long, and maintain a bullish bias.

What Happened Subsequently

On 19 September 2007, the Nifty broke out from 4,560 and soared on to a high of 5,260, making a gain of 700 points (*see* Figure 4.2 on page 310).

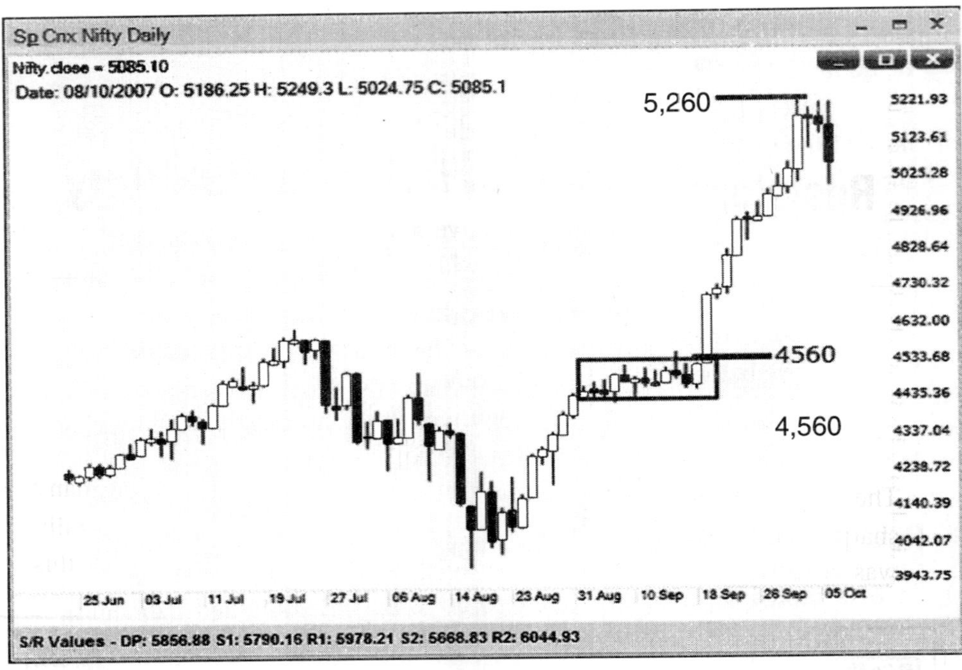

Figure 4.2: **Nifty daily chart: A breakout at 4,560 took the Nifty 700 points up.**

6 November 2007

Resistance at Higher Levels Pushes Nifty Below 5,900

More Downside Possible

The current bull market started in 2003. Since then we have seen many sharp rallies. The weekly chart given on next page shows how each rally was broadly contained by the upper line of the Bollinger Bands. But, this

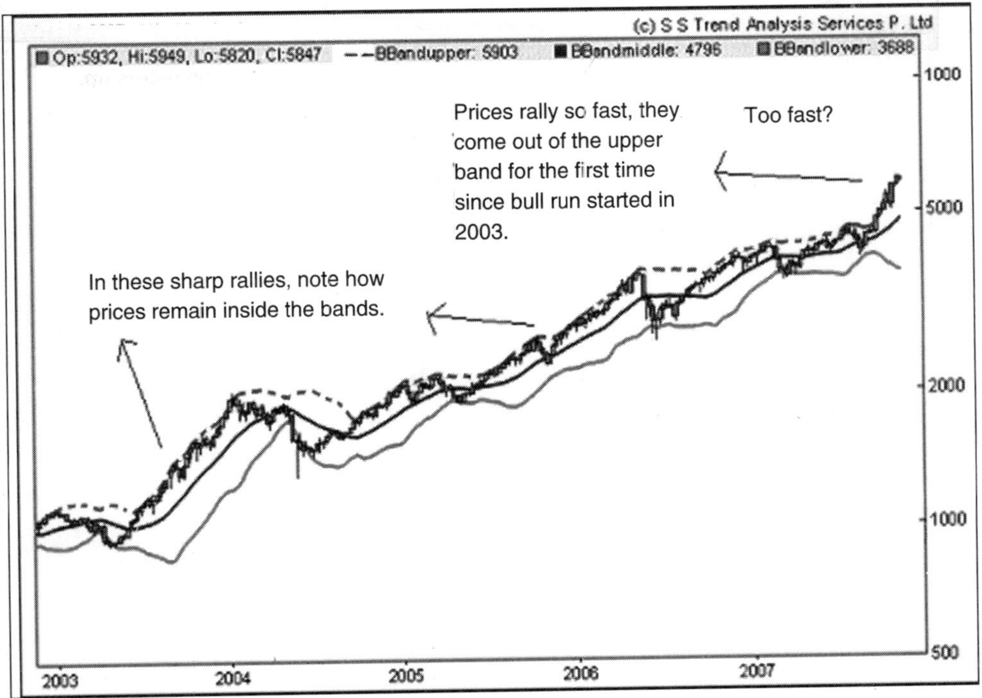

Figure 4.3: **Nifty weekly chart with Bollinger Bands.**

time, the rally has been so rapid, prices have gone above the bands. This may be an indication of unsustainable momentum.

The Nifty continued its roller coaster ride with large intra day swings — both up and down. For some reason, the Index disregarded American worries on Friday. Today (Monday), the market opened lower, then never really recovered from its gap down. A mid-afternoon sell off saw the Nifty go below 5,900, then reach 5,810, finally close at 5,847 with large losses over Friday's close.

So, what's happening? The Nifty chart tells us that the Index is in a trading range for the past five days. This trading range will eventually lead to a trending move — up or down is unknown. Taking the width of this range to be around 150 points (upper boundary = 5,950, lower = 5,800), if and when any of these boundaries break, we can look for a move to 5,650 on the downside or 6,100 on the upside.

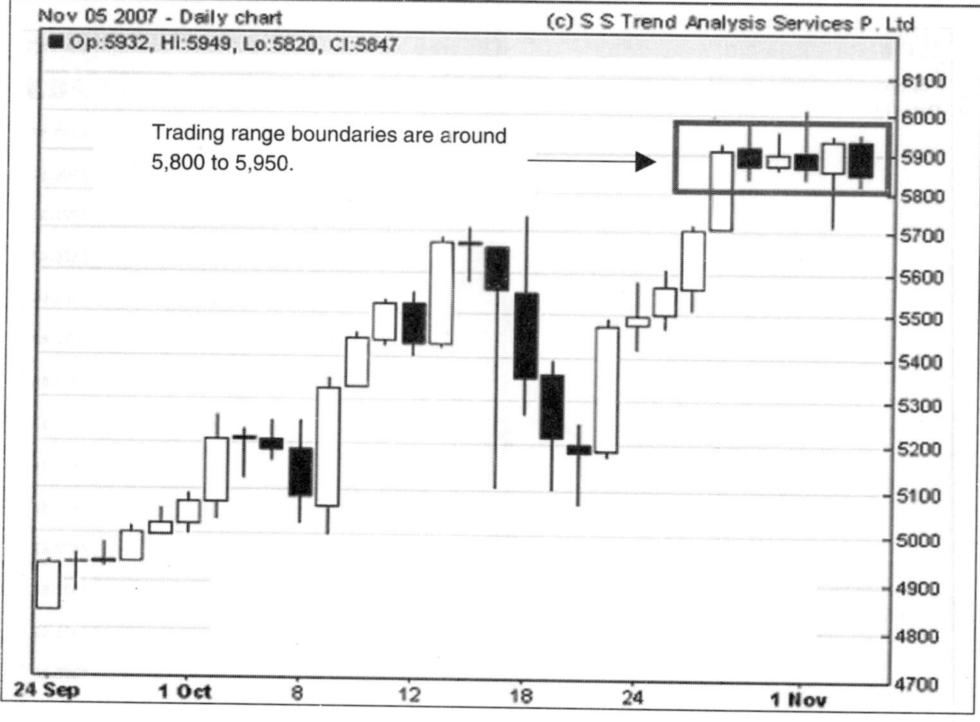

Figure 4.4: **Nifty spends five days in a trading range and may be ready for big move — up or down.**

The market is going through a period of increased volatility. This means that your stop losses must be wider than normal. If necessary, reduce volume. Avoid taking overnight positions that are losing money.

How Traders Can Use This Analysis

Short-term traders should reduce their long positions, swing traders can also take short positions with reduced volume. Traders should become alert on a buying opportunity after the expected dip.

What Happened Subsequently

On 6 November 2007, the Nifty broke down from 5,800, losing 333 points in 5 consecutive days. This low (5,477) may be a buying option for traders.

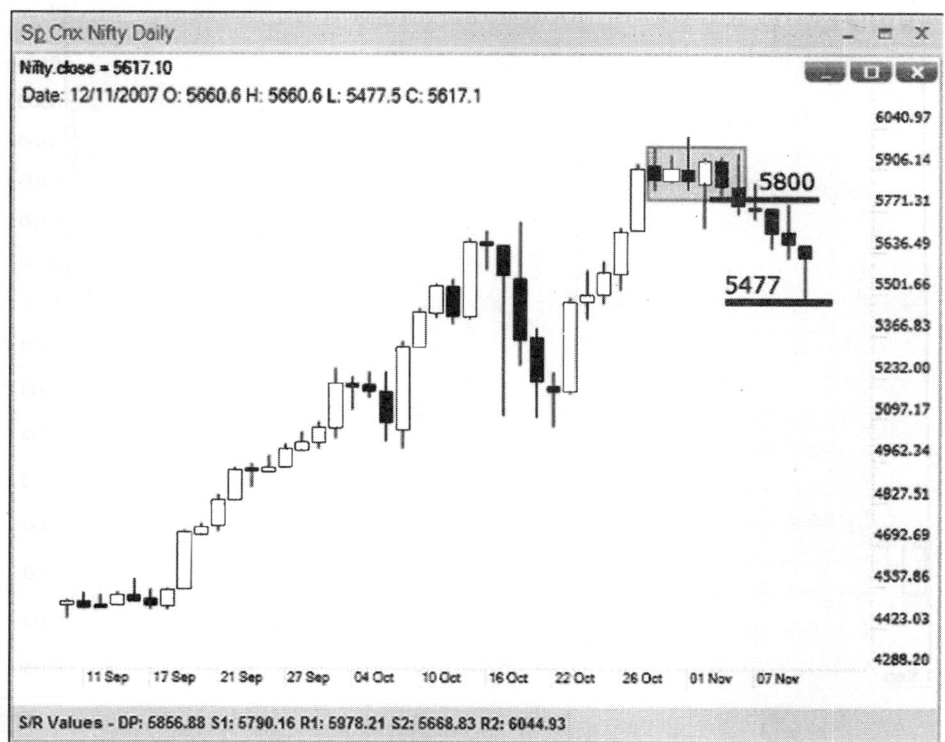

Figure 4.5: **Nifty daily chart: A breakdown at 5,800 took the Nifty at 5,477. A decrease of 333 points in 5 days.**

3 March 2008

The Budget Comes and Goes, Markets Remain Uncertain

Confused Index Continues Inside the 5,100-5,300 Range

Figure 4.6: **Nifty daily. Index continues inside a trading range. Buy above 5,300, avoid if Nifty falls below 5,100.**

Nifty Trend

The short term trend turned sideways, thanks to a sharp decline in the market on budget disappointments. This is the trend that traders should track. While the Index has turned sideways, more important is the trading range within which it is moving. The Nifty continues to move in:

1. A narrow daily range, and
2. Inside a well defined trading range — between 5,100 and 5,300.

The trend changes to down if and when the index closes below 5,100. The index had exhibited almost similar chart patterns in early January. What came after the narrow move was a big down thrust. Now, again the index is making a similar pattern. Again, the direction of the breakout is unknown. But traders should go with the flow, wherever it moves to.

The intermediate trend remains down. This is the trend that investors should track. Narrow range moves will eventually lead to big up moves. We have been suggesting that investors should buy, with the understanding that this is more of a trading entry. Keep tight stops. If Nifty falls below 5,100, then suspend any further buying. Also remember that March is usually a difficult month to trade. A new trend emerges in April.

How Traders Can Use This Analysis

Traders had two clear levels to trade with.

1. Buy the Nifty only if it crosses 5,300, and avoid buying below 5,100.
2. Professional traders could go short below 5,100.

By following these simple guidelines traders would have avoided buying inside the range.

What Happened Subsequently

On 3 March 2008, Nifty broke down below its lower trading range boundary of 5,100 which led to a downside move of 632 points in 11 days.

Figure 4.7: **Nifty daily chart. A breakout at 5,100 took the Nifty at a low at 4,468. A decrease of 632 points in 11 days.**

16 April 2008

Nifty Breaks Out Above a Minor Trading Range

This is a buy signal for short term traders. Buying should be done only on dips.

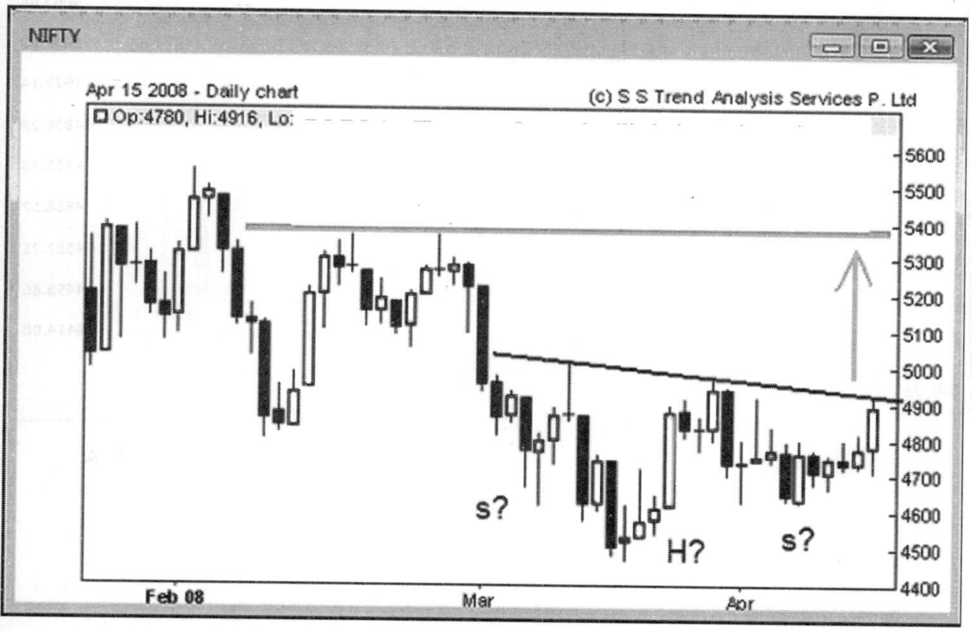

Figure 4.8: **Head and shoulder pattern plan? 5,350 is target for a bullish head and shoulder pattern, if the pattern is made and confirmed.**

Nifty Trend

We assume that this is a corrective rally in the downtrend. Counter-trend rallies during corrections are by no means a signal for new investments. Bear market rallies can be sharp to the upside and come back down even faster. If you look at the Nifty chart, notice how it has been repeatedly held back by its 50-day moving average which is acting as resistance. I might become more bullish if the Nifty can clear this line and stay above it with some convincing price / volume action.

Remember, markets can rally even with all the gloom and doom out there. It's their nature to fool the majority of the people.

Possible Scenario

The Nifty may be making a bullish head and shoulders pattern. A move above 4,950 will confirm this pattern and will give a target of 5,350 or thereabouts. While the Nifty may not reach these targets (if it crosses 4,950), an up move will represent a trading opportunity to go long. An eventual exhaustion of this up move may give a signal to go short. Thus, there are trades likely to be available now.

For long term investors, the trend remains down.

How Traders Can Use This Analysis

Short-term traders should position themselves to buy, as well as move out of short positions.

What Happened Subsequently

The Nifty broke out, taking the index from 4,910 to 5,298.

Figure 4.9: **Nifty daily chart. A breakout at 4,910 took the Nifty at 5,298.**

27 May 2008

Nifty Enters an Intermediate Downtrend

Figure 4.10: **Lower highs, lower lows confirmed. Nifty enters an intermediate downtrend again.**

The Nifty fell again, breaking the 4,950 support, and also printing a pattern of lower highs, lower lows. This is the sign of a resumption of the intermediate downtrend. All of this is worrying since a downtrend can extend in time as well as in price. We may be looking at a long, protracted bear market.

Worrying

Question: Is there a guarantee that the Nifty will fall?
Answer: Surely not. After making a pattern of lower highs, the Nifty can turn back and begin an up move again. No one can predict the markets. We can only work on the most probable scenario. Currently, the trend is down, with lower levels likely.

Correction in Terms of Time

The bull market that started in April 2003 lasted till January 2008 — i.e., for 4 years and 8 months. A one-third correction in time can mean 19 months — giving us a time target of September 2009 for the end of this bear market or correction.

Correction in Terms of Price

The bull market saw a rise from 920 to 6,350, i.e. a gain of 5,430 points. A one-third correction can see a decline of 1,810 points with a target of 4,540 points. The good news is that this correction has already taken place.

The bad news then is that to complete the correction in terms of time, the market may simply drift in a 1,000-point range for another one year. If this happens, brokers will become an endangered species while people will ask: What is CNBC ? Well, whatever will be, will be, will be. . .

How Traders Can Use This Analysis

The pattern of lower highs and lower lows was a strong warning of an impending downtrend. Traders as well as investors should have cut down on all trading positions.

What Happened Subsequently

This lower high, lower low pattern took the Nifty to a low of 3,790. The overall fall started from a high at 5,298 on 2 May 2008 to a low at 3,790 on 16 July 2008.

On 22 July 2008, this pattern ends when the Nifty broke above its earlier lower high at 4,215 and made a new high at 4,539 on 24 July 2008.

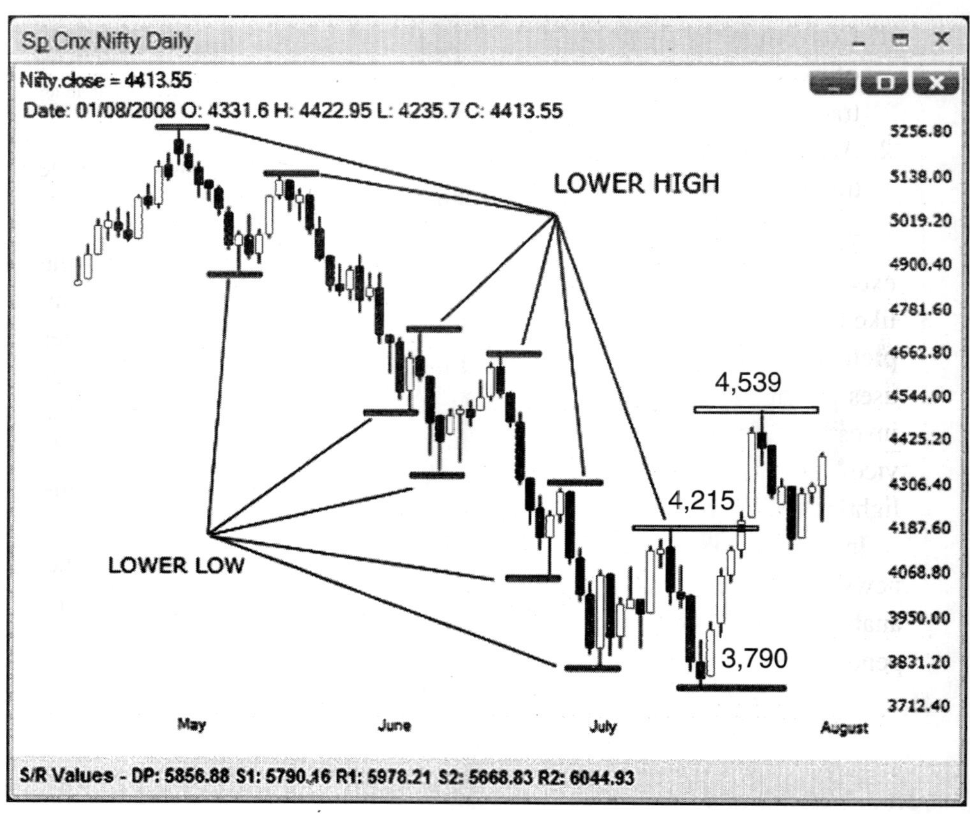

Figure 4.11: **Nifty daily chart.**

5 December 2008

Nifty Sees a Breakout

Maybe Looking at Higher Levels

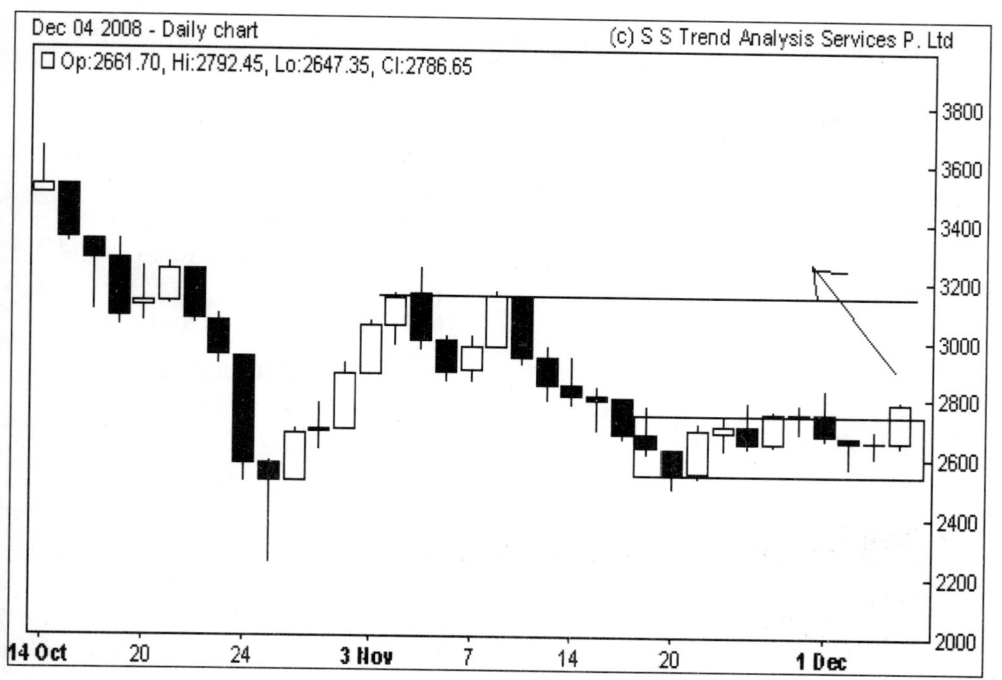

Figure 4.12: **Nifty breaks out of a trading range, closes above 2,750 resistance. Close below today's low 2,647 will cancel the breakout.**

One of the nice things about technical trading is flexibility. Rather than tell the market what it should do, technical traders follow the market. While this is difficult to do, in the long run, it pays money.

The Nifty was in a trading range between 2,555 and 2,755. A close above 2,755 today was a clear signal that the Index is breaking out from the range. The target for this breakout is 2,950. Traders should be long at close of trade today. What is the stop loss? It is 2,647, i.e. today's low, or, 2,555 the support line of the trading range. The two stops are for different trader profiles. The closer stop is for the swing trader, while the wider stop is for the position trader.

Is This the Start of the Bull Market?

Not really. It is possible that the Nifty may see a strong bear rally, reach 3,200, and then start a drift down to 2,000. I, of course, cannot say that this will happen, but there is a strong probability, so who knows?

We should also be open to the possibility that the Nifty may be building a base at current levels that is between 2,500 and 3,200. The Index could move inside this range for many weeks, or even months.

So, how do we trade?

The trading range breakout tells us to go long. Search for dips on intra day charts. Buy with proper stops. Maybe we will get a traditional year end rally; have fun!

How Traders Can Use This Analysis

Short-term traders should position themselves to buy, as well as move out of short positions.

What Happened Subsequently

The Nifty continued its up move, touching 3,000.

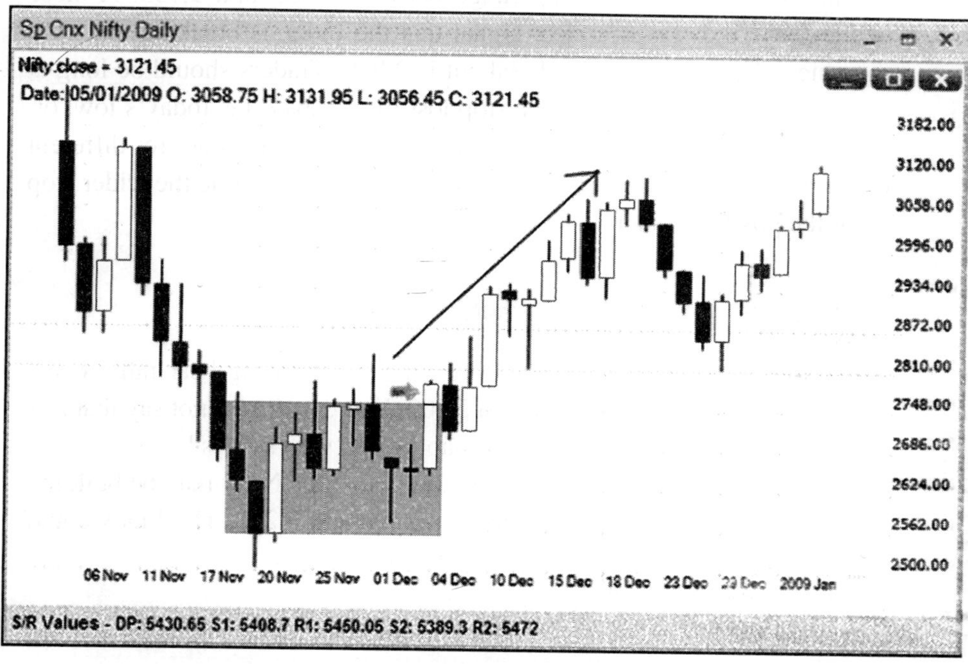

Figure 4.13: **Nifty daily chart. Breakout at 2,755 took the Nifty above 3,000.**

16 March 2009

Bulls Back in Action

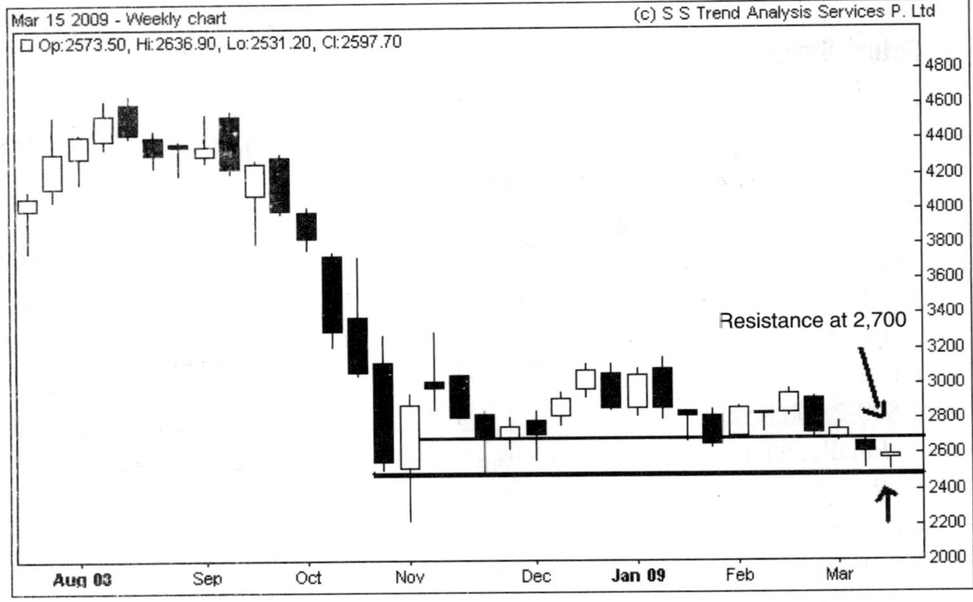

Figure 4.14: **Weekly chart of Nifty shows the index bouncing its support level of 2,500.**

The Nifty has broken out of a four-day consolidation between 2,580 and 2,620. This breakout suggests that the short-term trend is now up. A close above 2,800 is required to change the intermediate trend, which remains down as of now.

Traders should either step aside, or buy on dips. Conservative traders can consider buying if and when the intermediate trend changes to up. This will happen when the Nifty closes above 2,800.

Technically Bullish

On the weekly chart, a positive divergence between the Nifty and the 14-period RSI is now visible. The RSI is at 39.47, almost touching 40. I consider a move above 40 as a low risk buy signal — with proper stops. Many of these moves eventually end up in failure. Therefore, there is no way to suggest that the RSI signal will be a success. But traders may wish to take a buy on dips strategy. At worst, if the market falls, there will be small losses, and of course, non-participation in the decline.

Future Shock

Here are some scenarios:

Well, the Nifty could confound everyone by continuing to move up, quickly, reaching 3,500. All talk of 2,000 will then vanish as our friends will start talking of "fundamentally sound" companies and economy. Then, just before the election process starts, the markets could weaken, finally reaching 1,800 which, by then, everyone may have forgotten about.

Or, the market could do what everyone is suggesting — see a failure in the current rally, then fall below 2,500, and finally bottom out around the 1,800-2,000 levels.

Finally, the market could continue to drift between 2,550 and 2,800 .

Which scenario will work out? That is an answer only a fortune teller can give. My point is: depending on your trading profile, follow the market momentum. By going through a process of scenario building, we are not taken aback or shocked by what the market does. And, markets are unpredictable.

How Traders Can Use This Analysis

This change of trend came about almost at the lows of the bear market. Accordingly, traders should be going long while investors should begin buying once the Nifty closes above 2,800.

What Happened Subsequently

The Nifty entered a bull market, eventually going all the way to 6,350.

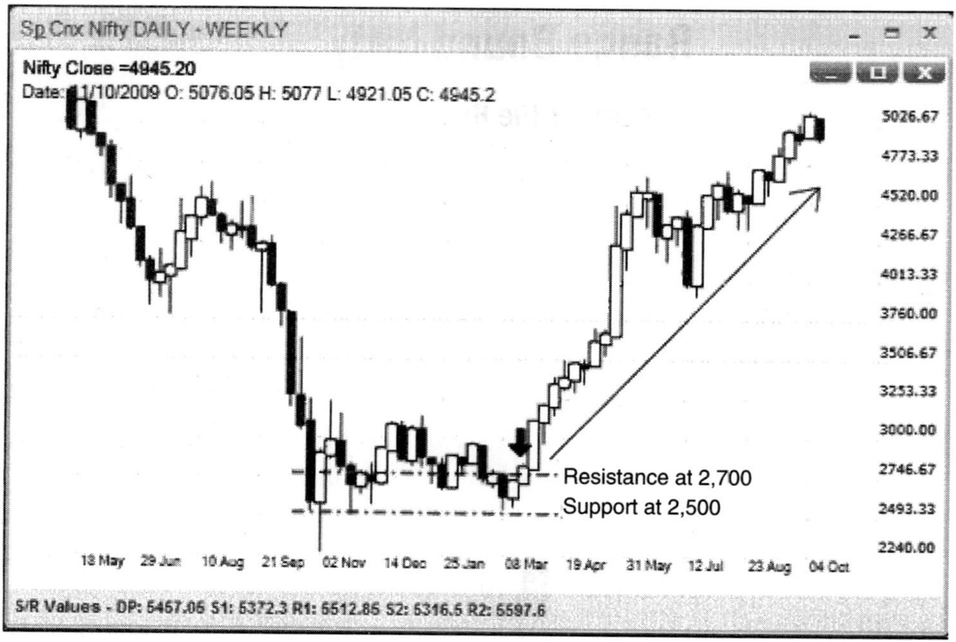

Figure 4.15: **Nifty daily-weekly chart. A breakout at its resistance starts the bull market.**

22 April 2009

Range Bound Nifty

Wait for the Big Move

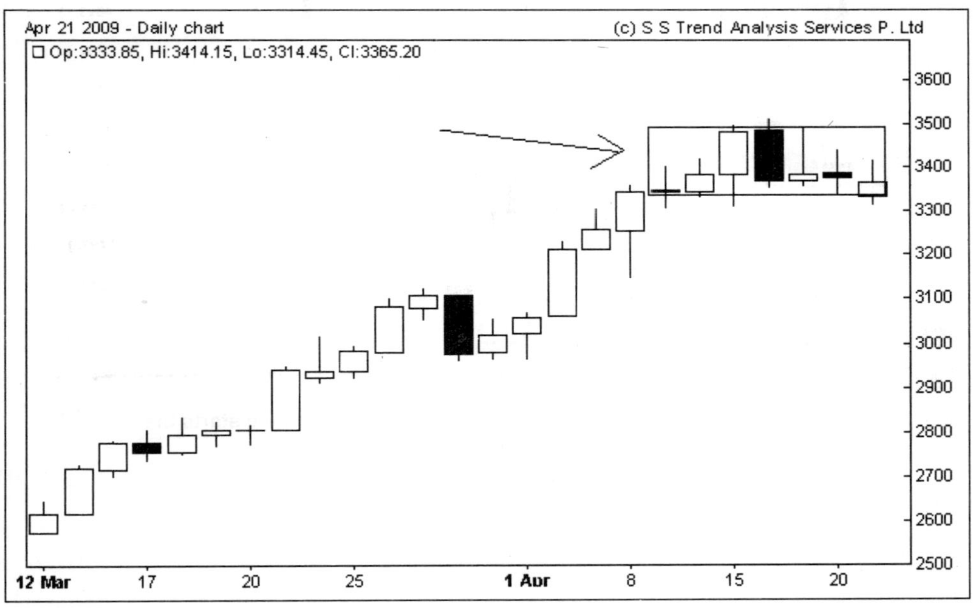

Figure 4.16: **The daily chart of 21 April 2009 shows Nifty in a trading range between 3,350 and 3,500. A move out of this range should provide a trend, wait patiently.**

The Nifty has now spent seven days inside a trading range between 3,350 and 3,500. This is in the nature of the Index. The Nifty goes through this process of expansion and contraction, regularly. After a big thrusting move beyond the 3,150 resistance level to 3,500, we now have the Index taking rest, moving inside a trading range. A move out of this range should be expected soon enough.

A close below 3,350 will tell us that the Nifty is ready for a correction. This down move should then go to 3,150 at the least. A close above 3,500, on the other hand, would suggest strength with more upside possible. We should then be looking at 3,800.

Nifty Support and Resistance

We have mentioned that Nifty has support at 3,350 and resistance at 3,500. For tomorrow's day trades we should expect support at 3,310 and resistance at 3,420.

How Traders Can Use This Analysis

This signal came in April 2009. Traders should maintain a bullish bias. Investors should continue to add to their positions.

What Happened Subsequently

The Nifty continued in its bull market, with a 1,000-point gain in the next one month.

Figure 4.17: **Nifty daily chart. A breakout took away Nifty.**

Chapter 5

The Close

Perils of Great Expectations

MOST BUSINESSMEN ARE WILLING TO WORK HARD TO DEVELOP THEIR business, happy to get whatever returns the business provides. Yet, when the same people enter the stock market, suddenly there are great expectations of abnormal, extraordinary returns from stocks. In his book *The Dow Theory*, author Robert Rhea quotes Charles Dow as saying "If people . . . would look upon trading in stocks as an attempt to get 12 per cent per annum on their money instead of 50 percent weekly, they would come out a good deal better in the long run."

The first step towards success in the stock market, whether as a trader or as an investor, comes when one understands the rewards and risks which the market offers. If the trader wants a return of 50 per cent per month, then she should be prepared to take the risk of losing 50 per cent in one month. Reward and risk go together, just like day and night.

That's not all.

Even if a trader is willing to lose 50 per cent in one month, her returns are not assured. The market gives what it wants to give. Sometimes the market movements are not enough to reward a trader with even 1 per cent return, let alone 50 per cent. Is it then possible for the trader to assume a risk of losing 50 per cent without having assurance of any gains? All risk and no reward becomes a foolish situation to be in.

Without the benefit of huge returns, what is the purpose of investing or trading in the market?

For the investor in equities, a number of studies have indicated out performance by the stock market over bank fixed deposits, in the long run. Over a period of many years, stocks generate an average inflation adjusted return of 8 per cent (Source: *The Four Pillars of Investing*, Bernstein). This number exceeds the returns on bank deposits which barely keep up with inflation. This data makes two points:

- First, stocks are a good investment for the long run, and
- Second, investors who expect lotteries from the stock market will be disappointed. Expectations must be reasonable.

For the stock market trader, trading is a business like any other business. People become doctors, lawyers, politicians, they run a dry cleaning business, or a steel factory, or a real estate brokerage. In the same way, some people become stock market traders. It is just one more profession. When a businessman opens a dry cleaning or a mobile handset shop, does he plan to obtain 50 per cent returns in one year? The answer is: absolutely not. But when a person starts out as a stock market trader, he considers 50 per cent returns per month his birth right. The trader puts in very little money in the trading business, thus remaining grossly undercapitalized. He takes large risks since he expects to earn large amounts from a small investment. This is a recipe for disaster. The trader should have expectations of returns which are similar to returns available in other business entities. If a person opens a small shop by investing ₹ 1 lakh, he can expect a return on the investment of ₹ 1 lakh. Suppose he says, my family expenses per month are ₹ 30,000, therefore I expect at least ₹ 40,000 per month to meet my expenses and also to give a return on my capital. After all, I am working full time so I expect a salary of ₹ 30,000 per month, the balance ₹ 10,000 per month is my return on investment. But, wait, no shopkeeper will expect ₹ 40,000 per month on an investment of ₹ 1 lakh! Business persons are smart and intelligent. They understand that returns are commensurate with their investment and effort.

Yet, when the same person becomes a stock market trader he demands from the market an income stream of ₹ 40,000 per month on an investment of ₹ 1 lakh. Such returns will not materialise.

Investors and traders who wish to make money from the stock market must have realistic expectations.

For investors, the target should be to obtain a return higher than the interest on bank fixed deposits. If the investor can get 4 per cent more every year than he does from bank fixed deposits, then over a period of 20 years his accumulated wealth will be significantly higher, since compounding works in his favour. Here is how it works:

Invest ₹ 1 lakh for 20 years.

Final Amount:

Bank Fixed Deposit: @ 9 per cent — ₹ 5,60,441.08
Stock Market Equity: @ 13 per cent — ₹ 11,52,308.78

Note that the returns more than double when compare to a bank fixed deposit. Also, there is a tax benefit since fixed deposits are subject to tax while capital gains in stocks are (currently) tax free.

As an investor, you should target a return of about 50 percent more than the bank fixed deposit rate. As you grow more skilled and experienced, you can get somewhat higher returns, but the expectation should be reasonable.

Let us consider an investor who can save ₹ 1 lakh per year for 30 years.
Final Amount:

Bank Fixed Deposit: @ 9 per cent — ₹ 1,48,57,521.7
Stock Market Equity: @ 13 per cent — ₹ 3,31,31,511.3

Now, let us consider the situation that you could actually get 18 per cent per year on your stock market investments. If you invested ₹ 1 lakh per year, at the end of 30 years you will then have ₹ 9,33,31,862.98. Most mutual funds will not be able to provide a track record that returns 18% for 30 years. A return of 18% per annum should be considered outstanding, while about 13% is a reasonable expectation.

Traders should treat stock market trading as a business. Like any other business, there are two expectations:

1. The business will provide a return on capital, and
2. The business will pay a salary to the trader.

The return on capital should be more than the bank fixed deposit rate. It should be more or less what an investor earns. The salary paid by the business to the trader must be commensurate with the capital employed in the business. If the capital employed is ₹ 2 lakh, then the trader cannot expect a salary of ₹ 30,000 per month, or ₹ 3.6 lakh per year. Probably, a business will pay a salary of ₹ 30,000 per month when it has a capital of, maybe, ₹ 20 lakh.

My point is simple: expectations of your own income (salary) have to be based on the money invested and not on your own needs.

Index